# Immigrant and Refugee Students in Canada

# Immigrant and Refugee Students in Canada

*Edited by Courtney Anne Brewer
and Michael McCabe*

Copyright © 2014 Courtney Anne Brewer and Michael McCabe

14 15 16 17 18 5 4 3 2 1

Excerpts from this publication may be reproduced under licence from Access Copyright, or with the express written permission of Brush Education Inc., or under licence from a collective management organization in your territory. All rights are otherwise reserved, and no part of this publication may be reproduced, stored in a retrieval system, or transmitted in any form or by any means, electronic, mechanical, photocopying, digital copying, scanning, recording, or otherwise, except as specifically authorized.

Brush Education Inc.
www.brusheducation.ca
contact@brusheducation.ca

Editorial: Leslie Vermeer, William Thorsen
Cover design: Dean Pickup; Cover image of pencils: ID 3143228 © Ljupco Smokovski, Dreamstime.com; Maple leaf: Dean Pickup
Book interior design: Carol Dragich, Dragich Design

Printed and manufactured in Canada
E-book edition available at brusheducation.ca, iBookstore, Kobo, Amazon, and other e-retailers

**Library and Archives Canada Cataloguing in Publication**
Immigrant and refugee students in Canada / Courtney Anne Brewer and Michael McCabe, editors.

Includes bibliographical references.
Issued in print and electronic formats.
ISBN 978-1-55059-548-2 (pbk.).—ISBN 978-1-55059-550-5 (mobi).—
ISBN 978-1-55059-551-2 (epub)

1. Immigrant children—Education—Canada.  2. Refugee children—Education—Canada.   I. Brewer, Courtney Anne, 1988-, editor of compilation   II. McCabe, Michael, 1964–, editor of compilation

LC3747.C3I45 2014     371.826'9120971 C2013-908294-8     C2013-908295-6

Produced with the assistance of the Government of Alberta, Alberta Media Fund. We also acknowledge the financial support of the Government of Canada through the Canada Book Fund for our publishing activities.

Government of Alberta ■   Canadian Heritage  Patrimoine canadien

# Dedication

*To my wonderful family and friends. Thank you for your unwavering support and encouragement every step of the way.*
—Courtney

*To Sarah, Rebecca, and Zachary. Thanks for leaving Daddy enough time for this!*
—Mike

# Contents

|   |   |   |
|---|---|---|
|   | *Acknowledgements* | ix |
| 1 | Introduction: Working together to navigate the Canadian education system<br>*Michael McCabe and Courtney Anne Brewer* | 1 |
| 2 | School readiness: A review of literature<br>*Courtney Anne Brewer and Michael McCabe* | 7 |
| 3 | Immigrant students' health: An overview of the need to improve our awareness and response to the health of immigrant children and their families within the educational context<br>*Taunya Wideman-Johnston* | 20 |
| 4 | School-based interventions for refugee children and youth: Canadian and international perspectives<br>*Marta Young and K. Jacky Chan* | 31 |
| 5 | Immigrant mothers' use of a discussion group in becoming school ready<br>*Courtney Anne Brewer and Michael McCabe* | 54 |
| 6 | Matching policies to needs in early childhood development programs in newcomer populations<br>*Linda Ogilvie, Darcy Fleming, Anna Kirova, Lucenia Ortiz, Sandra Rastin, Catherine Caufield, Elizabeth Burgess-Pinto, and Mahdieh Dastjerdi* | 65 |
| 7 | Cultural negotiations of sense of place through shared parent–child art-making in a preschool for immigrant children<br>*Anna Kirova, Patti Pente, and Christine Massing* | 89 |

| 8 | African refugee women's songs and stories: Possibilities for diversifying literacy practices in early childhood education | 112 |
|---|---|---|
| | *Christine Massing* | |
| 9 | Refugee families with preschool children: Looking back | 129 |
| | *Darcey M. Dachyshyn* | |
| 10 | Refugee students in Canadian schools: Educational issues and challenges | 147 |
| | *Samuel Tecle and Carl E. James* | |
| 11 | The value of language in refugee youth's construction of identity | 161 |
| | *Neda Asadi* | |
| 12 | The Accelerated Basic Literacy Education (ABLE) program in the Waterloo Region District School Board | 174 |
| | *Kimberly Hird-Bingeman, Michael McCabe, and Courtney Anne Brewer* | |
| 13 | Building community capacity to support Karen refugee youth in schools | 183 |
| | *Lisa Sadler and Nancy Clark* | |
| 14 | Fostering solidarity in the classroom: Creative expression workshops for immigrant and refugee students | 202 |
| | *Caroline Beauregard, Marie-France Gauthier, and Cécile Rousseau* | |
| 15 | "More than winning the lottery": The academic experiences of refugee youth in Canadian universities | 220 |
| | *Martha K. Ferede* | |
| 16 | Managing expectations through building cultural competencies | 249 |
| | *Ashley Korn, Michelle Manks, and Jacqueline Strecker* | |
| 17 | How do I get in? Exploring the underemployment of immigrant teachers in Canada | 261 |
| | *Christine L. Cho* | |
| | *Contributor biographies* | *273* |

# Acknowledgements

The editors of this book would like to extend thanks for and acknowledgement of a Language and Literacy Research Grant from Nipissing University's Schulich School of Education. Without this funding, projects such as this would not be possible. The editors would also like to thank Brush Education for recognizing the importance of this project and helping to make the research and ideas gathered from this collaborative initiative accessible to policy makers, educators, community service agencies, and the greater population. Furthermore, extensive gratitude is offered to each author who contributed to this project. The authors' passion for working with refugees and immigrants, as well as their dedication to research and deep desire to continue conversations in support of Canada's students in their educational journeys, is truly admirable.

# 1

# Introduction

## Working together to navigate the Canadian education system

*Courtney Anne Brewer and Michael McCabe*

This book is long overdue. Unique in its design, it is a truly collaborative effort of impassioned researchers and frontline workers from across Canada, exploring a plethora of programs aimed at assisting many of our immigrant and refugee families as they attempt to navigate the Canadian educational system. It also examines many of the issues that face this unique population as they begin to settle in Canada. Dewey (1907) considers schools to be "a miniature community, an embryonic society" (p. 32), one that reflects "the life of the larger society, and [is] permeated throughout with the spirit of art, history and science" (p. 45). Noddings (2007) states that schools are "mini-societies in which children learn through practice how to promote their own growth, that of others, and that of the whole society" (p. 39). The most effective strategies to promote learning are those that recognize differences in student experiences and that fit learning to individual students. Or, if we put it another way, the experience has to be built on or connected to prior experience. The programs explored here attempt to do exactly that.

This project is grounded in socio-cultural theory (Vygotsky, 1978) with influences from Freire's (1970/2000) *Pedagogy of the Oppressed*. We assume that both culture and context play a major role in the situations that refugee families experience. Refugee families are in unique situations in Canada, and as Lee (1988) suggests, having ties to two places in these situations can result in feeling a lack of place or identity. In each chapter, complex scenarios about how and why participants arrived in Canada exist for all participant groups. It is important to gain perspectives from across Canada, as experiences and interventions vary from region to region (Fantino & Colak, 2001; Pillay & Asadi, 2012). Understanding these contexts is crucial in building an understanding of the immigrant and refugee family experience, particularly as it pertains to adjusting to the Canadian educational system. Because Canada is a geographically large country that offers various approaches and services to immigrant and refugee families (Fantino & Colak, 2001), the socio-cultural lens becomes even more complex, yet more necessary. As Tecle and James explain in their chapter, "Many studies have demonstrated the ways in which racism and colonialism have influenced and informed both historical and contemporary Canadian society." The ongoing legacies of colonialism, capitalism, and racism affect individuals' experiences—particularly those of refugees. We draw on anti-colonial theory to understand colonialism and the indelible influence it has had on geopolitical conflict, forced migration of peoples, and persistent struggles (Dei & Asgharzadeh, 2001). Colonialism has had a role in territorial conflicts, ethnic disagreements, displacement of people, and, as a consequence, the creation of refugees. Colonialism also plays a role in the push and pull factors that make resettlement possible and necessary.

Initially, this book looks at overarching issues related to the lives of immigrants and refugees in Canada, namely school readiness and familiarity, health issues specific to the population we are investigating, and an overview of the types of programs available to this population. Each of these topics is repeated throughout chapters that follow because it is impossible to ignore these issues in a book like this one.

Brewer and McCabe review the literature related to school readiness and how readiness affects students, families, teachers, and schools. This investigation is taken up later with a look at a parent school-readiness program in the Kitchener-Waterloo region of Ontario. Wideman-Johnston looks at health issues specific to immigrants and refugees and relates them to the increasing body of research surrounding overall health and well-being in our student populations and the way they contribute to academic endeavours. Wideman-Johnston points to the need for increased attention in this area, particularly related to the complex discussions integrating physical, mental, and social health as it relates to academic success.

Young and Chan provide a thorough account of the types of programs that promote school-based interventions for refugee students. This chapter acts as an introduction to the remaining chapters of the book. As Young and Chan say, "Given that the majority of refugee children and adolescents attend school, the school setting is an optimal venue for interventions to be developed and implemented to address their psychosocial challenges. From an ecological standpoint, it is crucial that comprehensive school-based interventions include not only the students themselves but also their parents and teachers."

The second part of the book provides accounts of various research projects that focus on important issues related to interventions. It is divided into four general sections, namely early years, middle years, secondary education, and post-secondary education, according to the age of the students discussed. The early-years component deals with a broad spectrum of issues related to the process of children's early education. Using parental involvement and engagement in school as indicators of school readiness, Brewer and McCabe explore the process by which immigrant mothers prepare themselves and their children for school in Ontario. The immigrant mothers who participated in a school-readiness program provide accounts of barriers to and benefits of their participation. Ogilvie, Fleming, Kirova, Ortiz, Rastin, Caufield, Burgess-Pinto, and Dastjerdi use action research to generate policy-relevant data to evaluate the cultural appropriateness of assessment tools and practices used in early childhood development education programs with immigrant and refugee (newcomer) children. In the tradition of humanistic geographers, Kirova, Pente, and Massing explore how immigrant preschool teachers and their immigrant students and families investigate their bicultural identities through aesthetic explorations of sense of place, while recognizing the importance of the emotional realm of our human relationships with place and of the human ability to reflect and interpret such relationships through artistic representations.

Through two ethnographic studies, Massing investigates experiences from professional development sessions on communication and guidance for refugee women employed at an early childhood centre and for women in an early childhood certification program. In this chapter, the author concentrates on the women's recollections of the ways in which storytelling and songs were used in their families and cultures. In the final chapter in this section, Dachyshyn provides an account of data rooted in research undertaken with refugee families located in Canada, but also includes experiences and research from other locations that now inform the author's understandings of the complexities involved in refugee resettlement. We believe this perspective will open up opportunities for dialogue about the multifaceted nature of resettlement.

The next section deals with the middle-years school experiences of immigrants and refugees. Building on Sam Tecle's experiences as a child of Eritrean parents who grew up in a racially diverse, low-income urban neighbourhood, Tecle and James discuss the complexities, tensions, and challenges of students and teachers as they engage in the educational process—a process where students struggle to maintain a dual identity: that of being a Canadian while remaining true to "their" country of origin and by extension their "ethnic culture." Asadi reports on the importance of identity, the role of language in identity development and belonging, and the stance of public and educational policies. The focus here is on high dropout rates among students for whom English is a new language and a multitude of other factors such as discrimination, poverty, lack of ability to access resources, peer pressure, and the tendency to engage in criminal behaviour. Hird-Bingeman, McCabe, and Brewer look at the Accelerated Basic Literacy Education (ABLE) program operating in the Waterloo Region District School Board, which is for students ages 9 to 13 who have recently arrived in Ontario schools with limited prior schooling. Students enter the program through a referral process at any point between grades 4 and 8. The ABLE program is intended to help identified ESL/ELD students who have been in Canada for one to three years make significant gains in English-language development, literacy, numeracy, and academic skills and knowledge so they can successfully integrate into regular classroom programs.

Two chapters are dedicated to issues related to students and families in the secondary school years of their education. Sadler and Clark outline a collaborative approach to the integration of refugee youth into Canadian schools. They work with Karen refugee youth, who are one of Canada's newest and largest groups of government-assisted refugees resettled into a suburban community. Drawing on a strengths-based approach, the authors discuss some stories of success in which several community organizations play a role in supporting youths' access to education and ongoing resettlement needs. Beauregard, Gauthier, and Rousseau examine three programs of the Transcultural Research and Intervention Team, which focus on creative expression workshops for children and youth in multi-ethnic schools. One common feature of these programs is that they offer a space where fostering solidarity becomes possible through play and creative expression. The authors first discuss the rationale and theoretical framework structuring the workshops, and then describe the three programs using vignettes to illustrate the complexity of the relational dimension of these interventions.

The post-secondary section looks at academic experiences of refugees in Canadian universities, the building of cultural competencies, and the underemployment of immigrant teachers in Canada. Ferede investigates the academic experiences of refugees who were resettled directly into universities through the World University Service of Canada's Student Refugee Program from 2007 to 2011. Findings show that refugee students face tremendous pedagogical, curricular, and technical challenges that they overcome with institutional, faculty, staff, and peer-to-peer supports. Korn, Manks, and Strecker delve into refugee experiences with pre-departure orientations for university students. Using evidence from the experiences of the World University Service of Canada's Student Refugee Program, the authors conclude that such orientations are an essential aspect of any refugee-sponsorship program. Cho explores the under employment of immigrant teachers in Ontario. Drawing from a critical ethnographic project with immigrant teacher candidates juxtaposed with an information session at an immigrant counselling service, Cho's research exposes two challenges with getting hired as a teacher in Ontario: perceptions around language proficiency and the limitations of Canada's Multiculturalism Act.

The purpose of this book is to highlight services and interventions offered to immigrant and refugee students and families, not only to provide identification of problem areas but to offer meaningful solutions. It is important that Canadian information about immigrants and refugees becomes part of scholarly literature. If they understand these issues in a Canadian context, those in the field of education will be able to approach their practice with a more thoughtful and informed perspective. We hope this book will form the basis for discussion and future studies and courses in teacher education and social foundations programs.

This book will be instrumental in addressing several key themes pertaining to the education of children of immigrant and refugee families:

1. Common challenges faced by immigrant and refugee children and families with regards to the formal education system;
2. Common aspects of intervention that appear to assist immigrant and refugee children and families successfully;
3. What narratives from academics and frontline workers tell us about working with immigrant and refugee families.

We hope our efforts will act as a starting point for future discussion and a spark for future research.

## REFERENCES

Dei, G.J.S., & Asgharzadeh, A. (2001). The power of social theory: The anti-colonial discursive framework. *Journal of Educational Thought, 35*(3), 297–323.

Dewey, J. (1907). *The school and society*. Chicago, IL: University of Chicago Press.

Fantino, A.M., & Colak, A. (2001, Sep–Oct). Refugee children in Canada: Searching for identity. *Child Welfare, 80*(5), 587–596. Retrieved from http://search.ebscohost.com/login.aspx?direct=true&db=ehh&AN=5377635&site=ehost-live&scope=site Medline:11678416

Freire, P. (1970/2000). *Pedagogy of the oppressed*. (30th anniversary ed.). New York, NY: Continuum International Publishing.

Lee, E. (1988, Jun). Cultural factors in working with Southeast Asian refugee adolescents. *Journal of Adolescence, 11*(2), 167–179. http://dx.doi.org/10.1016/S0140-1971(88)80051-4 Medline:3403751

Noddings, N. (2007). *Philosophy of education* (2nd ed.). Boulder, CO: Westview Press.

Pillay, T., & Asadi, N. (2012). *Participatory action research and educational liberation for refugee youth in Canada*. The Canadian Society for the Study of Education Annual Conference, Waterloo, ON.

Vygotsky, L.S. (1978). *Mind in society: The development of higher psychological processes*. Cambridge, MA: Harvard University Press.

# 2

# School readiness

## A review of literature

*Courtney Anne Brewer and Michael McCabe*

## School readiness as a definition in different contexts

School readiness is often thought of in relation to students and their personal experience in terms of being prepared, or not, for attending formal schooling. According to the US National Education Goals Panel in 1997 (as cited in Dockett & Perry, 2009), school readiness includes the traditional notion of children being ready for school but goes beyond this to include the schools' readiness for children and the family, and community support services that benefit children in their transition into school. Even in terms of determining school readiness at the level of the individual student, concepts of school readiness have changed. At the student level, traditional understandings of school readiness often focus on knowing the alphabet, knowing how to count, and skills such as being able to hold a pencil properly. Now, however, ideas about school readiness, in terms of what will actually offer students an advantage upon arrival to school, are changing drastically. A study by Janus and Duku (2007) explains that the way students navigate the classroom—by being flexible, adaptable, cooperative with others, able to ask questions comfortably, and able to show respect for all aspects of the classroom—is much more important than the traditional understanding that curricular knowledge is primarily essential. Janus and Duku also explain that children do not automatically become ready for school just before beginning school; rather, being ready for school is an outcome of everything in a child's life. This point means that the role of the parents in exposing their children to things that will promote all aspects of being ready for school is immensely important. In addition, the need for promoting school readiness often focuses on children who are on the verge of entering formal school; Graue (2006) notes, however, that kindergarten is too late to start concentrating on school readiness. Graue suggests that readiness should focus on development of children from birth to five years. This idea of focusing on readiness early in life is repeated by Ramey and Ramey (2004), who identify seven types of experiences that are important in ensuring school readiness among children, based on brain and behavioural development. These experiences include "encouraging exploration, monitoring basic skills, celebrating developmental advances, rehearsing and extending new skills, being protected from inappropriate disapproval, teasing and punishment, communicating richly and responsively, and guiding and limiting behaviour" (p. 473).

One important issue to consider in school readiness, beyond what the research says about child development and essential skills needed to participate in the school environment, is the perception of school readiness that teachers and parents hold. Such perceptions are important because they influence school readiness at the human, practical level rather than from a removed and distant standpoint. Moreover, if perceptions differ, the needs of the child may not be completely met, as one ideal may be preferred over another, more optimal one. Piotrkowski, Botsko, and Matthews (2000) and Zhang, Sun, and Gai (2008) state that there are consistencies in ideas of readiness in terms of "physical well-being, the ability to concentrate, child rearing, self confidence, learning interests and engagement in class" (Zhang et al., 2008, p. 469). Discrepancies exist in terms of parents emphasizing the need for mastery of basic knowledge over mastery of learning skills, compared to kindergarten teachers, who saw less of a need to have a mastery of knowledge and more of a need for mastery of learning skills (Piotrkowski et al., 2000; Zhang et al., 2008). This discrepancy was also reported by Barbarin et al. (2008), who noticed that there was an emphasis on general knowledge and a lack of importance placed on inferential skills as an aspect of readiness. Piotrkowski et al. noted that among black and Hispanic parents who speak English, there was a belief that children should be able to communicate in English before entering kindergarten, which contrasts with views of kindergarten and preschool teachers. The discrepancies between what parents and teachers consider to be sufficient indicators of school readiness can complicate the ability of children to actually be ready for school.

It is important to see the many influences and items that encompass and conceptualize school readiness as well as the variety of perspectives from which these influences arise if we are to begin to improve school readiness among children, parents, and schools.

## The role that parents play in school readiness

The need for parents to be engaged in school readiness is intense, especially in the early years of a child's education. As Entwisle and Alexander (1995) note,

> Younger children are also more physically and emotionally dependent on their families. They need their parents to get them to school, provide the supplies they need, and see that they are properly dressed and groomed. Older students, by contrast, can visit libraries on their own, hold part-time jobs, and in various other ways make up for any shortfall of resources in the home. Older students are tied to their families too, but they have alternative sources of emotional support outside the home—in peer groups, for example—and they also have ways to earn money when income is insufficient. For these reasons, family influences on schooling are probably stronger for elementary than for secondary youngsters. (p. 400)

With this said, there are still a variety of issues related to school readiness in older grades, especially for immigrant teenagers. Despite this controversy over readiness based on age, parents remain essential to the readiness process. The role of the parent in school readiness is common in the research literature; however, this information does not often indicate the school-readiness needs of parents as reported by parents themselves (Giallo, Kienhuis, Treyvaud, & Matthews, 2008). Giallo et al. (2008) note that approximately 70% of parents wanted information about how to help their children prepare for starting school. They suggest that wanting information may be due to feeling unprepared for their child's transition into school despite their desire to make the transition as smooth as possible. Anderson and Minke (2007), drawing on Bandura's theory of self-efficacy (1977), explain that parents' efficacy "refers to parents' beliefs that their involvement in their children's schooling will positively affect their children's learning and school success" (Bandura, 1977; as cited in Anderson & Minke, 2007, p. 312). Anderson and Minke also note that parents with high efficacy in parental engagement believe they can participate in practices and behaviours that will result in positive academic outcomes for their children. It is important for parents to feel comfortable in being able to assist their children in becoming ready for school and in being prepared to become engaged with the school community themselves.

At the same time, a lack of comfort in schools may exist among parents for a variety of reasons, including negative personal experiences in school as a student, feeling inferior or intimidated by teachers and administration, or having no clearly defined role within the school community. Feeling comfortable and being engaged in the school as a parent are especially important. Englund, Luckner, Whaley, and Egeland (2004) noticed that the quality of a mother's instruction to her child when the child was 3.5 years old had a direct influence on the child's IQ and an indirect influence on the child's achievement in the first and third grades. They also found that higher academic achievement in the first grade led to higher expectations among parents and to more parental engagement and involvement. The combination of higher expectations and increased engagement is associated with the higher academic achievement that students experienced in the third grade (Englund et al., 2004). In a study of mothers and children who attended Head Start programs aimed at assisting low-income families during the early years of a child's life through various interventions, such as preschool and parenting programs, Parker, Boak, Griffin, Ripple, and Peay (1999) also note that "children whose parents spent more time helping them learn skills at home reported higher overall cognitive and language competencies" (p. 418). Parker et al. noticed similar results related to play and noted that "greater parent-initiated play was associated with increased receptive language in preschool-aged children ... when parents understand the importance of play in their child's development, it is likely to lead to positive gains for children's readiness for school" (p. 420). Further, in their study Parker et al. found that "the parent's ability to facilitate their child's learning was associated with increased sensory concept activation and increased independence in the classroom" (p. 420). On the other hand, Parker et al. noted, "the more school-related things parents do or talk about with their child, the less considerate and task-oriented their children were and the more depressed and distractible" (pp. 420–422). The study's explanation for this finding, however, was that a demanding parent, versus an encouraging parent, led to children feeling overwhelmed (p. 422). This point speaks to the need for parents to exercise balance and foresight when engaging with their children in school-readiness discussions and activities. Also, as previously stated, if parents are to engage in positive behaviours associated with school readiness, their perception of their ability to do this, Bandura (1977) suggests, must also be positive or at least must not act as a barrier to helping their children learn at home.

The role of the parent in school readiness can be determined not only by the active approaches that parents take but also by their nature as a parent. Chazan-Cohen et al. (2009) noticed that optimal approaches to learning were related to lower parenting stress when the child was 14 months old, a decrease in parenting stress over time, and an increasingly positive learning environment in the home. In terms of more traditional views of school readiness, parents who were less stressed when their child was 14 months tended to have children with higher vocabulary scores, which in turn were associated with better learning environments and supportive parenting during play (Chazan-Cohen et al., 2009).

Differences between mothers and fathers exist in terms of parental influences on school readiness. A study by Martin, Ryan, and Brooks-Gunn (2010) found that fathers' supportiveness was associated with children's school readiness only when the mothers lacked supportiveness. Mothers' supportiveness, on the other hand, was associated with children's school readiness when fathers scored low, average, or high on supportiveness. The study concludes that fathers may act as a buffer against unsupportive mother parenting and its association with school readiness (Martin et al., 2010).

The influence parents have on their children's school readiness should not be ignored. Parents' needs should be responded to, and their contributions should be noted and encouraged. Since parents are often thought to be a child's first teachers, keeping parents informed and engaged in the school-readiness process is essential.

## Effects of immigration on student success in secondary school

Immigration at a young age can be difficult for children, but the effects of not being well adjusted can carry over into secondary school, where students face a harsher academic environment. As well, many newcomers arrive when their children are old enough to be in high school, regardless of their school readiness or preparation for entering secondary schools.

Immigrant youth often need to learn a new set of norms and customs while also trying to adjust to the world of secondary school. They couple their experiences of a new school with disorientation and a lack of familiarity with readiness (Suárez-Orozco, 2000). Furthermore, secondary schools are often unable to meet the variety of needs that immigrant youth face each day (Suárez-Orozco, Onaga, & Lardemelle, 2010), and the ability to meet the needs of immigrant students becomes even more challenging because relocation may be taking place as families attempt to settle (Suárez-Orozco, Gaytán, Bang, Pakes, O'Connor, & Rhodes, 2010).

A longitudinal study in the United States by Suárez-Orozco, Gaytán, et al. (2010) classified immigrant youth according to various academic trajectories. Participants were recruited at 12 years of age, and data was collected for a five-year term. The researchers noticed five trajectories; of these, two groups improved their academic performance over time: High Achievers (which comprised 25% of the sample) and Improvers (which made up 11% of the sample). The remaining participants either did not improve or ended up declining in measured performance during the study. Of these, 25% were Slow Decliners, who often moved to more demanding schools during their academic career and failed to keep up with the increased expectations, while 27.8% were Precipitous Decliners. This group faced several hardships related to pre- and post-migration, went to lower-quality schools, and often dealt with psychological issues. Another group began with low academic performance and continued to decline in performance. Known as Low Achievers, this group made up 14.4% of the sample group and tended to attend the lowest-quality schools, was the least engaged, and often lived in poverty.

An Ontario study revealed that in the high school grades, "10% of responding schools reported that they had ESL students, but no ESL programs or teachers to support them, up from 4% in 2000/01" (People for Education, 2003, p. 27). The study also states, "In 2002, 63% of ESL students failed the test [Grade 10 Literacy Test], compared to a 25% failure rate for all students writing the test" (People for Education, 2003, p. 28). The study did not speculate on the role of integrated services in this phenomenon; a few issues may be occurring, however. First, it is possible that although integrated service centres may be useful, the transfer of school responsibility begins to falter once students enter the secondary grades. Second, it is possible that when immigrating as students eligible for secondary school, young people lack services geared toward learning English. The need for positive school-readiness experiences extends far beyond early learning and requires family engagement at all levels of schooling.

## Influences that make parents more vulnerable to being unprepared for school

Research focused on the need for parent engagement as an asset in school readiness has highlighted several issues that make it difficult for parents to be engaged. These barriers or predispositions hinder engagement and therefore preparedness. Parent engagement and involvement are important in terms of readiness because, although the child may be in school during parent "readying" activities, readiness operates on a continuum and parent readiness is important at all points throughout a child's schooling.

Huntsinger and Jose (2009) note that immigrant status influences both the nature and the level of parent involvement and engagement. Turney and Kao (2009) also support this idea, finding that barriers to parental engagement are more pronounced among minority immigrant parents compared to native-born parents. This difference is especially important given that when racial and ethnic differences are controlled, the gap in school readiness among children is reduced by 25 to 50% (Brooks-Gunn & Markman, 2005). Lahaie (2008) found that a gap in math scores between children of immigrant parents who do not speak English in the home and children of immigrant parents who do speak English in the home, who were entering kindergarten for the first time, was consistent with a variety of other indicators such as "the number of children's books in the home, the frequency of the child looking at picture books, going to centre-based care prior to kindergarten, going to private school, and that the parent had already met with the teacher at least once" (p. 698).

Levine-Rasky (2009) conducted research at an elementary school with a Caucasian population that had always existed in prominence and a newcomer population that lacked deep roots within the school. The study found that the non-immigrant mothers used elements of social capital to stay engaged in the school and in their child's fate within the school:

> Mothers ... and others quoted ... present the kind of disposition toward the school that enables effective relationships. Their practice and knowledge are "aligned" with the school. A chief manifestation of this is the warm, even personal, relationships they had with teachers and the principal. (Levine-Rasky, 2009, p. 335)

The study also noted that some of the mothers knew how to "work the system" (p. 335) to gain special attention for their children and to intervene to produce favourable conditions for their children (p. 336). In contrast, immigrant parents from Eastern Europe interviewed in the study said their purpose for communicating with teachers was not to manoeuvre situations to favour their children but rather to solve problems that concerned their children. Levine-Rasky notes,

> Like other immigrant parents, they have the same desire to see their children succeed at school and as immigrants. Yet they refer to no particular strategies in their relations with the school. They do not 'work the system' or follow the rules of the field as do the insiders. (p. 337)

This study demonstrates the implicit aspects of school readiness and the implicit disadvantage that many immigrant mothers may face. Carreón, Drake, and Barton (2005) further note that parents, particularly immigrant parents, enter schools where structures and norms have already been established, and so they find themselves powerless to influence change or define their role within the school. Social capital, such as relationship-building practices with school staff, may allow parents to provide advantages for their children; however, these strategies are not often a part of school discourse used by immigrant mothers.

Our Place Family Resource and Early Years Centre in Kitchener, Ontario, offers reasons that immigrant parents may find adjusting to sending their children to school or having their children be successful in school difficult. The Centre compiled a report that explains that being socially isolated, especially when immigrating to a new country, can be extremely difficult for parents to manage and can interfere with other aspects related to having a productive and satisfying life:

> Newcomers to Canada move through several stages of adaptation before reaching the final stage of equal participation in Canada's economic, cultural, social and political life. In Canada, an extensive system of government-funded settlement services exists to address the pressing needs of newcomers during the initial stage of adaptation to their new country. After three years' residency, newcomers are entitled to apply for Canadian citizenship. At the same time, they lose their access to support from settlement agencies. For new Canadian families, the complex process of adaptation and integration will continue over many years and even to the next generation. During this process, some families will encounter challenges that can inhibit integration and lead to marginalization, social detachment and even radicalization. These families need assistance to overcome the barriers that are keeping them isolated in parallel communities. (Kampijan & Snyder, 2011, p. 8)

This comment suggests not only that there is an urgent need to help new Canadian families facing challenges upon their arrival, but that these challenges can persist and new challenges can arise. Furthermore, these challenges may provide reasons that immigrant families are less likely to engage in school readiness behaviours and to be ready for school, based on a continuum that persists throughout the child's school career. Being socially isolated in one's country of residence does not provide a nurturing situation in which issues of school readiness can be effectively addressed. Further isolation occurs when the dominant language is not spoken. Panferov (2010) studied differences in parents who did not speak English and how this factor affected their children's school readiness and success. Panferov notes,

> In terms of the family home being specifically supportive for developing second language literacy skills, reading and writing exposure in the home is crucial, as building literacy in the home, in turn, supports school literacy, which is essential to academic success. (p. 110)

Further, the study notes that when parents are not fluent in the new language, children in immigrant and refugee families are often used as translators for discussions that are not necessarily appropriate for children (p. 110). This point demonstrates the need to have supports such as translation services linked with schools and available to support families outside of school situations. The study also noted that immigrant families often have different perceptions of the value of school attendance and that those who attend school more frequently, as per North American customs and values, tend to fare better academically (p. 110). Education about issues related to school readiness and school success must target immigrant parents so that these discrepancies can be reduced or avoided altogether.

In addition to immigrant status, Griffith (1998) found that parents with lower socio-economic status often had lower involvement in their children's schooling. Suggested reasons for this difference include time conflicts such as work schedules and "attitudes and practices within the school that suggest parents lack the abilities to help" (Griffith, 1998; as cited in Barnyak & McNelly, 2009, p. 39). Cooper, Crosnoe, Suizzo, and Pituch (2010) noticed the association between poverty and children's academic achievement based on different racial groups. Black, Hispanic, and white families living in poverty were more likely to experience a negative association between their poverty and their child's academic success, whereas for Asian families, poverty did not appear to affect academic success in kindergarten significantly. Other barriers associated with family poverty cited by Geenen, Powers, and Lopez-Vasquez (2001) include fatigue among parents, a lack of awareness of their rights and school policies, and limited opportunities to engage in the school. Geenen et al. also explain that often limitations such as a lack of transportation or child care can restrict school involvement, as can language barriers between the parent and the school or classroom teacher.

Parker et al. (1999) noted that the family dynamic can have an impact on school readiness as well. For example, mothers' age and education level are linked to child outcomes associated with school readiness. In this study, children who had older mothers tended to be more independent (Parker et al., 1999, p. 418). Also, children whose mothers had higher education tended to have better "overall cognitive and language competencies" (Parker et al., 1999, p. 418). This finding is also noted by Noddings (2006):

> There are also parents who are either too tired or just uninterested. Some are so poorly educated that they cannot help. Some are intimidated by teachers and schools. They are embarrassed when they don't understand the assignment. Better-educated parents may react to an unclear assignment with irritation, but parents who have a history of failure in school may interpret their lack of understanding as proof of their own incompetence. (p. 125)

Again, the idea of parental efficacy emerges clearly, this time related to parents helping their children to complete schoolwork.

Lack of engagement has also been related to factors beyond the direct control of the parent and has instead been linked to the practices of teachers and administrators. A study by Barnyak and McNelly (2009) investigated teachers' and administrators' practices related to parent engagement behaviours in an urban school district. The study looked at district/school level practices, teacher/administrator practices, and teachers' and administrators' beliefs about parent engagement. The study revealed that at the school level, parents were unsure of parent policy decision-making, opportunities related to parent learning, and opportunities for parents to volunteer in the local school. At the teacher/administrator level, the study found that teachers rarely used things like newsletters, emails, or websites and instead used parent–teacher conferences or special information sheets to communicate with parents. In contrast, however, teachers stated that they were frequently available to speak with parents before and after school and during their preparation time. In terms of their beliefs about parent engagement based on communication, most teachers and administrators agreed that a variety of tools and methods would be beneficial to keep parents informed about the school and their child's academic progress. When teachers and administrators reported their own efficacy beliefs about parent engagement, a mismatch occurred in the sense that the beliefs that teachers and administrators held about effective ways to keep parents informed and engaged were not put into practice.

In another study, by Joshi, Eberly, and Konzal (2005), a survey was conducted to discover teachers' perceptions concerning reasons for a lack of parental involvement. The survey found that other time commitments were the main reason cited by teachers. Teachers perceived that parents have a hard time providing the basic needs of the families and that parents have a hard time understanding the language used in the school. A further perception concerned educational constraints of the parents and their difficulty comprehending the culture of the school. These perceptions may indicate that teachers see parents having barriers to engagement that are difficult to overcome.

In addition to the staff at the school, the school environment and structure can also have an impact on parent engagement. Griffith (1998) found that parents who had a child enrolled in a gifted or talented program, had multiple children enrolled in the schools, or perceived a safe, empowering, and positive school climate were more likely to participate in school activities. In contrast, Griffith found that in addition to race and low socio-economic status, having a child in a special-education program or an ESL program was related to less participation in school activities by parents. This finding is of concern, given the benefits that parental engagement and involvement can have on school readiness and school achievement.

It is important for schools to take an active role in encouraging parents to become engaged in their child's schooling. As Panferov (2010) states, this is especially true for immigrant parents: "We need to continue to learn how to better encourage parental involvement in the community schools and improve ELL school readiness, especially if parents are not literate themselves, or have had little or no previous formal schooling" (pp. 111–112). Again, immigrant parents need to be especially targeted in school-readiness initiatives and structural issues, such as creating safe school environments, and need to be included in efforts to improve engagement and readiness.

Because there are so many barriers to school engagement and involvement, efforts must be made to mitigate them. These efforts may occur both at a policy level and at a practical level.

## Conclusions of literature

The cumulative findings of this review indicate that school readiness involves more than ensuring children know basic content for the curriculum. It involves interactions among parents, children, and community support services, it begins early in a child's life, and it requires varying degrees of social, emotional, physical, and intellectual competence. There are discrepancies in what parents and teachers believe school readiness means, and there are also differences in parents' practices of school readiness. Parents who are immigrants or who are considered to be low-income earners are at an increased risk for not preparing their children for school. This gap may be due to a variety of barriers, including a lack of information about schools and school readiness. Government websites offer some information to parents about navigating the school and its resources in Ontario, and many community programs have been created to target parents who may benefit from information about school readiness from a student, parent, teacher, and community perspective. Overall, these programs have been shown to be related to increases in school readiness based on a variety of indicators. Further research should focus on the specific curriculum of these readiness programs and on the perceptions that parents hold about these programs both before and after the programs take place.

To understand school readiness, we must understand the complexities of working with immigrant families in Canadian schools. When researchers (such as those featured in this book) describe observations and interventions related to immigrant students and their families, we must recall the initial stages of entering the realm of school and the importance of these events. If readers add *school readiness* as an implication to each unique study featured in this book, the concept may help to promote critical thinking toward and a more holistic comprehension of the issues that immigrant families and school stakeholders currently face.

## REFERENCES

Anderson, K.J., & Minke, K.M. (2007). Parent involvement in education: Toward an understanding of parents' decision making. *Journal of Educational Research, 100*(5), 311–323. http://dx.doi.org/10.3200/JOER.100.5.311-323

Bandura, A. (1977, Mar). Self-efficacy: Toward a unifying theory of behavioral change. *Psychological Review, 84*(2), 191–215. http://dx.doi.org/10.1037/0033-295X.84.2.191 Medline:847061

Barbarin, O.A., Early, D., Clifford, R., Bryant, D., Frome, P., Burchinal, M., ... & Pianta, R. (2008). Parental conceptions of school readiness: Relation to ethnicity, socioeconomic status, and children's skills. *Early Education and Development, 19*(5), 671–701. http://dx.doi.org/10.1080/10409280802375257

Barnyak, N.C., & McNelly, T.A. (2009). An urban school district's parent involvement: A study of teachers' and administrators' beliefs and practices. *School Community Journal, 19*(1), 33–58.

Brooks-Gunn, J., & Markman, L.B. (2005, Spring). The contribution of parenting to ethnic and racial gaps in school readiness. *The Future of Children, 15*(1), 139–168. http://dx.doi.org/10.1353/foc.2005.0001 Medline:16130545

Carreón, G.P., Drake, C., & Barton, A. C. (2005). The importance of presence: Immigrant parents' school engagement experiences. *American Educational Research Journal, 42*(3), 465–498. http://dx.doi.org/10.3102/00028312042003465

Chazan-Cohen, R., Raikes, H., Brooks-Gunn, J., et al. (2009). Low-income children's school readiness: Parent contributions over the first five years. *Early Education and Development, 20*(6), 958–977. http://dx.doi.org/10.1080/10409280903362402

Cooper, C., Crosnoe, R., Suizzo, M., & Pituch, K. (2010). Poverty, race, and parental involvement during the transition to elementary school. *Journal of Family Issues, 31*(7), 859–883. http://dx.doi.org/10.1177/0192513X09351515

Dockett, S., & Perry, B. (2009). Readiness for school: A relational construct. *Australasian Journal of Early Childhood, 34*(1), 20–26.

Englund, M.M., Luckner, A.E., Whaley, G.J.L., & Egeland, B. (2004). Children's achievement in early elementary school: Longitudinal effects of parental involvement, expectations, and quality of assistance. *Journal of Educational Psychology, 96*(4), 723–730. http://dx.doi.org/10.1037/0022-0663.96.4.723

Entwisle, D.R., & Alexander, K.L. (1995). A parent's economic shadow: Family structure versus family resources as influences on early school achievement. *Journal of Marriage and the Family, 57*(2), 399–409. http://dx.doi.org/10.2307/353693

Geenen, S., Powers, L.E., & Lopez-Vasquez, A. (2001). Multicultural aspects of parent involvement in transition planning. *Exceptional Children, 67*(2), 265–282.

Giallo, R., Kienhuis, M., Treyvaud, K., & Matthews, J. (2008). A psychometric evaluation of the parent self-efficacy in managing the transition to school scale. *Australian Journal of Educational & Developmental Psychology, 8*, 36–48.

Graue, E. (2006). The answer is readiness—Now what is the question? *Early Education and Development, 17*(1), 43–56. http://dx.doi.org/10.1207/s15566935eed1701_3

Griffith, J. (1998). The relation of school structure and social environment to parent involvement in elementary schools. *Elementary School Journal, 99*(1), 53–80. http://dx.doi.org/10.1086/461916

Huntsinger, C.S., & Jose, P.E. (2009). Parental involvement in children's schooling: Different meanings in different cultures. *Early Childhood Research Quarterly, 24*(4), 398–410. http://dx.doi.org/10.1016/j.ecresq.2009.07.006

Janus, M., & Duku, E. (2007). The school entry gap: Socioeconomic, family, and health factors associated with children's school readiness to learn. *Early Education and Development, 18*(3), 375–403. http://dx.doi.org/10.1080/10409280701610796a

Joshi, A., Eberly, J., & Konzal, J. (2005). Dialogue across cultures: Teachers' perceptions about communication with diverse families. *Multicultural Education, 13*(2), 11–15.

Kampijan, W., & Snyder, D. (2011). Project Summary Information. Project: Family resource centres: Community settings that support social inclusion—Focus group for new Canadian families: Report (pp. 1–14). Unpublished: Canadian Association of Family Resource Programs.

Lahaie, C. (2008). School readiness of children of immigrants: Does parental involvement play a role? *Social Science Quarterly, 89*(3), 684–705. http://dx.doi.org/10.1111/j.1540-6237.2008.00554.x

Levine-Rasky, C. (2009). Dynamics of parent involvement at a multicultural school. *British Journal of Sociology of Education, 30*(3), 331–344. http://dx.doi.org/10.1080/01425690902812604

Martin, A., Ryan, R.M., & Brooks-Gunn, J. (2010, Apr). When fathers' supportiveness matters most: Maternal and paternal parenting and children's school readiness. *Journal of Family Psychology, 24*(2), 145–155. http://dx.doi.org/10.1037/a0018073 Medline:20438190

Noddings, N. (2006). *Critical lessons: What our schools should teach.* Cambridge: Cambridge University Press. http://dx.doi.org/10.1017/CBO9780511804625

Panferov, S. (2010). Increasing ELL parental involvement in our schools: Learning from the parents. *Theory into Practice, 49*(2), 106–112. http://dx.doi.org/10.1080/00405841003626551

Parker, F.L., Boak, A.Y., Griffin, K.W., Ripple, C., & Peay, L. (1999). Parent-child relationship, home learning environment, and school readiness. *School Psychology Review, 28*(3), 413–425.

People for Education. (2003). *The 2003 secondary school tracking report: Diminishing support in a harsher environment.* Retrieved October 10, 2010, from http://www.peopleforeducation.com/tracking/summrpts/second/03/full.PDF

Piotrkowski, C.S., Botsko, M., & Matthews, E. (2000). Parents' and teachers' beliefs about children's school readiness in a high-need community. *Early Childhood Research Quarterly, 15*(4), 537–558. http://dx.doi.org/10.1016/S0885-2006(01)00072-2

Ramey, C.T., & Ramey, S.L. (2004). Early learning and school readiness: Can early intervention make a difference? *Merrill-Palmer Quarterly, 50*(4), 471–491. http://dx.doi.org/10.1353/mpq.2004.0034

Suárez-Orozco, C. (2000). Identities under siege: Immigration stress and social mirroring among the children of immigrants. In A. Robben & M. Suárez-Orozco (Eds.), *Cultures under siege: Collective violence and trauma* (pp. 194–226). Cambridge, UK: Cambridge University Press.

Suárez-Orozco, C., Gaytán, F.X., Bang, H.J., Pakes, J., O'Connor, E., & Rhodes, J. (2010, May). Academic trajectories of newcomer immigrant youth. *Developmental Psychology, 46*(3), 602–618. http://dx.doi.org/10.1037/a0018201 Medline:20438174

Suárez-Orozco, C., Onaga, M., & Lardemelle, C. (2010). Promoting academic engagement among immigrant adolescents through school–family-community collaboration. *Professional School Counseling, 14*(1), 15–26.

Turney, K., & Kao, G. (2009). Barriers to school involvement: Are immigrant parents disadvantaged? *Journal of Educational Research, 102*(4), 257–271. http://dx.doi.org/10.3200/JOER.102.4.257-271

Zhang, X., Sun, L., & Gai, X. (2008). Perceptions of teachers and parents regarding school readiness. *Frontiers of Education in China, 3*(3), 460–471. http://dx.doi.org/10.1007/s11516-008-0030-6

# 3

# Immigrant students' health

*An overview of the need to improve our awareness and response to the health of immigrant children and their families within the educational context*

*Taunya Wideman-Johnston*

Health and health-related issues are often neglected when we consider the education of children. As schools are called upon to become more dynamic in their approaches to promoting the well-being of the whole child rather than just the academic lives of students, health care needs to be added to the conversation. When students are healthy, they are better able to engage in all aspects of the schooling experience, including those aspects that can assist in other areas of overall well-being such as access to community resources, meeting social needs, and developing societal norms. When health is compromised, not only are students unable to participate fully in important academic experiences, but they and their families can miss out on important community connections and interactions. This literature review is intended to provide an overview of some of the health issues that immigrants face as they settle in Canada. Readers will be able to use this information to add further dimension to the research studies discussed in this book. As we build an understanding of immigrants in the Canadian school context, we can refer to the role of health care, health promotion, and illness prevention as these issues pertain to several dimensions in Canadian education.

Canada is among the most diverse countries in the world. Close to 20% of Canada's population was born in another country, and the number of immigrants arriving in Canada increases every year (Gushulak, Pottie, Hatcher Roberts, Torres, & DesMeules, 2010;

Statistics Canada, 2008). The Canadian Council on Social Development (2006) estimates that by 2016, 25% of Canadian children will have immigrated to Canada from a different country. Populations of immigrant, refugee, ethno-cultural, and racialized (IRER) groups within Canada live throughout the country, all coming from different places with different needs and experiences. The diverse experiences of immigrants living in Canada, as well as differences in population sizes, contribute to the challenges in addressing the needs of IRER groups. Inconclusive, limited literature exists in regards to social determinants, mental health prevalence, and obstacles involved with access to care for IRER populations. In Canada, research being conducted in British Columbia, Ontario, and Quebec suggests that IRER groups have increased exposure to social determinants that result in mental health issues and illnesses in combination with migration, prejudice, and language barriers (Hansson, Tuck, Lurie, & McKenzie, 2009).

In addition, the limited information on refugee children entering Canada contributes to difficulty in determining their health needs. When immigrant children are not accompanied by their parent(s) or guardian(s), it is even more difficult to determine their health needs. Strategies to meet children's needs and protect them sufficiently may be lacking. Crowe (2006) explains the significance of the issue by saying that we must ask immigrant children to tell practitioners what they need.

## Implemented health policies for immigrant families

Health issues for immigrants arriving in Canada differ from the health needs of Canadian-born people. The prevalence of diseases differs in immigrants due to exposure, trauma, susceptibilities, migration, living conditions, social stratification, access to services and treatments, and genetics (Canadian Collaboration for Immigrant and Refugee Health, 2011). Immigration legislation in Canada requires that all permanent residents (refugees, refugee claimants, and some temporary residents) have a medical exam. The medical examination is considered a primary-care practice to assess potential medical issues, potential public health risks, and surveillance (Canadian Collaboration for Immigrant and Refugee Health, 2011). The following is an overview of the health policies that relate to immigrant families.

### Interim Federal Health Plan

The Interim Federal Health Plan (IFHP) provides temporary health coverage for certain immigrants (mostly refugees) until they are settled and qualify for coverage from the provincial health plan. The

IFHP is available only for emergency and critical health care needs and is usually available for only 12 months. The IFHP applies to the following health services:
- Only essential and emergency health services for the treatment and prevention of serious medical conditions and the treatment of emergency dental conditions;
- Contraception, prenatal and obstetrical care;
- Essential prescription medications; and
- Costs related to the Immigration Medical Examination by a designated medical practitioner. (Citizenship and Immigration Canada, 2001, 2012; for more information see http://www.cic.gc.ca/english/refugees/outside/arriving-healthcare.asp)

Services not covered by the IFHP include expensive medications, allergy and sensitivity testing, regular medical examinations and assessments, counselling, and more than one psychiatric consultation (Citizenship and Immigration Canada, 2001, 2012). Although immigrants and refugees have access to provincial health care and child benefit programs once their permanent residency is established, no programs specifically address the vulnerable situation of immigrant and refugee children (Crowe, 2006). Furthermore, in April 2012, the Canadian federal government announced a series of changes to the IFHP effective as of June 2012. The IFHP changes include the following:
- All refugees (excluding government-assisted refugees) no longer have access to medication coverage and vision and dental care;
- Individuals from designated countries of origin no longer have access to health care for urgent and essential care;
- All refugees are covered for the following medical conditions: issues related to public health concerns that are on the Public Health Agency diseases list and involve human transmission, and issues that concern public security where there is a danger to others. (Canadian Doctors for Refugee Care, 2013)

Health care workers across Canada have united to oppose these government health cuts, as many refugees are suffering or will suffer without access to medications and are at further risk for complications. There is also much concern for people from designated countries of origin having no access to care, which may, in turn, increase health costs (Canadian Doctors for Refugee Care, 2013).

### United Nations
The United Nations High Commission for Refugees (UNHCR) office in Canada, the Child Welfare League of Canada, and International

Social Service Canada (ISSC) hosted the National Roundtable on Separated Children Seeking Asylum in Canada in 2001. Participants included provincial and federal governments, child welfare authorities, and civil society. This roundtable was a strategy to address the issue of meeting the best interests of refugee children in Canada. A primary concern of this roundtable was refugee children separated from their parents and the support these children receive while in Canada. Little is known about child asylum seekers, and what is known is not favourable for the child. Child asylum seekers have a lower rate of success in claiming asylum than children coming to Canada with their parent(s) and also have a lower removal or deportation rate. So these children remain in host countries without access to support and adequate protection. The best-interest principle needs to include the whole child: health, psychosocial stability, family, education, legal representation, and access to the immigration and refugee process. With regards to the health of these children, further training and sensitization is needed. Many of these children have experienced trauma and, without adequate support, are at risk for further trauma. The roundtable was intended to start a conversation that needs to continue. It recognized that increased participation of the children being affected is needed and that a model for these children must be developed (Kumin & Chaikel, 2001).

## Canadian Collaboration for Immigrant and Refugee Health

The Canadian Collaboration for Immigrant and Refugee Health (CCIRH) is a national partnership that includes specialists, health practitioners, researchers, policy leaders, and immigrant community leaders who all support improving the health of immigrants and refugees. CCIRH also has a Knowledge Exchange Network (KEN), a translation project centred in improving the health of immigrants and refugees by providing evidence-based recommendations and resources to the medical community and immigrant community. The central focus of the CCIRH Guideline Project is to develop evidence-based recommendations for preventable health issues for immigrants and refugees (Canadian Collaboration for Immigrant and Refugee Health, 2012).

At present, the Canadian federal government is investigating the number of refugees entering Canada with high health care needs. Citizenship and Immigration Canada has been asked to explore strategies to lower the number of high-needs refugees in order to relieve strain on Canada's health care system. Citizenship and Immigration Canada has implemented an approach by placing a cap on refugees with specific health problems and moving from a global settlement approach to focusing on three to five refugee populations. Further limiting refugees with health needs entering Canada is extremely concerning as it puts the most vulnerable at risk. This concern is especially pronounced when considering that in April 2012, cuts had already been made to refugee and refugee claimant health care and services (Canadian Doctors for Refugee Care, 2013; Keung, 2013; Shingler, 2013).

## Healthy development for immigrant children

Healthy childhood development requires a supportive family, a safe environment, having nutritional needs met, education, and access to health care (Hanvey, 2002). Being able to attend school and participate in schooling activities is critical to creating positive student involvement and development within the school environment (Thies, 1999; Wideman-Johnston, 2010). Pushor (2011) describes the need for educators to look inward and stand with families, rather than standing apart from them. Immigrant children may have lost their sense of security because of the adversity and instability many of them have faced. Not only are they coping with the day-to-day struggles of growing up, but they are learning a new way of life in a new country. Economically, the family may be struggling, may speak no or limited English, and may not know what living in Canada involves. It is important to note that the majority of immigrant children speak another language at home (Organisation for Economic Co-operation and Development, 2012). If these children experienced trauma in their home country, it can affect their development and may produce mental health ailments (Cook, 2006). Depending on their situation, these children may have had no experience in formal schooling and may be illiterate. A different language may not be the main challenge within the family; rather, different health care beliefs, expectations, and preventive measures may affect the health care of immigrants (Canadian Collaboration for Immigrant and Refugee Health, 2011; Hamilton, Marshall, Rummens, Fenta, & Simich, 2011; Hyman, 2007). All of these issues affect the health of immigrant students, and when students are not healthy, educational achievement is difficult. When they lack access to health resources and services, immigrants are at greater risk for health issues compared to Canadian-born children (Alberta Health Services, 2009). A gap remains in research with regards to immigrant students' health, school context, and adjustment (Blake, Ledsky, Goodenow, & O'Donnell, 2001).

## Immigrant students' health and the school environment

We know the school environment affects children's lives (Hamilton et al., 2011). Research reveals the importance of nurturing school environments and the promotion of positive mental health to influence children positively. Further research indicates that negative parental views of school can affect the child's mental health. Entering school as an immigrant student can be a difficult transition, filled with obstacles that may be overwhelming. Immigrant children enter a new school system that includes different learning styles and expectations, and they may not have any experience with formal schooling. Children are exposed to a new language; they may have little or no knowledge of Canada's official languages and may lack literacy in their first language (Cook, 2006; Hamilton et al., 2011). With specific relation to their health and well-being, immigrant students may be exposed to pathogens that they lack resistance to, as well as dietary differences that can lead to food allergies (Alberta Health Services, 2009). Oxman-Martinez, Gagnon, Gravel, Lacroix, and Lefebvre (2005) explored the mental and physical health of immigrant and refugee children in Montreal, Quebec. Sixty-six percent of these children were living with an income level below the poverty line, and 25% had not accessed health care services in the past year. Schools and school boards have requested further resources that are necessary to aid families and schools during the settlement period (Cook, 2006; Crowe, 2006).

Immigrant students are at risk for poor health that may further impede their overall school experience and success. Health issues cited in the United States that can further impede educational experiences and outcomes include the following:

- Low socio-economic status and poverty contributing to poor health outcomes;
- Higher mortality and morbidity for immigrant children than for US children born to immigrant parents;
- Family separation;
- Political violence, extreme hardships;
- Malnutrition, overweight, and obesity;
- Lower levels of physical activity;
- Asthma;
- Emotional well-being (anxiety, depression, substance abuse);
- ADHD and conduct disorders;
- Iron deficiency anemia. (Canadian Collaboration for Immigrant and Refugee Health, 2011; Perreira & Ornelas, 2011)

Hamilton, Marshall, Rummens, Fenta, and Simich's (2011) research revealed a significant association between immigrant parents' perception of school, child behaviour, and emotional health.

Further, it indicated that a child's behaviour and emotional health may be influenced by the school environment through parental perceptions and involvement. Creating relationships between parents and the school contributes to the social supports available to the family and may assist with positive emotional health and behaviour. Knowledge regarding immigrant children's health is critical for the school community to provide health policies and programs to support these students.

## Immigrant students' mental health and the school environment

Mental health depends on a multitude of factors that pertain to the individual, the family, and the community with respect to both past and present experiences. The IRER population is at risk for mental health problems and illness as a result of the stress and traumatic experiences individuals may have endured; such experiences may foster resilience or may lead to day-to-day struggles (Hansson et al., 2009). Compounding the issue of potential mental health challenges is the lack of resources available to this population. Specifically within mental health, immigrants are at risk for post-traumatic stress disorder (PTSD) (Alberta Health Services, 2009; Canadian Mental Health Association, 2003). Approximately 9% of refugees suffer from PTSD; for children, the prevalence of PTSD is 11%. PTSD symptoms include somatic symptoms, sleep disorders, and further mental health issues such as depression and panic disorders (Rousseau, Pottie, Thombs, Munoz, & Jurick, 2011). If PTSD is not adequately treated, approximately a third of individuals will have further mental health challenges. For this reason, it is essential that recommendations be put forward that children with PTSD be treated with cultural sensitivity in a safe and trustworthy environment Having an interpreter to support family communication is another helpful strategy. Educators who provide empathy, reassurance, and advocacy are also essential to the recovery process of PTSD. The research exploring PTSD and children is limited, and further research and further support are needed with regards to culturally adapted psychological interventions (Rousseau, Pottie, Thombs, Munoz, & Jurick, 2011; White, Tutt, Rude, Mutwiri, & Senevonghachack, 2011).

The support of the educational community, including both classmates and teachers, is crucial in providing protection against mental health issues among immigrant students (Oppedal & Roysamb, 2004). Research has also linked parental involvement in school and positive perspectives about the school atmosphere (Griffith, 1998;

Hamilton et al., 2011; Soodak & Erwin, 2000). Research reveals that immigrant parents may be less involved in schools than non-immigrant parents (Hamilton et al., 2011).

The extent to which education interacts with the overall health needs of immigrant students has yet to be thoroughly explored and documented (Blake, Ledsky, Goodenow, & O'Donnell, 2001). For instance, the support and role modelling of teachers in the lives of immigrant students needs to be further explored. It has yet to be determined whether educators are further sources of institutional discrimination or whether immigrant students who are facing health issues are already experiencing stress when educators become involved (Oppedal, Roysamb, & Sam, 2004). Further research exploring the involvement of friends and classmates with regards to bullying and disrespect of immigrant students both within and outside of their ethnic culture is also needed (Oppedal, Roysamb, & Sam, 2004).

## Discussion and recommendations

Educational implications for immigrant students and their health are multi-faceted and remain difficult to access with the limited information available. Better understanding of acculturation and migration is necessary (Perreira & Ornelas, 2011). Much emphasis remains on the need for further funding and coverage of health care for immigrant students and their families (Canadian Doctors for Refugee Care, 2013).

To begin to improve the health status of immigrants, we need increased collaboration and communication among stakeholders to inform both health programs and policy (Hamilton et al., 2011; Hansson et al., 2009). To further understand the needs of immigrant students, we must continue to focus on child-centred services and resources within communities with further research to develop and support these programs and services. The improved resources and services must include social, emotional, mental health, language, and recreation programs (Canadian Collaboration for Immigrant and Refugee Health, 2011; Crowe, 2006; Hamilton et al., 2011). Within these resources and programs, we must be sensitive to the needs of immigrant families and children. To ensure needs are met, stakeholders must collaborate to continue to develop programs for immigrant families. Sensitivity to needs also includes an increase in multilingual health care professionals and increased cultural knowledge among them, with an emphasis on the needs of immigrant children (Perreira & Ornelas, 2011). Within health, further research is required in perceptions of health and patterns of health in different areas where there are immigrant children so that we can develop further preventive health and treatment programs (Canadian Collaboration for Immigrant and Refugee Health, 2011; Perreira & Ornelas, 2011). Specifically within education, educators need to collaborate and ensure the academic, emotional, and social needs of immigrant students and families are being met (Pushor, 2011). Unless we take a holistic approach to the education of immigrant students, ill health may occur. Healthy, positive development for immigrant students requires the complex integration of many facets of mainstream society (Oppedal, Roysamb, & Sam, 2004). With further exploration and the incorporation of further research regarding health knowledge and resources for immigrant students, their families, and educators, we can achieve more prevention-oriented health care (Blake, Ledsky, Goodenow, & O'Donnell, 2001).

Unfortunately, a double standard appears to be occurring here. We often rely on statistical information to develop public policy. Some research (Canadian Collaboration for Immigrant and Refugee Health, 2011; Canadian Doctors for Refugee Care, 2013; Crowe, 2006; Hyman, 2007; Hamilton et al., 2011) finds that immigrant populations are less likely to access public health resources in Canada; but with a closer look, one can certainly argue that immigrant populations may be less familiar with, and thus less likely aware of, all the resources available to them. In addition, cultural barriers related to mental health issues may prevent immigrant populations from seeking the required assistance from our Eurocentric processes. It is important to also consider the severe limitations and lack of coverage in Canada's health policy for refugees. Refugees are not able to access health care fully, and consequently their health needs are not on record. Of course, when it is convenient for policy-makers, this lack may be interpreted as indicating fewer needs in these populations.

## Conclusion

If children do not have opportunities to maintain well-being, their health, education, and future employment all face potential consequences. Healthy growth and development are essential not only to maintaining health but to our future economic well-being (Perreira & Ornelas, 2011). With the present health obstacles immigrant families face, students are at a disadvantage in achieving optimal development, an outcome that affects their academic journey. Government officials, health professionals, and educators must collaborate to ensure that immigrants' health needs are being met with improved research, programs, and policy development. The required information and conversations must begin with immigrant families. When immigrants lack access to adequate health care, we simply know too little about their health status and needs.

# REFERENCES

Alberta Health Services. (2009). *Diversity and Alberta health services: Diversity resources.* Retrieved from http://www.crha-health.ab.ca/programs/diversity/diversity_resources/health_div_pops/immigrants.htm

Blake, S.M., Ledsky, R., Goodenow, C., & O'Donnell, L. (2001, Mar). Receipt of school health education and school health service among adolescent immigrants in Massachusetts. *Journal of School Health, 71*(3), 105–113. http://dx.doi.org/10.1111/j.1746-1561.2001.tb07302.x Medline:11314274

Canadian Collaboration for Immigrant and Refugee Health. (2011). Evidence-based clinical guidance for immigrants and refugees. *Canadian Medical Association Journal.* http://dx.doi.org/10.1503/cmaj.090313

Canadian Council on Social Development (CCSD). (2006). *The progress of Canada's children and youth.* Ottawa: Renouf. Retrieved from http://www.ccsd.ca/pccy/2006/pdf/pccy_2006.pdf

Canadian Doctors for Refugee Care. (2013). *The issue.* Retrieved from http://www.doctorsforrefugeecare.ca/the-issue.html

Canadian Mental Health Association. (2003). *Immigrant and refugee mental health.* Retrieved from http://www.cmha.ca/public_policy/immigrant-and-refugee-mental-health-backgrounder/#.Uua6tnn0BO0

Citizenship and Immigration Canada. (2001). *Interim Federal Health Program: Information handbook for health care providers.* Edmonton: FAS Bennett Administration. Retrieved from http://wiki.straightjacketstudio.com/images/7/7e/IFHProvidersHandbook.pdf

Citizenship and Immigration Canada. (2012). *Health care – Refugees.* Retrieved from http://www.cic.gc.ca/english/refugees/outside/arriving-healthcare.asp

Cook, S. (2006). Canadian School Boards Association on meeting the language learning and settlement needs of immigrant children and youth in Canada's school systems: CSBA consultation paper on second language learning. Prepared by Alberta School Boards Association, British Columbia Trustees Association, Ontario Public School Boards' Association. Retrieved from http://www.opsba.org/index.php?q=system/files/CSBA_Draft_Consultation_SLL.pdf

Crowe, S. (2006). Immigrant and refugee children in middle childhood: An overview. Prepared for the Middle Childhood Initiative of the National Children's Alliance. Retrieved from http://www.nationalchildrensalliance.com/nca/pubs/2006/Immigrant%20and%20Refugee%20Children%20in%20their%20Middle%20Years.pdf

Griffith, J. (1998). The relation of school structure and social environment to parent involvement in elementary schools. *Elementary School Journal, 99*(1), 53–80. http://dx.doi.org/10.1086/461916

Gushulak, B.D., Pottie, K., Hatcher Roberts, J., Torres, S., & DesMeules, M. (2010). Migration and health in Canada: Health in the global village. [Epub ahead of print]. *Canadian Medical Association Journal.* Medline:20584934

Hamilton, H.A., Marshall, L., Rummens, J.A., Fenta, H., & Simich, L. (2011, Jun). Immigrant parents' perceptions of school environment and children's mental health and behavior. *Journal of School Health, 81*(6), 313–319. http://dx.doi.org/10.1111/j.1746-1561.2011.00596.x Medline:21592126

Hansson E., Tuck A., Lurie S., & McKenzie K., for the Task Group of the Services Systems Advisory Committee, Mental Health Commission of Canada. (2009). Improving mental health services for immigrant, refugee, ethno-cultural and racialized groups: Issues and options for service improvement. Retrieved from http://www.mentalhealthcommission.ca/SiteCollectionDocuments/Key_Documents/en/2010/Issues_Options_FINAL_English%2012Nov09.pdf

Hanvey, L. (2002, Jun). Middle childhood: Building on the early years: A discussion paper. Ottawa: National Children's Alliance.

Hyman, I. (2007). *Immigration and health: reviewing evidence of the healthy immigrant effect in Canada*. CERIS Working Paper No. 55. Toronto: Joint Centre of Excellence for Research on Immigration and Settlement.

Keung, N. (2013, Jun 17). Toronto really urges Ottawa to reverse refugee health cuts. *The Toronto Star*. Retrieved from http://www.thestar.com/news/gta/2013/06/17/toronto_rally_urges_ottawa_to_reverse_refugee_health_cuts.html

Kumin, J., & Chaikel, D. (2001). Taking the agenda forward: The roundtable on separated children seeking asylum in Canada. *Refuge: Canada's Periodical on Refugees, 20*(2), 73–77. Retrieved from http://pi.library.yorku.ca/ojs/index.php/refuge/article/viewFile/21257/19928

Oppedal, B., & Roysamb, E. (2004, Apr). Mental health, life stress and social support among young Norwegian adolescents with immigrant and host national background. *Scandinavian Journal of Psychology, 45*(2), 131–144. http://dx.doi.org/10.1111/j.1467-9450.2004.00388.x Medline:15016267

Oppedal, B., Roysamb, E., & Sam, D.L. (2004). The effect of acculturation and social support on change in mental health among young immigrants. *International Journal of Behavioral Development, 28*(6), 481–494. Retrieved from http://www.randf.co.uk/journals/pp/01650254.html. http://dx.doi.org/10.1080/01650250444000126

Organisation for Economic Co-operation and Development. (2012). Untapped skills: Realising the potential of immigrant students, *Programme for International Student Assessment*. Retrieved from: http://www.oecd.org/edu/Untapped%20Skills.pdf

Oxman-Martinez, J., Gagnon, A., Gravel, S., Lacroix, M., & Lefebvre, C. (2005). *A comparative study of Immigrant and refugee children and youth in Quebec (IRCYQ)*. Quebec, QC: Fond Québécois de Recherche Société et Culture [FQRSC].

Perreira, K.M., & Ornelas, I.J. (2011, Spring). The physical and psychological well-being of immigrant children. *Future of Children, 21*(1), 195–218. http://dx.doi.org/10.1353/foc.2011.0002 Medline:21465861

Pushor, D. (2011, September). Looking out, looking in: A partnership approach respects the strengths and knowledge of families. *Educational Leadership, 69*(1), 65–68.

Rousseau, C., Pottie, K., Thombs, B., Munoz, M., & Jurick, T. (2011). *Appendix 11: Post traumatic stress disorder: Evidence review for newly arriving immigrants and refugees*. Canadian Collaboration for Immigrant and Refugee Health. Retrieved from www.cmaj.ca/content/suppl/2010/06/07/cmaj.090313.DC1/imm-ptsd-11-at.pdf. http://dx.doi.org/10.1503/cmaj.090313

Shingler, B. (2013, Sep 3). Canadian government examined limiting refugees with health policies. *The Toronto Star*. Retrieved from http://www.thestar.com/news/canada/2013/09/03/canadian_government_examined_limiting_refugees_with_health_problems.html

Soodak, L.C., & Erwin, E.J. (2000). Valued member or tolerated participant: Parents' experiences in inclusive early childhood settings. *Journal of the Association for Persons with Severe Handicaps, 25*(1), 29–41. http://dx.doi.org/10.2511/rpsd.25.1.29

Statistics Canada. (2008). *Canada's ethnocultural mosaic, 2006 census*. Statistics Canada Catalogue no. 97562XIE2006001. Ottawa April 2. Analysis Series, 2006 Census.

Thies, K.M. (1999, Dec). Identifying the educational implications of chronic illness in school children. *Journal of School Health, 69*(10), 392–397. http://dx.doi.org/10.1111/j.1746-1561.1999.tb06354.x Medline:10685375

White, J., Tutt, S., Rude, D., Mutwiri, B., & Senevonghachack, O. (2011). Executive summary: Post traumatic stress disorder: The lived experience of immigrant, refugee and visible minority women. Retrieved from http://www.pwhce.ca/ptsd-immigrant.htm

Wideman-Johnston, T. (2010). *The academic journey of students with chronic gastrointestinal illness: Narratives from daughters and their mothers* (Unpublished master's thesis). Nipissing University, North Bay, ON.

# 4

# School-based interventions for refugee children and youth

## Canadian and international perspectives

*Marta Young and K. Jacky Chan*

Canada has a long history of being a sanctuary for refugees (Kaprielian-Churchill, 1996), dating back to the American Revolution in the 1700s. The United Nations High Commissioner for Refugees has recently estimated that there are more than 200,000 refugees in Canada (UNHCR, 2013), half of them children or adolescents. Of further relevance, the number of refugee children and adolescents living in Canada is projected to increase significantly over the next decades (Citizenship and Immigration Canada, 2012). It is thus imperative that key stakeholders—such as educators, social service providers, and mental health professionals—gain a comprehensive understanding of the psychosocial challenges faced by refugee children and adolescents as they resettle in Canada. In this chapter, we provide an overview of the issues and challenges faced by refugee children and adolescents pre- and post-migration. We then review international and Canadian school-based intervention programs.

Given that the majority of refugee children and adolescents attend school, the school setting is an optimal venue for interventions to be developed and implemented to address psychosocial challenges. From an ecological standpoint, it is crucial that comprehensive school-based interventions include not only the students themselves but also their parents and teachers (Bronfenbrenner, 1979). We conclude this chapter by discussing the factors that facilitate or hinder the successful delivery of such interventions.

## Traumatic events and stressors experienced by refugee children and youth

Before we explore the issues and challenges refugee children and adolescents face, we must emphasize that their experiences vary greatly. Depending on the particular contexts, the extent and types of traumatic events survived will differ within and across refugee groups. For children, the following factors have been found to affect their individual experiences: age at flight, gender, country of origin, culture, religion, and socio-economic status (Kaprielian-Churchill, 1996). The current literature groups the challenges and stressors faced by refugee children and adolescents into three main stages: pre-flight (i.e., still living in the country of origin), flight (the journey to a safe haven), and finally resettling in a new country (Fazel & Stein, 2002; Lustig et al., 2004).

Refugee children from war-torn or unstable socio-political regions are typically forced to flee their homes, often at a moment's notice, to escape persecution and violence (Fazel & Stein, 2002). These children often witness the murders and/or mass killings of family members, neighbours, and friends (Lustig et al., 2004). For instance, in a sample of 500 refugee children fleeing conflicts in Mozambique, 77% reported witnessing murders and/or mass killings (Boothby, Upton, & Sultan, 1991). Similarly, among a group of 364 internally displaced children in Bosnia, 40% reported seeing a parent or a sibling killed or seriously injured (Goldstein, Wampler, & Wise, 1997).

Increasingly, in addition to experiencing horrific violence, a significant number of children and adolescents, in countries such as Sierra Leone and the Democratic Republic of Congo, are engaged in combat or commit other acts of interpersonal violence (Betancourt, McBain, Newnham, & Brennan, 2013; Hecker, Hermenau, Maedl, Hinkel, Schauer, & Elbert, 2013). Non-governmental organizations, such as Child Soldiers International (2001), have estimated that more than 300,000 children under the age of 18 have fought worldwide. Although many are abducted and forced by government military forces or other armed groups to take up arms, some children join in search of a relatively more *stable* life amidst chaos. For some, it is a means of securing food or meeting the need to belong. This reasoning is especially the case for children who are orphaned due to war. The reality of being a child soldier is harsh, however, and many are victims and/or witnesses of significant neglect and/or physical, emotional, and/or sexual abuse (Lustig et al., 2004). These acts of abuse may take many forms and typically include indoctrination, physical beatings, torture, sexual assault, or rape (Betancourt, Agnew-Blais, Gilman, Williams, & Ellis, 2010).

In addition to traumatic events experienced in their country of origin, many refugee children encounter additional hardships and trauma during flight (Lustig et al., 2004). The journey itself is often physically and emotionally exhausting, often made with little food or adequate shelter. In many cases, refugees are confronted by dangerous situations and, as a result, experience further acts of abuse or violence (e.g., physical or sexual assaults of self or others, death of loved ones, or being thrust again into a war zone).

It is also important to highlight that a significant number of refugee children and adolescents become separated from their parents, family members, or caretakers either in the country of origin or during flight (Fazel & Stein, 2002). The separations are often due to the chaotic circumstances of war when family members get lost in crowds or are not together when a sudden, mass exodus begins. In other cases, children and youth are separated from their parents due to death or serious injury. In some situations, parents make the difficult decision not to accompany their children due to lack of funds to pay smugglers for all family members or because they believe their children will have a greater chance of surviving and being accepted in a safe country (Fazel & Stein, 2002). Regardless of the reasons, unaccompanied minors are more likely to endure abuse during flight and, not surprisingly, have significantly more difficulties during resettlement (Stewart, 2011).

Many refugee children and youth encounter additional trauma and hardship while living in refugee camps and in detention centres for asylum seekers (Lustig et al., 2004). Living conditions in refugee camps are typically poor, with inadequate water, food, and medical care (Harrell-Bond, 2000; Paardekooper, de Jong, & Hermanns, 1999). In addition, refugee camps are often unsafe; witnessing or experiencing acts of violence (e.g., attacks, rapes, deaths by suicide) is common (Rothe, Lewis, Castillo-Matos, Martinez, Busquets, & Martinez, 2002). Detention centres in Australia (Mares, Newman, Dudley, & Gale, 2002), the United Kingdom (Lorek et al., 2009), and the United States (Welch & Schuster, 2005) have also been criticized for their inhumane and harsh living conditions. Furthermore, children are often forcibly separated from their parents, putting them at greater risk for physical and emotional neglect (Mares et al., 2002). We note too that the issue of detaining refugee children and adolescents in Canada has recently gained significant attention in the media as the federal government moves forward with its agenda to expand the use of detention centres for refugee claimants (Canadian Broadcasting Corporation [CBC], 2012).

## Psychological impact of trauma

Given the multiple traumas and adversities faced by many refugee children and youth pre-migration and during flight, it is not surprising that a significant number exhibit mental health issues and adjustment difficulties once in Canada (Fazel & Stein, 2002; Stewart, 2011). The traumatic experiences survived before resettling in Canada often elicit immediate and intense psychological responses in refugee children and adolescents (Lustig et al., 2004), including a general sense of insecurity, anxiety, anger, and/or avoidance. As a result, they may develop emotional coping strategies that, while appropriate in the immediate contexts, are maladaptive in the long run (Lustig et al., 2004).

Resettlement is also fraught with several acculturative challenges that some view as "secondary trauma" (Fazel & Stein, 2002). Many refugee children and adolescents describe feelings of disconnection and isolation from their new cultural surroundings during the initial stages of adjustment (Lustig et al., 2004). These feelings are further complicated as the children mourn their loss of homeland, family, friends, and material possessions left behind. In a sample of Montreal refugee families, close to 40% of refugee children interviewed described experiencing difficulties in adapting to living in Montreal two years post-migration (Morantz, Rousseau, & Heymann, 2012).

Refugee children and youth who have participated in combat as child soldiers are particularly at risk (de Silva, Hobbs, & Hanks, 2001; Macksoud & Aber, 1996). Many develop a distorted sense of self due to combat experiences and abuses suffered in the camps. In addition, child soldiers often believe that their violent behaviours were justified. In a sample of Mozambican child soldiers, Boothby, Upton, and Sultan (1991) found a significant correlation between time spent in combat and difficulties refraining from morally wrong behaviours.

Not surprisingly, refugee children and adolescents exhibit symptoms of post-traumatic stress disorder (PTSD). Symptoms specific to children include disorganized or agitated behaviours, repetitive play about the trauma (in younger children), nightmares, trauma-specific re-enactment, avoidance behaviours, flashbacks, and symptoms of hyper-arousal (American Psychiatric Association, 2000). High PTSD prevalence rates have been documented in children and adolescents living in war-torn countries. For instance, researchers found that close to 25% of children living in regions of Palestine with active military conflicts suffered from PTSD (Thabet, Abed, & Vostanis, 2002). They also found that the PTSD prevalence rate increased to 60% for Palestinian children who had had personal exposure to severe acts of violence and losses (Thabet et al., 2002). In Iraq, up to 80%

of children suffered from PTSD (Dyregrov, Gjestad, & Raundalen, 2002). Very similar prevalence rates were observed among children and youth in Rwanda (Schaal & Elbert, 2006) and Sudan (Morgos, Worden, & Gupta, 2007).

A significant proportion of refugee children and adolescents also develop co-morbid psychological difficulties, such as symptoms of depression and/or anxiety. A high co-morbidity rate between PTSD and depression was found for children (Thabet, Abed, & Vostanis, 2004) and adolescents (Elbedour, Onwuegbuzie, Ghannam, Whitcome, & Abu Hein, 2007) as for adults. Among children, symptoms of anxiety typically included dependent behaviours, such as clinging to parents, fear of falling asleep in the dark, and fear of being alone (Montgomery & Foldspang, 2005).

## Challenges experienced by refugee families

Adjustment challenges faced by refugee families also have a significant effect on the well-being of refugee children and adolescents. It is well documented, for example, that parental distress is closely associated with problematic behaviours and emotional difficulties in refugee children (Almqvist & Broberg, 1999; McCloskey & Southwick, 1996; Pawliuk, Grizenko, Chan-Yip, Gantous, Mathew, & Nguyen, 1996; Short & Johnston, 1997). Similarly, a diagnosis of PTSD in either parent is a significant risk factor for the mental health of refugee children and adolescents (Kinzie, Sack, Angell, Manson, & Rath, 1986). Prolonged parental unemployment has also been identified as a risk factor for a child's psychological well-being (Tousignant, Habimana, Biron, Malo, Sidoli-LeBlanc, & Bendris, 1999).

Differential acculturation trajectories between parents and children have been consistently identified as a source of conflict in refugee families (Hyman, Vu, & Beiser, 2000; Morantz et al., 2012; Stewart, 2011). In many families, refugee children assimilate and adapt to the Canadian culture more rapidly than their parents. Refugee parents tend to keep transnational ties with family members still residing in their country of origin (Morantz et al., 2012). Refugee parents are also more likely to socialize with members of their own ethno-cultural group, whereas refugee children and adolescents tend to acquire the behaviours and values of peers from diverse ethnocultural groups, especially within the school context. Given cultural differences in communication styles and underlying cultural values, conflicts often occur between refugee parents and their children on issues related to academic expectations, acceptable social and sexual behaviours (e.g., family obligations, dating), and discipline (Dumbrill, 2009; Hyman et al., 2000; Merali, 2005).

Research has also shown that parental involvement in refugee children's education has a positive influence on their school behaviour and academic achievement (Hamilton, 2004). Parental involvement in the school setting also facilitates, to a certain extent, parents' acculturation to Canadian society (Rousseau & Guzder, 2008). We should underline, however, that refugee parents often face significant barriers in terms of their ability to engage in their children's education. Literacy issues and language proficiency have been repeatedly cited as important obstacles to parental involvement (Kanu, 2008; Merali, 2005; Weine, 2008). Other barriers include heavy parental work schedules, unfamiliarity with formal education systems, and a sense of embarrassment and failure when parents discuss their children's academic struggles (Weine, 2008). Furthermore, some parents carry culturally specific notions where teachers are viewed as the experts, and thus parental engagement in the school setting is seen as disrespectful. Although many parents have high hopes for their children's education, they often lack a sense of self-efficacy as parents (Dumbrill, 2009; Weine, 2008).

## Challenges experienced by refugee children and youth in the school system

In the school setting, refugee children and adolescents often experience academic and interpersonal difficulties (Kanu, 2008; Stewart, 2011; Yau, 1995). For many, academic difficulties are related to language barriers. Schools that have implemented programs designated for English-language learning (ELL) or *français langue seconde* (FLS) are found to be helpful in assisting students acquire English or French proficiency (Kanu, 2008; Yau, 1995). Other difficulties are related to the fact that refugee students may have experienced a disrupted flow in their formal education in their country of origin or in refugee camps, leading to lacunae in basic literacy and/or numeracy (Stewart, 2011). In Canada, some refugee children who do not have official refugee status do not attend school as their parents fear deportation (Yau, 1995). In other cases, refugee children are placed in a particular grade level based on age and not their actual academic abilities (Kanu, 2008). The impact of a disrupted education becomes particularly problematic when students are in high school and decisions are being made in terms of their placement in different academic streams (i.e., university, college, or workplace bound). A significant proportion of refugee students are placed in the workplace-bound stream, even though many have clear aspirations to attend post-secondary institutions (Yau, 1995).

Additional factors that hinder the academic performance of refugee students include their heightened frustration when their parents do not empathize with their academic difficulties or are unable to help due to their limited education and lack of proficiency in English or French (Kanu, 2008; Stewart, 2011). Unaccompanied refugee minors are at a much greater risk of dropping out of school (Stewart, 2011; Yau, 1995). For instance, the emotional distress associated with being separated from parents and family members has been found to be a significant impediment to their academic performance (Kanu, 2008). In addition, unaccompanied refugee minors often have difficulties concentrating at school and completing their homework due to the fact that they work long hours at unskilled jobs to support themselves financially (Kanu, 2008; Stewart, 2011).

A significant number of refugee students also experience interpersonal difficulties, especially with peers. In particular, they experience challenges in developing and/or maintaining social relationships (Stewart, 2011). Refugee students often develop feelings of isolation and marginalization within the school setting given their academic, emotional, and language difficulties (Hyman et al., 2000). These feelings are particularly prominent among students who attend schools that are less culturally and linguistically diverse. Furthermore, issues related to bullying and racial discrimination were also found to be common for refugee students (Yau, 1995). In many cases, refugee students attributed their experiences of being bullied or discriminated against to their refugee status or their cultural origins.

## Protective factors and resilience

Although a significant number of refugee children and adolescents struggle during resettlement, several protective mechanisms have been identified (Fazel & Stein, 2002; Lustig et al., 2004). At the individual level, connections with the child's heritage culture act as a protective factor against psychological distress (Lustig et al., 2004). For instance, religious beliefs, active community involvement, and a sense of solidarity with members of the same heritage culture were found to be inversely correlated with psychological distress among a group of Tibetan refugee children displaced in India (Servan-Schreiber, Le Lin, & Birmaher, 1998). A positive personality disposition also acted as a key factor in fostering resilience among refugee children and adolescents (Fazel & Stein, 2002).

At the family level, the emotional well-being of parents, as described previously, is an important protector for refugee children's well-being (Almqvist & Broberg, 1999). Similarly, social support from a familiar and trusted adult (e.g., parent, friend of the family, older sibling) has been found to promote well-being during difficult times among refugee children (Melville & Brinton Lykes, 1992). Outside of the home, positive relationships with peers are associated with refugee children's sense of self-worth and social adjustment (Almqvist & Broberg, 1999). Furthermore, positive experiences in school, such as a perceived sense of safety and belonging, have also been identified as important (Fazel, Reed, Panter-Brick, & Stein, 2012). In particular, a sense of belonging is positively correlated with a positive self-concept, greater social skills, and higher academic achievement, and negatively correlated with depression, social distress, and social rejection among refugee students (Kia-Keating & Ellis, 2007).

## Barriers to accessing services

Various support services exist for refugee children and youth, ranging from support groups in resettlement organizations to programs offered by community-based mental health services and local hospitals (Chiumento, Nelki, Dutton, & Hughes, 2011; O'shea, Hodes, Down, & Bramley, 2000). However, several barriers to access have been identified in the literature (Ellis, Miller, Baldwin, & Abdi, 2011; Lustig et al., 2004).

A major barrier is the lack of trust many refugee families have in authority and government officials (Palmer, 2006; Scuglik, Alarcón, Lapeyre, Williams, & Logan, 2007). Many refugee families have had negative prior experiences with governmental organizations in their country of origin, especially families who experienced government-sanctioned violence, torture, and persecution. Furthermore, many refugee families had first-hand experiences with being marginalized and disempowered given their socio-cultural minority status both in their country of origin and in Canada (Hundley & Lambie, 2007; Scuglik et al., 2007). This legacy of distrust hinders some refugee families from seeking support services for their children.

The stigma attached to mental health issues is another major obstacle for parents (Murphy, Ndegwa, Kanani, Rojas-Jaimes, & Webster, 2002; Palmer, 2006; Scuglik et al., 2007). For some cultural groups, mental health is considered a taboo topic and is therefore not discussed publicly. For other groups, mental health concerns are conceptualized differently compared to Western perspectives. Regardless of the rationale, the stigma of mental illness deters a significant number of refugee children and adolescents from receiving appropriate mental health services.

For those refugee parents who do seek mental health care for their children, the issue of limited language proficiency tends to be another obstacle (Gong-Guy, Cravens, & Patterson, 1991; Singh, McKay, & Singh, 1999). In some instances, parents recognize the psychological difficulties that their children are experiencing, but they do not have the language capacity either to locate the appropriate services or to engage with the treatment offered by service providers. Although culturally sensitive mental health care providers offer language interpreters and cultural brokers, some refugee families are still reluctant to use the services (Singh et al., 1999). This reluctance relates back to the stigma attached to mental health in specific cultural communities, in particular among tightly knit communities. Many refugee families expressed concerns that the language interpreters and cultural brokers, who are often members of their ethnocultural community, will breach confidentiality and let others in the community know about their struggles (Singh et al., 1999).

Finally, refugee families typically do not have the time or the resources to access mental health services for their children, especially when they are juggling multiple responsibilities to survive (Murphy et al., 2002; Palmer, 2006). Many refugee parents, especially during early resettlement, are either working multiple jobs or spending time dealing with social welfare agencies to ensure that they have the necessary financial resources to cover basic living costs (e.g., food, rent, clothes). It is only when basic needs are met that parents are more able to spend the time and resources to access support services for their children (Murphy et al., 2002).

### Need for school-based interventions

Given the host of barriers to accessing mental health services among refugee children and adolescents, schools have been identified as the optimal setting for the design and implementation of effective interventions (Chiumento et al., 2011; Rolfsnes & Idsoe, 2011). For example, when offered a similar treatment model in two settings, close to 80% of the refugee students eligible for interventions chose the school-based intervention over a program offered at a community clinic (Chiumento et al., 2011). O'shea, Hodes, Down, and Bramley (2000) also found low utilization rates for a community-based mental health program designed and implemented for refugee children and adolescents. Another advantage of school-based interventions is that they tend to be more holistic in nature (Fazel & Stein, 2002). Service providers have the opportunity to consult with teachers to monitor students' academic progress and behavioural issues, to facilitate peer relationships, and to instill a sense of belonging and identity. Thus, school-based interventions provide an anchor point for stable social support for refugee students. Subsequent sections will review current school-based interventions for refugee students in Canada and internationally.

## Interventions addressing the psychological impact of trauma in refugee children and youth

Several school-based interventions have been developed internationally, most notably in the United States and the United Kingdom. Most of these interventions integrate elements of individual or group cognitive-behavioural therapy (CBT). Most outcome studies have used the Strength and Difficulties Questionnaire (SDQ; Goodman, 1997). The SDQ is a brief questionnaire that assesses children's emotional symptoms, conduct problems, hyperactivity/inattention, peer relationship problems, and pro-social behaviours.

In Boston, Project SHIFA is a school-based mental health intervention designed specifically for Somali refugee students attending public middle school (Ellis et al., 2011). Researchers found that those who received CBT-based individual psychotherapy were more likely to remain engaged in therapy compared to a community sample, and they experienced a reduction in symptoms. Similarly, in both of the other two studies that took place in London (O'shea, Hodes, Down, & Bramley, 2000) and Oxford in the UK (Fazel, Doll, & Stein, 2009), refugee students who received CBT therapy experienced a decrease in SDQ scores. In the Oxford sample, a decrease in the following domains was observed: emotional symptoms, hyperactivity/inattention, and peer relationships (Fazel et al., 2009). A recent meta-analysis corroborates these findings (Rolfsnes & Idsoe, 2011). In particular, school-based CBT intervention programs were found to be an effective treatment option for PTSD in school-age refugee children and adolescents.

Group-based treatment approaches have also been found to alleviate the emotional and psychological impact of trauma among refugee students (Ehntholt, Smith, & Yule, 2005). Using the *Children and War: Teaching Recovery Techniques* manual, a six-week group CBT program was delivered to secondary school refugee students who had experienced war-related trauma (Smith, Dyregrov, Yule, Perrin, Gjestad, & Gupta, 2000). The sessions covered topics such as typical reactions to stress, sleep hygiene, imagery and relaxation techniques, and activity scheduling for leisure activities. Post-intervention participants exhibited a significant reduction in both PTSD symptoms and behavioural difficulties (as measured by the SDQ). Similar outcomes were found for an eight-week Spanish CBT group targeting traumatized Latino children in Los Angeles (Kataoka et al., 2003). This program covered common reactions to stress, relaxation techniques, links between thoughts and behaviours, avoidance and coping, social skills development, and exposure to traumatic memory. In this Latino sample, a significant reduction in PTSD and depression symptoms was evident post-intervention.

Still within the international context, there is evidence suggesting that art-therapy groups can be beneficial in reducing the psychological distress refugee students experience. One exemplar program is the Haven Project in Liverpool, UK (Chiumento et al., 2011). In this program, collaborations were forged between mental health professionals, various community artist groups, and seven schools already offering school-based support groups. In each of the schools, groups of refugee students were formed based on their artistic interests. Possible options included art psychotherapy, psychodrama, filmmaking, poetry writing, and horticultural activities. Post-intervention, students from six of the seven schools in the project experienced significant improvements in terms of their emotional and behavioural functioning, as measured by the SDQ.

Within the Canadian context, school-based programs that target the mental health needs of refugees specifically are more limited. Notable exceptions are the intervention programs offered by the Transcultural Research and Intervention Team (TRIT) in Montreal. Using techniques from art- and play-based therapy, the TRIT team offered interventions to a wide range of refugee children (Rousseau & Guzder, 2008). For preschool children, a 10-week sand-play group was offered, during which participants played with peers in recreating their perceptions of the world using sand trays and figurines. The evaluation of the sand-play group suggested that the intervention improved the children's overall functioning (Lacroix et al., 2007).

Elementary school students participated in creative workshops that included verbal (e.g., storytelling) and non-verbal (e.g., painting a picture) components (Rousseau & Heusch, 2000). Activities included sharing myths and tales from the students' heritage culture and storytelling about the student's pre- and post-immigration experience. After the intervention, students reported experiencing significant improvements in self-esteem and emotional and behavioural symptoms compared to a control group (Rousseau & Heusch, 2000).

For high school students, a 12-week drama-based therapy group was offered (Rousseau et al., 2007). Using techniques from improvisational theatre, under the guidance of a director, students recreated scenes from their own personal stories with the goal of building connections between the past and the present. Compared to the control group, participants in this drama-based intervention reported a diminished sense of impairment in their emotional and behavioural symptoms, as well as improved academic performance (Rousseau et al., 2007).

Although documented school-based programming to support refugee children's and youth's psychological needs is currently limited in Canada, there is a more diverse range of services offered in community settings. In many Canadian urban centres with a large number of refugees, community-based health clinics have developed programs within a multidisciplinary health care team that target refugees' physical and mental health (Fowler, 1998; White et al., 2009). For instance, in a community health centre in Hamilton, Ontario, distressed refugee children and youth were screened by clinic doctors and received individual counselling sessions with a linguistically matched psychologist (Fowler, 1998). Similarly, a Regina, Saskatchewan, community health centre adopted a group support model that provided group counselling to refugee youth and their families to help them cope with the psychological impact of trauma (White et al., 2009). In the Greater Vancouver Area, a community settlement centre offered a one-on-one support program to connect refugee youth with peer support workers who had themselves struggled with mental health issues (DIVERSEcity Community Resources Society, 2012). As a result of the sessions, refugee youth were able to gain social and practical skills to better cope with living with a mental health concern.

### Interventions addressing challenges in refugee families

As mentioned previously, family-related challenges have a detrimental impact on the well-being of refugee children and adolescents. Various chapters in this book touch on parental distress in refugee families in schools. Further, several school-based programs in the UK and the US have included family therapy as part of their interventions (Fazel et al., 2009; Garrison, Roy, & Azar, 1999; O'shea, Hodes, Down, & Bramley, 2000). In these programs, refugee parents played an active role. As part of the intake process, mental health professionals assessed parents with respect to their challenges and difficulties. Family therapy sessions were then offered to the parents along with their children to address the effects of parental distress. Of particular interest, Latino parents in the AMIGO program were invited to participate in culturally sensitive play therapy with their children, given the evidence suggesting that play therapy is a highly effective modality among Latino families (Garrison et al., 1999). Furthermore, at-home psychotherapy sessions, with culturally and linguistically matched therapists, were also offered in two of the intervention projects cited above (Fazel et al., 2009; Garrison et al., 1999). Post-intervention, parents were referred to appropriate community-based mental health service providers for follow-up.

In addition to overall parental distress, acculturation-related stress is another major source of conflict for refugee families (Hyman et al., 2000; Stewart, 2011). In Toronto, a creative approach to address such difficulties is the Building Bridges Program, which organizes panel discussion groups for parents of refugee students (Cole, 2000). With the assistance of translators and cultural interpreters, discussions focus on parents' expectations of their children. Parents are given the opportunity to discuss the acculturative issues they face with their children and to generate strategies to resolve these conflicts. In addition, parents receive detailed settlement-related information, and referrals are made to relevant community service agencies (Cole, 2000).

The use of panel discussion groups and educational workshops for parents coping with acculturative stress was also adopted in a US-based program (Garrison et al., 1999). In the AMIGO program cited above, more than 20 free educational workshops and support groups in Spanish were offered per year in the community (e.g., public libraries, community centres). The workshops were offered at flexible times and provided on-site child care to support as much access as possible. A wide range of issues was discussed, such as acculturative challenges, parenting techniques, and strategies to engage more fully in children's schools. Workshops ranged from one-session workshops for parents with limited time to eight-session discussion groups.

Some programs have targeted refugee parents in particular with the aim of increasing their participation in the school system (Hamilton, 2004; Rousseau & Guzder, 2008). Both internationally and in Canada, parental discussion groups have been found to be useful in increasing refugee parents' awareness of the importance of being involved and exploring the barriers that prevent them from becoming more active (Cole, 2000; Garrison et al., 1999). A US-based school outreach program was found to be effective in engaging parents within the school setting (Ellis et al., 2011). Project SHIFA, targeting Somali refugee parents, identified that the lack of parental engagement was related to cultural expectations with respect to parents' involvement within schools (i.e., it is perceived as being disrespectful) (Ellis et al., 2011). To address this barrier, Project SHIFA developed an outreach strategy for parents to facilitate a cultural shift. One strategy was to encourage Somali parents to participate in a school-based computer literacy class designed for all school parents regardless of cultural origin. With the facilitation of project staff, Somali parents became more comfortable interacting with school officials/teachers while acquiring a valuable skill. The use of training programs, such as literacy classes or computer skills training, for refugee parents has consistently been found to be a meaningful and effective way of increasing refugee parental engagement in schools, in both the Canadian (Stewart, 2011) and international (Hamilton, 2004) contexts.

## Interventions addressing refugee children and youth's challenges at school

Within the school setting, refugee students typically experience challenges, especially with respect to academic achievement and interpersonal relationships (Kanu, 2008; Stewart, 2011; Yau, 1995). To address academic issues related to the lack of proficiency in English or French, several excellent programs, based on sound pedagogical theories, have been implemented in Canada. Examples of ELL programs include the Literacy Enrichment Academic Program (LEAP) implemented throughout the Toronto District School Board (TDSB, 2010) and the Accelerated Basic Literacy Education (ABLE) program that was adopted in the Waterloo Region District School Board.

In contrast, Canadian efforts dealing with the interpersonal challenges experienced by refugee children and youth with their peers are far more limited. One exception is the Hope Project, which uses art-based interventions to help refugee students deal with peer-related difficulties (Yohani & Larsen, 2009). The Hope Project is based on the premise that by embedding hope in the interpersonal context, participants can achieve more nurturing and connected relationships to others (Yohani, 2008). The 10-week program included taking photographs, making a quilt, and drawing pictures. During these activities, Yohani and Larsen (2009) observed that talking about hope was an important step in helping refugee children explore the possibility of relating to peers in a different cultural context. Facilitators were able to help foster new relationships within the school context, thereby decreasing refugee children's sense of isolation and loneliness.

Along similar lines, the TRIT team in Montreal developed a classroom drama therapy program for refugee high school students. Participants were encouraged to share stories regarding their lives in their country of origin and the challenges they face during resettlement. Through re-enactment, they were able to assign different meanings to these experiences and generated new coping strategies. Participants reported better social adjustment post-intervention (Rousseau et al., 2007).

International research exploring art-based therapy programs has also found them to be effective in fostering peer relationships among refugee students (Ingleby & Watters, 2002). The Pharos Program was developed in the Netherlands for elementary and secondary schools with a significant proportion of refugee students (Ingleby & Watters, 2002). Elementary students participated in eight sessions in which they were encouraged to make a book about their experiences. Topics discussed included their sense of self and family, their sense of belongingness to their school, their relationships with peers, and their overall adjustment to the Netherlands. High school students participated in a 21-session art-therapy group. They covered the same topics outlined above with the addition of leisure activities and future plans. A qualitative evaluation study found positive results for all program participants, especially with respect to self-reported sense of well-being, belongingness, and interpersonal relationships with peers.

Other approaches have provided refugee students in the UK with individual and group CBT sessions to help them with peer adjustment (Ehntholt et al., 2005; Fazel et al., 2009). Refugee students who were part of the individual CBT intervention experienced a significant reduction in relationship difficulties with peers (Fazel et al., 2009). Refugees in a group CBT intervention study were found to experience a decreasing trend in peer relationship problems post-intervention (Ehntholt et al., 2005).

## Barriers experienced by teachers in supporting refugee children and youth

Teachers interact with refugee students on a daily basis and are thus in a key position to observe the difficulties experienced by refugee students across different domains, such as academic challenges and difficulties in interpersonal relationships (Alisic, Bus, Dulack, Pennings, & Splinter, 2012; Yau, 1995). Furthermore, teachers often act as role models for refugee students and their peers, and they are able to facilitate links between refugee families and social service providers (Hamilton, 2004). Teachers reported difficulties supporting their refugee students, however. In particular, over 25% of teachers surveyed stated that it was difficult for them to determine which problematic behaviours required intervention, and they were often unfamiliar with available community resources (Alisic et al., 2012). Teachers also commented on the challenges of balancing the needs of traumatized refugee children with the needs of other children in the classroom (Alisic et al., 2012; Hamilton, 2004; Yau, 1995).

Although many teachers expressed a genuine desire to help their refugee students, they also expressed concerns for their own personal well-being, especially given their lack of training and support

(Alisic et al., 2012; Yau, 1995). In particular, teachers shared that they were afraid they would become too emotionally involved and risked becoming vicariously traumatized. These findings clearly suggest that teachers working with refugee students would benefit from in-service training and consultation opportunities.

## Interventions targeting teachers of refugee students

In Canada, panel discussion groups and educational workshops have been found to be valuable in supporting teachers in their work with refugee students (Cole, 2000). For example, the Toronto-based Building Bridges program organized discussion panels for teachers that dealt with various issues, including how to conduct a needs assessment in the classroom, identifying students' strengths and challenges, and forming working collaborations with community service providers. In-service training workshops were also offered to teachers, providing them with concrete classroom activities to create inclusive classrooms for refugee students and to facilitate social skills and pro-social behaviours among students (Cole, 2000). Examples of helpful activities included developing peer-buddy programs, using games and art-based activities, and providing storytelling workshops. An evaluation of this program found that refugee students experienced an improved sense of self-esteem, a greater number of friends, more positive peer relationships, and a clearer sense of self. The students were also better able to integrate their past traumatic experiences with positive visions of the future (Cole, 2000).

Internationally, several interventions have adopted a consultation model whereby community-based mental health professionals link up with teachers and provide them with assistance and resources (Fazel et al., 2009; O'shea, Hodes, Down, & Bramley, 2000). Teachers have weekly consultation meetings during which they discuss with a health care provider the challenges they face with their refugee students. Teachers were provided with direct individual and class-based behaviour-management strategies to address identified difficulties. One of the programs provided teachers with additional training on how to use classroom observations to identify those refugee students who may be experiencing behavioural and emotional issues (Fazel et al., 2009). At the conclusion of these intervention projects, the mental health team provided teachers with information on how to make referrals to the appropriate social and mental health services (Fazel et al., 2009; O'shea, Hodes, Down, & Bramley, 2000).

Other approaches have advocated the value of having a designated refugee support teacher within the school setting (Bolloten & Spafford, 1998). In the UK, several schools in London hired a refugee support teacher to act as a liaison between refugee students and their teachers. Refugee support teachers are often responsible for the delivery of language training to immigrant students (i.e., ELL teachers) and have significant experience and/or training in working with refugee students (Bolloten & Spafford, 1998). As refugee support teachers, they have the ability to provide peer support and consultation to other teachers in the school. In addition, many refugee support teachers are also able to offer concrete classroom-management strategies and community referrals to other teachers based on their training and experiences (Bolloten & Spafford, 1998).

## Putting the pieces together: Practical implications and conclusions

This review of the literature suggests that there is a fairly wide range of school-based interventions available to support refugee children and adolescents. In many of the interventions discussed, there is empirical evidence that they are effective in reducing refugee students' behavioural, emotional, and interpersonal difficulties. In several interventions, an integrative approach was adopted that targeted refugee students, their parents, and their teachers. An integrative approach is often more effective in promoting refugee students' overall well-being. Providing support to refugee parents increases their adjustment, which in turn benefits the well-being of their children. Similarly, integrative interventions that provide support and skills to teachers provide another source of support for refugee children and youth.

Despite the merits of integrative approaches, school-based interventions designed for one specific target group were also found to be effective. Refugee students who participated in interventions designed specifically to deal with post-trauma difficulties tended to have positive outcomes, such as a reduction in emotional and behavioural difficulties, improved sense of self-esteem, and enhanced peer relationships. Interventions targeted at refugee parents provided them with additional skills to resolve conflicts with their children and resources for both themselves and their children to promote their well-being. Interventions that focused on teachers' needs in the classroom were also found to empower teachers with respect to classroom management, as well as to educate them with respect to available community resources.

It is important to highlight, however, that Canadian school-based interventions for refugee children and adolescents remain limited compared to interventions developed in other countries, such as the UK and the US. There is also a need in the Canadian context to gather and analyze outcome data using more rigorous experimental methods and designs, such as quasi-experimental trials. Furthermore, none of the Canadian interventions we reviewed were integrative in nature—that is, targeting the needs of students, parents, and teachers—within a given intervention. Current intervention programs in Canada would no doubt benefit from adopting components of programs developed internationally. It would be important, however, that modifications to existing programs take into account Canada's unique socio-political reality and that rigorous outcome research be undertaken to ascertain their effectiveness within the Canadian context.

Various community researchers have cited the lack of funding and resources as an important impediment to the development of more comprehensive and effective interventions for refugee children and youth, both in Canada and internationally. O'shea, Hodes, Down, and Bramley (2000) explicitly commented in their evaluation report about the difficulties in securing funding. Given tightened school budgets, the needs of refugee children and youth within the school system will be met only if government agencies and/or private foundations specifically earmark funds to deal with their particular realities. Some program developers/researchers have suggested that the development and implementation of manual-based interventions and programs that focus on capacity-building within schools (i.e., training for teachers regarding identifying behaviours that are problematic) may be more cost effective and sustainable in the long term (Ehntholt et al., 2005; Fazel et al., 2009).

## REFERENCES

Alisic, E., Bus, M., Dulack, W., Pennings, L., & Splinter, J. (2012, Feb). Teachers' experiences supporting children after traumatic exposure. *Journal of Traumatic Stress, 25*(1), 98–101. http://dx.doi.org/10.1002/jts.20709 Medline:22354512

Almqvist, K., & Broberg, A.G. (1999, Jun). Mental health and social adjustment in young refugee children 3 1/2 years after their arrival in Sweden. *Journal of the American Academy of Child and Adolescent Psychiatry, 38*(6), 723–730. http://dx.doi.org/10.1097/00004583-199906000-00020 Medline:10361791

American Psychiatric Association (2000). *Diagnostic and statistical manual of mental disorders* (4th ed., text rev.). Washington, DC: Author.

Betancourt, T.S., Agnew-Blais, J., Gilman, S.E., Williams, D.R., & Ellis, B.H. (2010, Jan). Past horrors, present struggles: The role of stigma in the association between war experiences and psychosocial adjustment among former child soldiers in Sierra Leone. *Social Science & Medicine, 70*(1), 17–26. http://dx.doi.org/10.1016/j.socscimed.2009.09.038 Medline:19875215

Betancourt, T.S., McBain, R., Newnham, E.A., & Brennan, R.T. (2013, Mar–Apr). Trajectories of internalizing problems in war-affected Sierra Leonean youth: Examining conflict and postconflict factors. *Child Development, 84*(2), 455–470. http://dx.doi.org/10.1111/j.1467-8624.2012.01861.x Medline:23002719

Bolloten, B., & Spafford, T. (1998). Supporting refugee children in East London primary schools. In J.R.C. Jones (Ed.), *Refugee education: Mapping the field* (pp. 107–123). Oakhill, UK: Trentham Books.

Boothby, N., Upton, P., & Sultan, A. (1991). *Children of Mozambique*. Washington, DC: US Committee for Refugees.

Bronfenbrenner, U. (1979). *The ecology of human development: Experiments by nature and design*. Cambridge: Harvard University Press.

Canadian Broadcasting Corporation (2012, Dec 13). Detention centres no place for migrant children, critics argue. CBC News. Retrieved from http://www.cbc.ca/news/canada/detention-centres-no-place-for-migrant-children-critics-argue-1.1169993

Child Soldiers International (2001). Who are child soldiers? Retrieved from http://www.child-soldiers.org/about_the_issues.php

Chiumento, A., Nelki, J., Dutton, C., & Hughes, G. (2011). School-based mental health service for refugee and asylum seeking children: Multi-agency working, lessons for good practice. *Journal of Public Mental Health, 10*(3), 164–177. http://dx.doi.org/10.1108/17465721111175047

Citizenship and Immigration Canada (2012). The refugee systems in Canada. Retrieved from http://www.cic.gc.ca/english/refugees/canada.asp

Cole, E. (2000). Supporting refugee and immigrant children: Building bridges programme of the International Children's Institute in Canada and overseas. *Refuge: Canada's Periodical on Refugees, 18*(6), 41–45.

de Silva, H., Hobbs, C., & Hanks, H. (2001). Conscription of children in armed conflict—A form of child abuse. A study of 19 former child soldiers. *Child Abuse Review, 10*(2), 125–134. http://dx.doi.org/10.1002/car.669

DIVERSEcity Community Resources Society (2012). *Child and Youth Mental Health: Refugee Peer Support Program*. Retrieved from https://www.surreyschools.ca/departments/BDEV/Community_Information/Events_Organizations/Documents/DIVERSEcity%27s%20Refugee%20Peer%20Support%20Program.pdf

Dumbrill, G.C. (2009). Your policies, our children: Messages from refugee parents to child welfare workers and policymakers. *Child Welfare, 88*(3), 145–168. Medline:20084822

Dyregrov, A., Gjestad, R., & Raundalen, M. (2002, Feb). Children exposed to warfare: A longitudinal study. *Journal of Traumatic Stress, 15*(1), 59–68. http://dx.doi.org/10.1023/A:1014335312219 Medline:11936723

Ehntholt, K.A., Smith, P.A., & Yule, W. (2005). School-based cognitive-behavioural therapy group intervention for refugee children who have experienced war-related trauma. *Clinical Child Psychology and Psychiatry, 10*(2), 235–250. http://dx.doi.org/10.1177/1359104505051214

Elbedour, S., Onwuegbuzie, A.J., Ghannam, J., Whitcome, J.A., & Abu Hein, F. (2007, Jul). Post-traumatic stress disorder, depression, and anxiety among Gaza Strip adolescents in the wake of the second Uprising (Intifada). *Child Abuse & Neglect, 31*(7), 719–729. http://dx.doi.org/10.1016/j.chiabu.2005.09.006 Medline:17631959

Ellis, B.H., Miller, A.B., Baldwin, H., & Abdi, S. (2011). New directions in refugee youth mental health services: Overcoming barriers to engagement. *Journal of Child & Adolescent Trauma, 4*(1), 69–85. http://dx.doi.org/10.1080/19361521.2011.545047

Fazel, M., Doll, H., & Stein, A. (2009, Apr). A school-based mental health intervention for refugee children: An exploratory study. *Clinical Child Psychology and Psychiatry, 14*(2), 297–309. http://dx.doi.org/10.1177/1359104508100128 Medline:19293324

Fazel, M., Reed, R.V., Panter-Brick, C., & Stein, A. (2012, Jan 21). Mental health of displaced and refugee children resettled in high-income countries: Risk and protective factors. *Lancet, 379*(9812), 266–282. http://dx.doi.org/10.1016/S0140-6736(11)60051-2 Medline:21835459

Fazel, M., & Stein, A. (2002, Nov). The mental health of refugee children. *Archives of Disease in Childhood, 87*(5), 366–370. http://dx.doi.org/10.1136/adc.87.5.366 Medline:12390902

Fowler, N. (1998, Aug 25). Providing primary health care to immigrants and refugees: The North Hamilton experience. *Canadian Medical Association Journal, 159*(4), 388–391. Medline:9732723

Garrison, E.G., Roy, I.S., & Azar, V. (1999, Mar). Responding to the mental health needs of Latino children and families through school-based services. *Clinical Psychology Review, 19*(2), 199–219. http://dx.doi.org/10.1016/S0272-7358(98)00070-1 Medline:10078420

Goldstein, R.D., Wampler, N.S., & Wise, P.H. (1997, Nov). War experiences and distress symptoms of Bosnian children. *Pediatrics, 100*(5), 873–878. http://dx.doi.org/10.1542/peds.100.5.873 Medline:9346989

Gong-Guy, E., Cravens, R.B., & Patterson, T.E. (1991, Jun). Clinical issues in mental health service delivery to refugees. *American Psychologist, 46*(6), 642–648. http://dx.doi.org/10.1037/0003-066X.46.6.642 Medline:1952423

Goodman, R. (1997, Jul). The Strengths and Difficulties Questionnaire: A research note. *Journal of Child Psychology and Psychiatry, and Allied Disciplines, 38*(5), 581–586. http://dx.doi.org/10.1111/j.1469-7610.1997.tb01545.x Medline:9255702

Hamilton, R. (2004). Schools, teachers and education of refugee children. In R. Hamilton & D. Moore (Eds.), *Educational interventions for refugee children: Theoretical perspectives and implementing best practice* (pp. 83–96). New York: Routledge.

Harrell-Bond (2000). Are refugee camps good for children? Working paper (29). Cairo: American University of Cairo. Retrieved from http://www.unhcr.org/3ae6a0c64.html

Hecker, T., Hermenau, K., Maedl, A., Hinkel, H., Schauer, M., & Elbert, T. (2013, Feb). Does perpetrating violence damage mental health? Differences between forcibly recruited and voluntary combatants in DR Congo. *Journal of Traumatic Stress, 26*(1), 142–148. http://dx.doi.org/10.1002/jts.21770 Medline:23319373

Hundley, G., & Lambie, G.W. (2007). Russian speaking immigrants from the Commonwealth of Independent States in the United States: Implications for mental health counselors. *Journal of Mental Health Counseling, 29*(3), 242–258.

Hyman, I., Vu, N., & Beiser, M. (2000). Post-migration stress among South Asian refugee youth in Canada: A research note. *Journal of Comparative Family Studies, 31*(2), 281–293.

Ingleby, D., & Watters, C. (2002). Refugee children at school: Good practices in mental health and social care. *Education for Health, 20*(3), 43–45.

Kanu, Y. (2008). Educational needs and barriers for African refugee students in Manitoba. *Canadian Journal of Education, 31*(4), 915–940.

Kaprielian-Churchill, I. (1996). Refugees and education in Canadian schools. *International Review of Education, 42*(4), 349–365. http://dx.doi.org/10.1007/BF00601096

Kataoka, S.H., Stein, B.D., Jaycox, L.H., et al. (2003, Mar). A school-based mental health program for traumatized Latino immigrant children. *Journal of the American Academy of Child and Adolescent Psychiatry, 42*(3), 311–318. http://dx.doi.org/10.1097/00004583-200303000-00011 Medline:12595784

Kia-Keating, M., & Ellis, B.H. (2007, Jan). Belonging and connection to school in resettlement: Young refugees, school belonging, and psychosocial adjustment. *Clinical Child Psychology and Psychiatry, 12*(1), 29–43. http://dx.doi.org/10.1177/1359104507071052 Medline:17375808

Kinzie, J.D., Sack, W.H., Angell, R.H., Manson, S., & Rath, B. (1986). The psychiatric effects of massive trauma on Cambodian children: I. The children. *Journal of the American Academy of Child and Adolescent Psychiatry, 25*(3), 370–376. http://dx.doi.org/10.1016/S0002-7138(09)60259-4

Lacroix, L., Rousseau, C., Gauthier, M.-F., Singh, A., Giguere, N., & Lemzoudi, Y. (2007). Immigrant and refugee preschoolers' sandplay representation of the tsunami. *Arts in Psychotherapy, 34*(2), 99–113. http://dx.doi.org/10.1016/j.aip.2006.09.006

Lorek, A., Ehntholt, K., Nesbitt, A., et al. (2009, Sep). The mental and physical health difficulties of children held within a British immigration detention center: A pilot study. *Child Abuse & Neglect, 33*(9), 573–585. http://dx.doi.org/10.1016/j.chiabu.2008.10.005 Medline:19811830

Lustig, S.L., Kia-Keating, M., Knight, W.G., et al. (2004, Jan). Review of child and adolescent refugee mental health. *Journal of the American Academy of Child and Adolescent Psychiatry, 43*(1), 24–36. http://dx.doi.org/10.1097/00004583-200401000-00012 Medline:14691358

Macksoud, M.S., & Aber, J.L. (1996, Feb). The war experiences and psychosocial development of children in Lebanon. *Child Development, 67*(1), 70–88. http://dx.doi.org/10.2307/1131687 Medline:8605835

Mares, S., Newman, L., Dudley, M., & Gale, F. (2002). Seeking refuge, losing hope: Parents and children in immigration detention. *Australasian Psychiatry, 10*(2), 91–96. http://dx.doi.org/10.1046/j.1440-1665.2002.00414.x

McCloskey, L.A., & Southwick, K. (1996, Mar). Psychosocial problems in refugee children exposed to war. *Pediatrics, 97*(3), 394–397. Medline:8604277

Melville, M.B., & Brinton Lykes, M. (1992, Mar). Guatemalan Indian children and the sociocultural effects of government-sponsored terrorism. *Social Science & Medicine, 34*(5), 533–548. http://dx.doi.org/10.1016/0277-9536(92)90209-9 Medline:1604360

Merali, N. (2005). A comparison of Hispanic refugee parents' and adolescents' accuracy in judging family cultural values. *Alberta Journal of Educational Research, 51*(4), 342–353.

Montgomery, E., & Foldspang, A. (2005, Jun). Seeking asylum in Denmark: Refugee children's mental health and exposure to violence. *European Journal of Public Health, 15*(3), 233–237. http://dx.doi.org/10.1093/eurpub/cki059 Medline:15923213

Morantz, G., Rousseau, C., & Heymann, J. (2012). The divergent experiences of children and adults in the relocation process: Perspectives of child and parent refugee claimants in Montreal. *Journal of Refugee Studies, 25*(1), 71–92. http://dx.doi.org/10.1093/jrs/fer025

Morgos, D., Worden, J.W., & Gupta, L. (2007). Psychosocial effects of war experiences among displaced children in southern Darfur. *Omega, 56*(3), 229–253. http://dx.doi.org/10.2190/OM.56.3.b Medline:18300649

Murphy, D., Ndegwa, D., Kanani, A., Rojas-Jaimes, C., & Webster, A. (2002). Mental health of refugees in inner-London. *Psychiatric Bulletin, 26*(6), 222–224. http://dx.doi.org/10.1192/pb.26.6.222

O'shea, B., Hodes, M., Down, G., & Bramley, J. (2000). A school-based mental health service for refugee children. *Clinical Child Psychology and Psychiatry, 5*(2), 189–201. http://dx.doi.org/10.1177/1359104500005002004

Paardekooper, B., de Jong, J.T.V.M., & Hermanns, J.M.A. (1999). The psychological impact of war and the refugee situation on South Sudanese children in refugee campus in Northern Uganda: An exploratory study. *Child Psychology and Psychiatry, 40*(4), 529–536. http://dx.doi.org/10.1111/1469-7610.00471

Palmer, D. (2006). Imperfect prescription: Mental health perceptions, experiences and challenges faced by the Somali community in the London Borough of Camden and service responses to them. *Primary Care Mental Health, 4*(1), 45–56.

Pawliuk, N., Grizenko, N., Chan-Yip, A., Gantous, P., Mathew, J., & Nguyen, D. (1996, Jan). Acculturation style and psychological functioning in children of immigrants. *American Journal of Orthopsychiatry, 66*(1), 111–121. http://dx.doi.org/10.1037/h0080161 Medline:8720648

Rolfsnes, E.S., & Idsoe, T. (2011, Apr). School-based intervention programs for PTSD symptoms: A review and meta-analysis. *Journal of Traumatic Stress, 24*(2), 155–165. http://dx.doi.org/10.1002/jts.20622 Medline:21425191

Rothe, E.M., Lewis, J., Castillo-Matos, H., Martinez, O., Busquets, R., & Martinez, I. (2002, Aug). Posttraumatic stress disorder among Cuban children and adolescents after release from a refugee camp. *Psychiatric Services (Washington, D.C.), 53*(8), 970–976. http://dx.doi.org/10.1176/appi.ps.53.8.970 Medline:12161671

Rousseau, C., Benoit, M., Gauthier, M.-F., Lacroix, L., Alain, N., Viger Rojas, N., ... Bourassa, D. (2007). Classroom drama therapy program for immigrant and refugee adolescents: A pilot study. *Clinical Child Psychology and Psychiatry, 12*(3), 451–465. http://dx.doi.org/10.1177/1359104507078477 Medline:17953131

Rousseau, C., & Guzder, J. (2008, Jul). School-based prevention programs for refugee children. *Child and Adolescent Psychiatric Clinics of North America, 17*(3), 533–549, viii. http://dx.doi.org/10.1016/j.chc.2008.02.002 Medline:18558311

Rousseau, C., & Heusch, N. (2000). The trip: A creative expression workshop project for refugee and immigrant children. *American Journal of Art Therapy, 17*(1), 31–40. http://dx.doi.org/10.1080/07421656.2000.10129434

Schaal, S., & Elbert, T. (2006, Feb). Ten years after the genocide: Trauma confrontation and posttraumatic stress in Rwandan adolescents. *Journal of Traumatic Stress, 19*(1), 95–105. http://dx.doi.org/10.1002/jts.20104 Medline:16568463

Scuglik, D.L., Alarcón, R.D., Lapeyre, A.C., III, Williams, M.D., & Logan, K.M. (2007, Dec). When the poetry no longer rhymes: Mental health issues among Somali immigrants in the USA. *Transcultural Psychiatry, 44*(4), 581–595. http://dx.doi.org/10.1177/1363461507083899 Medline:18089640

Servan-Schreiber, D., Le Lin, B., & Birmaher, B. (1998, Aug). Prevalence of posttraumatic stress disorder and major depressive disorder in Tibetan refugee children. *Journal of the American Academy of Child and Adolescent Psychiatry, 37*(8), 874–879. http://dx.doi.org/10.1097/00004583-199808000-00018 Medline:9695450

Short, K.H., & Johnston, C. (1997, Jun). Stress, maternal distress, and children's adjustment following immigration: The buffering role of social support. *Journal of Consulting and Clinical Psychology, 65*(3), 494–503. http://dx.doi.org/10.1037/0022-006X.65.3.494 Medline:9170773

Singh, N.N., McKay, J.D., & Singh, A.N. (1999). The need for cultural brokers in mental health services. *Journal of Child and Family Studies, 8*(1), 1–10. http://dx.doi.org/10.1023/A:1022949225965

Smith, P., Dyregrov, A., Yule, W., Perrin, S., Gjestad, R., & Gupta, L. (2000). *Children and war: Teaching recovery techniques.* Bergen, Norway: Foundation for Children and War.

Stewart, J. (2011). *Supporting refugee children: Strategies for educators.* Toronto: University of Toronto Press.

Thabet, A.A., Abed, Y., & Vostanis, P. (2002, May 25). Emotional problems in Palestinian children living in a war zone: A cross-sectional study. *Lancet, 359*(9320), 1801–1804. http://dx.doi.org/10.1016/S0140-6736(02)08709-3 Medline:12044374

Thabet, A.A., Abed, Y., & Vostanis, P. (2004, Mar). Comorbidity of PTSD and depression among refugee children during war conflict. *Journal of Child Psychology and Psychiatry, and Allied Disciplines, 45*(3), 533–542. http://dx.doi.org/10.1111/j.1469-7610.2004.00243.x Medline:15055372

Toronto District School Board (TDSB; 2010). LEAP program for the Toronto District School Board. Retrieved from http://www.tdsb.on.ca/HighSchool/YourSchoolDay/EnglishasaSecondLanguage.aspx

Tousignant, M., Habimana, E., Biron, C., Malo, C., Sidoli-LeBlanc, E., & Bendris, N. (1999, Nov). The Quebec Adolescent Refugee Project: Psychopathology and family variables in a sample from 35 nations. *Journal of the American Academy of Child and Adolescent Psychiatry, 38*(11), 1426–1432. http://dx.doi.org/10.1097/00004583-199911000-00018 Medline:10560230

United Nations High Commissioner for Refugees (2013). *2013 UNHCR Regional Operations Profile—North America and the Caribbean.* Retrieved from http://www.unhcr.org/pages/49e491336.html

Weine, S. (2008, Jul). Family roles in refugee youth resettlement from a prevention perspective. *Child and Adolescent Psychiatric Clinics of North America, 17*(3), 515–532, vii–viii. http://dx.doi.org/10.1016/j.chc.2008.02.006 Medline:18558310

Welch, M., & Schuster, L. (2005). Detention of asylum seekers in the US, UK, France, Germany, and Italy: A critical view of the globalizing culture of control. *Criminology & Criminal Justice, 5*(4), 331–355. http://dx.doi.org/10.1177/1466802505057715

White, J., Franklin, D., Gruber, K., Hanke, C., Holzer, B., Nayyar, J., ... Weighill, C. (2009). The Moving Forward project: Working with refugee children, youth, and their families. In S. McKay, D. Fuchs, & I. Brown (Eds.), *Passion for action in child and family services: Voices from the Prairies* (pp. 143–164). Regina, SK: Canadian Plains Research Centre.

Yau, M. (1995). *Refugee students in Toronto schools: An exploratory study. (Research Services No. 211).* Toronto: Toronto Board of Education.

Yohani, S.C. (2008). Creating an ecology of hope: Arts-based intervention with refugee children. *Child & Adolescent Social Work Journal, 25*(4), 309–323. http://dx.doi.org/10.1007/s10560-008-0129-x

Yohani, S.C., & Larsen, D.J. (2009). Hope lives in the heart: Refugee and immigrant children's perception of hope and hope-engendering sources during early years of adjustment. *Canadian Journal of Counselling, 43*(4), 246–264.

# 5

# Immigrant mothers' use of a discussion group in becoming school ready

*Courney Anne Brewer and Michael McCabe*

Current understandings of school readiness identify the complexity and constancy of how children prepare for school (Dockett & Perry, 2009; Janus & Duku, 2007; Ramey & Ramey, 2004). The role of the parent or guardian in this process is exceptionally important and can be the difference between being prepared and not being prepared for school. In the school-readiness process, parents must also prepare themselves for school and be able to navigate the system to prepare their children and advocate on their behalf when needed. As studies show, a major indicator of school readiness is parents' engagement and involvement in their child's education (Anderson & Minke, 2007; Chazan-Cohen et al., 2009; Englund, Luckner, Whaley, & Egeland, 2004; Entwisle & Alexander, 1995; Giallo, Kienhuis, Treyvaud, & Matthews, 2008; Parker et al., 1999). Standing in the way of progress in school readiness are a variety of barriers that are more pronounced among immigrant populations (Brooks-Gunn & Markman, 2005; Huntsinger & Jose, 2009). However, several agencies and resources are available to mitigate these barriers so that the transition into Ontario schools can be a positive experience.

This chapter explores the process by which immigrant mothers prepare themselves and their children for school in Kitchener, Ontario, while attending a local discussion group. Data from qualitative interviews with study participants reveals the importance of the discussion group in this process and provides details about the complexity and interrelatedness of aspects related to school readiness. Recommendations for further action combine information obtained from this study with the existing literature to show the need for more holistic approaches, such as discussion groups, to preparing immigrant parents and their children for school.

## Methodology

This chapter is heavily grounded in socio-cultural theory (Vygotsky, 1978) with influences from *Pedagogy of the Oppressed* (Freire, 2000). We assume that both culture and context play a major role in the various situations that immigrant and refugee families experience. Immigrant and refugee families are in unique situations in Canada, and as Lee (1988) suggests, having ties to two places can result in feeling a lack of place or identity. Complex scenarios about how and why participants arrived in Canada exist for all participants, and although we may draw commonalities, consideration of these various contexts is crucial in building an understanding of the immigrant and refugee experience, particularly as it pertains to preparing children for the Canadian educational system.

Our study adopts a phenomenological approach. According to Starks and Brown Trinidad (2007), phenomenology uses thick and rich description. Meaning is created through understanding a lived experience where the researcher works closely with participants and carefully analyzes data within the context of the experience. In this study, thick description is used to help inform understandings of school readiness from immigrant mothers' perspectives.

We gathered the perspectives of immigrant mothers living in a southern Ontario city who attended Parenting in a New Society, a weekly drop-in discussion group. The discussion group was intended for immigrant mothers, although the time at which immigration took place was not restricted within the program. All participants self-identified as immigrant mothers, and there was no process to ensure the accuracy of this identification or to impose parameters regarding participation other than requiring that all participants be female. The discussion group was facilitated by Focus for Ethnic Women, a local advocacy group that relies on grants to run programming for immigrant women in the community. An Ontario Early Years Centre also co-facilitated the program. Focus for Ethnic Women provided the Parenting in a New Society curriculum, and the Ontario Early Years Centre provided a school-readiness program for children to attend while mothers attended the discussion group. Each agency also provided a co-facilitator for the Parenting in a New Society program. In a single one-on-one interview, participating mothers were asked about their experiences in immigrating to Canada, their experiences with the Ontario school system, and their views on preparing themselves and their children for school in Ontario. As well, mothers were asked to comment on their use of the Parenting in a New Society program in relation to their immigration experience and in relation to becoming school ready and preparing their children to be school ready in Ontario.

Similar discussion groups organized and facilitated by the same agencies operate out of local community centres and churches; this particular group was unique, however, because it took place in a local elementary school. Being in a local school provided easy and direct access to engagement opportunities and to the children's teachers, which made school-readiness efforts more efficient. The Parenting in a New Society discussion group requires no formal registration but does follow a loose curriculum of topics that relate to parenting practices in Canada (including ways to engage in school readiness and educational activities), the immigration experience, and available resources and supports for parents to access. Immigrant women facilitate the program, allowing participants to feel comfortable discussing their experiences. This rich and authentic discussion with a facilitator who shares a common experience not only promotes the goal of the program (to support immigrant mothers holistically) but also provides a unique opportunity for participants to gain fluency in English as they are encouraged to explain their feelings and contribute their ideas to the group.

## Participants

All mothers in this study agreed to participate and provided informed consent before any data collection. As well, all participants were asked to provide a pseudonym to protect their identity. Our study includes the stories of six mothers who were considered to be recent immigrants (in Canada for no more than five years) at the time the study took place. Countries of origin for these participants include Iraq, Jordan/Syria, Kurdistan, Morocco, Romania, and the United Arab Emirates. In addition, all participants had at least one child engaged in the school-readiness process either by preparing to attend school when he/she was old enough or by attending elementary school while negotiating new norms and practices within the school. Immigrant mothers attended the Parenting in a New Society discussion group voluntarily and regularly. The discussion group took place one morning each week in a program room in the local school. Participants were typically referred to the group through a school settlement worker or found out about it through various advertisements at the local Ontario Early Years Centre and from other participants.

## Data collection and analysis

Before we started data collection, this study underwent ethical review and permission to collect data was granted. To gain entry and build rapport with participants, the researcher acted as a participant-observer. Brief notes were taken during Parenting in a New Society sessions where only study participants attended the discussion group. The field notes were used to inform further research as this study progressed. As well, document review was used to gain insight into the Parenting in a New Society discussion group and into the mandates of both co-operating agencies. Document review sources included the Parenting in a New Society Facilitator's Guide, as well as agency websites that were available to the public, and any materials that were distributed to participants during Parenting in a New Society discussion sessions. Data used to form conclusions and suggest further study came from semi-structured one-on-one qualitative interviews. Participants were asked a variety of questions related to their experiences of immigrating and preparing for school in a new country with a direct relationship to the research questions listed above. A translator was provided in situations where a participant was uncomfortable with speaking English for the duration of the interview.

We reviewed literature related to Parenting in a New Society, Focus for Ethnic Women, and the local Ontario Early Years Centre to inform our research. The main source of data collected in this study was the one-on-one interviews with the participants. Interviews were transcribed, and open coding was used to form an understanding of each interview. A second round of coding was used to clarify information and to ensure consistency of codes in and among each transcription. Codes were clustered and re-clustered among all transcripts until overarching themes and subthemes emerged.

## Findings

Three main themes associated with the Parenting in a New Society discussion group emerged as a result of this study, along with several related subthemes. These main themes include issues related to immigration, involvement/engagement in school and community, and perceptions of school readiness. All themes relate directly to the importance of the discussion group.

### Issues related to immigration

As participants reflected on their experiences, whether they were speaking directly about their immigration experience or were discussing school-readiness practices and perceptions, immigration was always central to their discussion. Participants listed many reasons for immigrating to Canada, which included a desire for a better life, wanting to be closer to family who had previously immigrated to Canada, escaping conflict in their home country, and wanting citizenship or landing status. These circumstances were generally associated with feelings of stress, which place these mothers at a disadvantage in preparing their children for school and which must be dealt with before the school-readiness process can even be considered: "We came from Iraq. There was a war in Iraq so we had to escape to Syria, and from Syria we came here" (Asmahan). Immigration-related issues participants had faced included stress and insecurity. Stress was related to the actual move from one country and culture to another while trying to adjust to sending their children to school in Ontario. Stress was also related to being away from other family and friends who did not immigrate to the area. Insecurity involved language insecurity and cultural insecurity. Regardless of their level of English fluency, all participants expressed a desire to become better speakers of English and hoped that their children would be proficient in English as well: "I always used to worry about how she [daughter] would go to the bathroom or how she could change her clothes at school, because she can't explain or talk, until now" (Rana). As well, cultural insecurity was related to the clothing and practices that were part of the participants' religion and culture:

> Because we have hijab, sometimes we have to face problems with people we are with.... Whatever is written about us and whatever people have learned about us, I want to prove that it's wrong, we are also good human beings too, like all of you. (Maryam)

Participants used the Parenting in a New Society discussion group to help mitigate their insecurity and stress. The group provided a forum for participants to discuss their immigration experience with others who were going through similar situations:

> This group, it helped a lot. You see some people who like to help you, who feel with you, and who try to make this all easier for you, of course you can see you are not alone. There are some people with you, you are not alone, so you can feel comfortable. It's not stressed anymore, the stress will be away. (Rana)

### Involvement/engagement in school and community

Involvement/engagement in the school and wider community was a central theme in this study. Outside of school, participants in this study described taking their children to programs at community centres and at the local Ontario Early Years Centre. As well, parents remained engaged by reading with their children at home, reviewing homework and practising concepts together, and talking with their children about how the school day went. Participants noted that they were more formally involved in the school through attending the Parenting in a New Society discussion group program, visiting and speaking with the teachers and the school settlement worker, attending some of the evening programs offered at the school such as a dinner program and a literacy program, and volunteering in their child's class: "I helped with the milk program and pizza program. I was in the lunch program at Christmas, for kids, giving lunch to all of the kids before Christmas. And I was over there [Parenting in a New Society program], of course!" (Claudette). Participants also recognized how their involvement in the program assisted in their preparedness in other aspects of their lives:

> Kitchener was a very new place for me and she (worker) gave me so much information about the addresses and she gave me so many papers, she explained so many centres for me, some for education, some for papers like any kind of papers, even if I ask about ID, about health cards, citizenship, whatever, and she told me, anyway that I can go to YMCA. (Rana)

It is clear that the perceived benefits of participating in this discussion group are far reaching and extend beyond academic and knowledge-based preparedness.

### INVOLVEMENT BARRIERS

Consistent with other research (Huntsinger & Jose, 2009; Lahaie, 2008; Turney & Kao, 2009), parents also described a variety of barriers that prevented or hindered involvement/engagement behaviour. These barriers included needing to work or attend school themselves and therefore having less time to become involved/engaged:

> I only go to this program because it's every Tuesday ... because I go to school everyday so it's enough for me. And there's nobody to help me at home. This is the reason, I have to come and feed them (her children) and clean. And I like it, I like school so much, more and more and more, I like education, even with computers and English, with everything but it's hard for me to get the chance to volunteer when I go to school, you know? (Rana)

Furthermore, illness, needing to care for other children at home, and needing to care for the house were mentioned as barriers to involvement. One participant described a lack of transportation to the local school as a barrier: "You must have a car and time to go with your kids around the town" (Claudette). Not being able to speak English fluently was a commonly cited barrier among participants in this study: "When my English develops I would like to volunteer there [the school]" (Halah). It is important to recognize barriers that do exist in terms of parents being involved in schooling, activities, and behaviours concerning their children so that these barriers can be reduced. For example, it may be important to have approachable school staff who help parents to be more comfortable in approaching the school for assistance and for involvement opportunities. Careful planning should also be used when considering the location and timing of programs since participants may not have transportation or time to devote to program sessions.

## LANGUAGE INSECURITY: THE CATALYST TO VALUABLE SUPPORTS

When we looked at the barriers to involvement, there were barriers that prevented involvement, as we expected, but there were also barriers that actually led to more involvement. We call these barriers *catalyst barriers*. Within barriers to school readiness, language insecurity was discovered to act more as a catalyst barrier than as a traditional barrier. It appears that, in an effort to reduce language insecurity, mothers joined the Parenting in a New Society discussion group as a way to practise conversing in English:

> I need some listeners, those who can listen to me and I can listen to them, so that's why I joined the program, and I also wanted to improve my English because back home, I don't speak any English, because it's totally Urdu and Arabic, so I wanted to improve my English. (Maryam)

Further, a participant explained: "I joined this program to make new friends, to improve my English, and for my daughter, to go with other children" (Lina). In essence, participants attended the Parenting in a New Society discussion group to practise speaking in English while gaining social support. While language fluency was one of their initial intents, participants were also exposed to support from community agencies and services that could help in preparing their children for school:

> When we were starting this program on Tuesday, I think [the program facilitator] told us there is another program for language in the community centre.... She told us about sharing day, from the community centre, and she told us about the Leisure card from City Hall. (Claudette)

Participants received a presentation about a local community centre and some events and programs it was running, public health services for families, and local community supports such as the regional police. Mothers also received information about child development and how to promote learning in the home:

> I can get stuff from the community centre that I need at home, or whatever. So it was so so many things you know, even about the kids or if there is a program or an activity, always I can get information. (Maryam)

Since the discussion group took place in the school their children attended, participants were exposed to involvement and engagement opportunities from simply being in the school. For example, one mother noticed a reading program for students that took place in the school and decided to join as a volunteer when she believed she could speak enough in English to do so. Another participant needed information on housing and was therefore connected with the school settlement worker. Because participants wanted to improve their English language skills, they joined Parenting in a New

Society and subsequently gained access to a plethora of information and resources associated with school readiness as well as a variety of engagement and involvement opportunities.

## Perceptions of school readiness

Mothers commented on how they prepared themselves and their children for school in Canada and the way they used the Parenting in a New Society discussion group in this process. Participants were asked what they believed was important for their children to know before entering school. Responses were both consistent and inconsistent with current literature, which states that immigrant parents are more likely to attribute academic mastery skills as an indicator of school readiness rather than social skills or learning process skills (Barbarin et al., 2008; Piotrkowski et al., 2000; Zhang et al., 2008). Participants explained that from their perspectives, school readiness included being able to care for oneself, feeling comfortable in the school, being able to socialize with others, knowing the school structure, valuing education, and knowing basic academic information such as the alphabet and how to count. To address readiness needs, parents did a variety of things including participating in extra-curricular activities and reading with their children at home.

Participants were also asked what they, as mothers, needed to be ready to send their children to school in Ontario. Participants stated that they needed to feel comfortable in the school, to know the school structure, and to know the basic curriculum. For example, one participant stated, "They [immigrant parents] have to know that their kids will only go for three days a week, or full-time, it depends. Because many schools [kindergartens] are not full-time. So first they have to know this!" (Maryam). Parents also engaged in behaviours associated with satisfying these readiness needs such as speaking with their child's teacher, talking with the school settlement worker, and attending the Parenting in a New Society discussion group:

> If you are confident, I think you can talk to their teachers, the kids' teachers, more frequently. So, now I feel better that I can talk to their teacher. If they have some problem, I can ask them "What is this happening?" and "This shouldn't be happening" or something like this. (Claudette)

When participants were asked what they believed to be the most important aspect of preparing their children for school and preparing themselves for school, they consistently identified English-language fluency as crucial: "I think it's very important for me to improve my English to help her, yes to help her at school, and I think this is very important for me" (Rana). Again, joining the discussion group helped participants manage language-insecurity concerns as well as access other language-education resources outside of the program.

## Discussion

When considering school readiness for parents, the literature consistently explains that immigrant parents are less likely to prepare their children adequately for school (Brooks-Gunn & Markman, 2005; Carreón, Drake, & Barton, 2005; Huntsinger & Jose, 2009; Kampijan & Snyder 2011; Lahaie, 2008; Levine-Rasky, 2009; Turney & Kao, 2009). Parental involvement is frequently cited as an indicator of parental readiness for school and of parents' ability to prepare their children for school (Geenen, Powers, & Lopez-Vasquez, 2001; Panferov, 2010; Parker et al., 1999).

In understanding parental involvement, we must also consider barriers that impede parental involvement, especially barriers that pertain specifically to immigrant parents. These barriers include language barriers (Panferov, 2010), parental stress (Chazan-Cohen et al., 2009), low self-efficacy (Anderson & Minke, 2007; Bandura, 1997), lack of information regarding school structure and the opportunities for involvement that exist (Giallo et al., 2008), lack of resources (Lahaie, 2008), and lack of social capital (Carreón, Drake, & Barton, 2005; Levine-Rasky, 2009), among others. We found some similar barriers, such as parental stress and language barriers. In addition, some barriers acted as catalysts, meaning that although they may stifle involvement, they may also motivate involvement.

We recommend that discussion groups such as Parenting in a New Society continue to exist in the school setting as a way for parents to gain support as they begin to manoeuvre the complexities of preparing their children and themselves for school in a new country. Mothers had been refraining from participating in other activities within the school due to their language insecurity. However, in an effort to reduce this language insecurity, they joined the Parenting in a New Society discussion group and were thus connected with a variety of other engagement opportunities and language support.

An important aspect of Parenting in a New Society is that it addresses issues related to motherhood and parenting in a holistic manner from the perspectives of newcomers to Canada. Issues of adjusting to a new country, forming social connections, and being connected with resources (community agencies, English language classes, food assistance programs, counselling agencies, local libraries, and activities for children) are addressed in the discussion group and influence the school-readiness process.

## Conclusion

Our research indicates that the Parenting in a New Society program plays a central role in the school readiness of immigrant mothers in the Kitchener region. Providing a safe place for immigrant parents to discuss issues about themselves and about their children is consistent with Carreón, Drake, and Barton (2005), who state that there is an "urgency of creating practices and structures that promote dialogue among immigrant parents themselves and among immigrant parents and school actors" (p. 495). Hosting this program in the school building is appealing to program participants because it allows them to feel safe and to be close to their children and other supports, such as the school settlement worker and school administration.

It is clear that this method of implementation is convenient. From the perspective of agencies, it is becoming increasingly important to incorporate strategies to assist in dealing with the stresses of immigrating to a new country. Many of these stresses (language insecurity, cultural insecurity, financial issues, health problems) can take extended time to access and overcome. Other stresses, such as the place and time that assistance and support are offered, are very much under the control of agencies and easily accommodated. The widespread support of our research participants points to the direct and tangential benefits of having this program housed directly in the school their children attend or will attend.

---

### REFERENCES

Anderson, K.J., & Minke, K.M. (2007). Parent involvement in education: Toward an understanding of parents' decision making. *Journal of Educational Research, 100*(5), 311–323. http://dx.doi.org/10.3200/JOER.100.5.311-323

Bandura, A. (1997). *Self-efficacy: The exercise of control.* New York: Freeman.

Barbarin, O.A., Early, D., Clifford, R., Bryant, D., Frome, P., Burchinal, M., ... & Pianta, R. (2008). Parental conceptions of school readiness: Relation to ethnicity, socioeconomic status, and children's skills. *Early Education and Development, 19*(5), 671–701. http://dx.doi.org/10.1080/10409280802375257

Brooks-Gunn, J., & Markman, L.B. (2005, Spring). The contribution of parenting to ethnic and racial gaps in school readiness. *Future of Children, 15*(1), 139–168. http://dx.doi.org/10.1353/foc.2005.0001 Medline:16130545

Carreón, G.P., Drake, C., & Barton, A.C. (2005). The importance of presence: Immigrant parents' school engagement experiences. *American Educational Research Journal, 42*(3), 465–498. http://dx.doi.org/10.3102/00028312042003465

Chazan-Cohen, R., Raikes, H., Brooks-Gunn, J., et al. (2009). Low-income children's school readiness: Parent contributions over the first five years. *Early Education and Development, 20*(6), 958–977. http://dx.doi.org/10.1080/10409280903362402

Dockett, S., & Perry, B. (2009). Readiness for school: A relational construct. *Australasian Journal of Early Childhood, 34*(1), 20–26.

Englund, M.M., Luckner, A.E., Whaley, G.J.L., & Egeland, B. (2004). Children's achievement in early elementary school: Longitudinal effects of parental involvement, expectations, and quality of assistance. *Journal of Educational Psychology, 96*(4), 723–730. http://dx.doi.org/10.1037/0022-0663.96.4.723

Entwisle, D.R., & Alexander, K.L. (1995). A parent's economic shadow: Family structure versus family resources as influences on early school achievement. *Journal of Marriage and the Family, 57*(2), 399–409. http://dx.doi.org/10.2307/353693

Freire, P. (1970/2000). *Pedagogy of the oppressed* (30th anniversary ed.). New York, NY: Continuum International Publishing.

Geenen, S., Powers, L.E., & Lopez-Vasquez, A. (2001). Multicultural aspects of parent involvement in transition planning. *Exceptional Children, 67*(2), 265–282.

Giallo, R., Kienhuis, M., Treyvaud, K., & Matthews, J. (2008). A psychometric evaluation of the parent self-efficacy in managing the transition to school scale. *Australian Journal of Educational & Developmental Psychology, 8*, 36–48.

Huntsinger, C.S., & Jose, P.E. (2009). Parental involvement in children's schooling: Different meanings in different cultures. *Early Childhood Research Quarterly, 24*(4), 398–410. http://dx.doi.org/10.1016/j.ecresq.2009.07.006

Janus, M., & Duku, E. (2007). The school entry gap: Socioeconomic, family, and health factors associated with children's school readiness to learn. *Early Education and Development, 18*(3), 375–403. http://dx.doi.org/10.1080/10409280701610796a

Kampijan, W., & Snyder, D. (2011). Project Summary Information. *Project: Family resource centres: Community settings that support social inclusion—Focus group for new Canadian families: Report* (pp. 1–14). Unpublished: Canadian Association of Family Resource Programs.

Lahaie, C. (2008). School readiness of children of immigrants: Does parental involvement play a role? *Social Science Quarterly, 89*(3), 684–705. http://dx.doi.org/10.1111/j.1540-6237.2008.00554.x

Lee, E. (1988, Jun). Cultural factors in working with Southeast Asian refugee adolescents. *Journal of Adolescence, 11*(2), 167–179. http://dx.doi.org/10.1016/S0140-1971(88)80051-4 Medline:3403751

Levine-Rasky, C. (2009). Dynamics of parent involvement at a multicultural school. *British Journal of Sociology of Education, 30*(3), 331–344. http://dx.doi.org/10.1080/01425690902812604

Panferov, S. (2010). Increasing ELL parental involvement in our schools: Learning from the parents. *Theory into Practice, 49*(2), 106–112. http://dx.doi.org/10.1080/00405841003626551

Parker, F.L., Boak, A.Y., Griffin, K.W., Ripple, C., & Peay, L. (1999). Parent–child relationship, home learning environment, and school readiness. *School Psychology Review, 28*(3), 413–425.

Piotrkowski, C.S., Botsko, M., & Matthews, E. (2000). Parents' and teachers' beliefs about children's school readiness in a high-need community. *Early Childhood Research Quarterly, 15*(4), 537–558. http://dx.doi.org/10.1016/S0885-2006(01)00072-2

Ramey, C.T., & Ramey, S.L. (2004). Early learning and school readiness: Can early intervention make a difference? *Merrill-Palmer Quarterly, 50*(4), 471–491. http://dx.doi.org/10.1353/mpq.2004.0034

Starks, H., & Brown Trinidad, S. (2007, Dec). Choose your method: A comparison of phenomenology, discourse analysis, and grounded theory. *Qualitative Health Research, 17*(10), 1372–1380. http://dx.doi.org/10.1177/1049732307307031 Medline:18000076

Turney, K., & Kao, G. (2009). Barriers to school involvement: Are immigrant parents disadvantaged? *Journal of Educational Research, 102*(4), 257–271. http://dx.doi.org/10.3200/JOER.102.4.257-271

Vygotsky, L.S. (1978). *Mind in society: The development of higher psychological processes.* Cambridge, MA: Harvard University Press.

Zhang, X., Sun, L., & Gai, X. (2008). Perceptions of teachers and parents regarding school readiness. *Frontiers of Education in China, 3*(3), 460–471. http://dx.doi.org/10.1007/s11516-008-0030-6

# 6

# Matching policies to needs in early childhood development programs in newcomer populations

*Linda Ogilvie, Darcy Fleming, Anna Kirova, Lucenia Ortiz, Sandra Rastin, Catherine Caufield, Elizabeth Burgess-Pinto, and Mahdieh Dastjerdi*

Links between early childhood development (ECD) and educational success are acknowledged through public funding of Head Start (a government program that provides comprehensive education, health, nutrition, and parent-involvement services to low-income children and their families) and similar programs globally. Both child development and education are important determinants of health (Commission on the Social Determinants of Health, 2008), and the emerging field of epigenetics (Murgatroyd & Spengler, 2011) substantiates and maps the pathways through which both the fetal response to maternal stress and a child's response to stress may lead to chronic disease in adulthood. Stresses related to relocation to a new country are well documented in the immigration literature and include social isolation, separation from family, difficulty finding adequate employment and housing, difficulty accessing appropriate health services, and language and cultural differences (Simich & Jackson, 2010). Supporting families with young children in the settlement process, therefore, may be key to newcomer child health and development. Funding of ECD programs, however, tends to stipulate a child focus for activities that precludes adequate attention to the family and social contexts in which the newcomer (immigrant and refugee) children are situated (Bernhard, 2012). Our action-research project explored ECD assessment issues in newcomer children and revealed the tensions between what frontline workers saw being required by funders and what they believed the newcomer children and their families needed. Our primary intent was to yield policy-relevant data.

## Risks to early childhood development in newcomer populations

A recent study mapping kindergarten skills in children in Edmonton, Alberta, suggests that as many as 32% of the children struggle in one or more areas of development ("Kindergarten skills lacking," 2012). Areas of concern include communication skills, general knowledge, emotional maturity, physical health and well-being, social competence, thinking, and language skills. While not all children experiencing difficulty will be newcomers or the children of newcomers, it is immigrant and refugee children for whom accurate assessment of development is often most difficult. Before conducting our study, we knew that 35% of children participating in Head Start programs in Edmonton spoke a language other than English in their home (Lucenia Ortiz, personal communication). If health, social work, and education professionals accept that promotion of child health is an important goal, then they need awareness of child-development assessment issues in newcomer children. As frontline professionals, nurses need to advocate for policy-level changes as warranted (Reutter & Kushner, 2010). Policy-makers need reliable evidence on which to base funding decisions.

### Assessing development in newcomer toddlers and preschoolers

While our research was conducted in 2004 and 2005, current review of the literature confirms that our findings remain relevant today both in Canada and in other immigrant-receiving societies (Educational, Audiovisual and Culture Executive Agency, European Commission, 2009; Hernandez, Denton, & Macartney, 2008; Karoly & Gonzalez, 2011; Leseman, 2007; Shewbridge, Kim, Wurzburg, & Hostens, 2010; Taguma, Shewbridge, Huttova, & Hoffman, 2009). Prior to initiation of our study, 63 newcomer families with preschool children in Edmonton participated in research to explore their transition between cultures. This research focused on elements that enhanced or detracted from adjustment to their new national context and how such factors affected their ability to parent (Multicultural Health Brokers Co-op, 2004). Findings were congruent with other research that revealed significant differences in experiences of immigrant versus refugee families, with refugee families tending to experience significantly more mental health stress (Abu-Laban et al., 1999; Beiser, 2005).

Publicly funded programs are facing increasing pressure to assess young children formally, both to justify investments in ECD education programs and to apply best practices, which include assessing need and monitoring progress. Several articles, however, question the validity of using standardized tests normed on Western populations to assess culturally different groups (Greenfield, 1997; Suske & Swanson, 1997; Willgerodt, 2003; Williams & Williams, 1987). Policy documents published by the US National Institute for Early Education point to the potential for subjectivity in all ECD assessment (Epstein, Schweinhart, Parecki-DeBruin, & Robin, 2004). These documents reveal particular concern in newcomer children as current standardized tests are designed to measure proficiency in a predetermined set of tasks that are grounded in Western developmental norms. Newcomer children's diverse knowledge is often marginalized and devalued in comparison to the privileged knowledge associated with norms promoted by the dominant discourse within the field of early childhood education. Consequently, "the power base which determines which people are more likely to be successful in life is uneven right from the start as children start school with hugely different amounts of the 'right' kind of cultural capital" (O'Connor, 2011, p. 117).

Four articles highlighted cultural differences in parenting that could affect the validity of standardized tests of child development (Dreher & Hayes, 1993; Lewis, 2000; Pachter & Dworkin, 1997; Rogoff, Mosier, Mistry, & Goncu, 1993). For example, in a study of four cultures, mothers were asked to identify ages at which children achieve specific milestones. While responses related to gross motor skills and language were similar, those related to social and personal competency differed. The differences appeared to be related to child-rearing practices (Pachter & Dworkin, 1997).

An association between socio-economic status and health, cognitive, and socio-emotional outcomes in children is well established (Bradley & Corwyn, 2002; Maggi, Hertzman, Kohen, & D'Angiulli, 2004). Poverty in the Canadian immigrant population in 2004 was 20% compared to 10% for other Canadians (Simich & Jackson, 2010). Similar income discrepancies in newcomer populations are reported in the United States (Hernandez, Denton, & Macartney, 2008) and across Europe (Educational, Audiovisual and Culture Executive Agency, European Commission, 2009). Such income inequality reinforces the potential for increased developmental risk in immigrant children, although Canadian research suggests that poverty in newcomer families may have fewer adverse effects on child educational and behavioural outcomes than poverty in native-born families (Beiser, 2005). Congruent with what is happening in Europe (Educational, Audiovisual and Culture Executive Agency, European Commission, 2009), research in the US reveals that enrolment of newcomer children in early childhood education programs lags behind enrolment of American-born children except in states with universal, fully funded access for all children (Clements, Barfield, Kotelchuk,

& Wilber, 2008; Greenberg & Khan, 2011; Karoly & Gonzalez, 2011). Fiscal barriers, language differences, and lack of transportation are partial explanations, but the issues of lack of parental recognition of possible problems that could affect school success, inadequate assessment of developmental delays, bureaucratic complexity, parental distrust of government programs, and parental preference to keep young children at home were also raised (Karoly & Gonzalez, 2011).

The barriers reported in the international literature also emerged in our research and have been articulated in Canadian literature that tends to be less focused on the child and more focused on the family (Community–University Partnership for the Study of Children, Youth, and Families, 2006; Dotsch, 1999; Navabi, 2011). In a media report of a new study of three western Canadian cities, Kelly Ng, a co-director of the report and director of SUCCESS Family and Youth Services in British Columbia, states that "different cultures can hold different interpretations of what values should be ingrained in a child, and that those differences are not reflected in ECD programs in the Lower Mainland" (Lupick, 2009). An Australian author made the point that with globalization and increasing international mobility, the possibility of "hybridized parenting," related to adaptation of parenting to life in a new culture, must be considered (Sanagavarapu, 2010, p. 36). Another Australian article proposed action research as a means to analyze programs and pose solutions (Razum, Görgen, & Diesfeld, 1997). What was not discussed adequately in the literature was the difficulty of assessing whether newcomer child performance in a standardized test reflects the child's difficulty in achieving milestones or parenting differences. Identified lags in child development may be the result of language, environmental, or parenting differences or an issue intrinsic to the child regardless of home environment. While interventions in both situations may appear similar, long-term potential and needs for intervention can be very different, and avoidance of inappropriate "labelling" of children is critical.

Finally, of relevance to our interests, a study of Haitian "boat people" revealed "paranoia" related to circumstances of arrival that made them "suspicious of participating in research of any kind" (de Santis, 1990, p. 361). This reluctance matched a concern of settlement agency researchers in our study as they were concerned that signed consents for child assessment and for participation in ECD education programs were perceived as risky by some parents.

## The research process

Our research emerged as a follow-up to the 2004 Multicultural Health Brokers Co-op study mentioned above. Administrators of

ECD programs were concerned that child-assessment tools and practices mandated by provincial government policies related to funding opportunities were not in line with the realities encountered by frontline staff in their work with newcomer children and families. Government decision-makers were sympathetic but needed initial and ongoing child assessments and outcome data to validate the provision of funds. Research to evaluate the assessment tools used in practice and to suggest culturally responsive revisions seemed the best approach to meet the need for changes that would be congruent with an evidence-based funding policy. Because of the need to make and validate changes as part of the research process, an action-research approach was chosen.

### Research objectives and design

The decision to use action research is congruent with current research trends when change is sought. Collaboration is critical, and cultural skills are essential. Ongoing data collection, analysis, change, and repetition of the cycle are envisioned, and knowledge translation is conceptualized as part of the research process (Baum, MacDougall, & Smith, 2006; Burgio, 2010; Hills, Mullett, & Carroll, 2007; Kelly, 2005; Minkler, 2010; Oscós-Sánchez, Lesser, & Kelly, 2008; Ragsdell, 2009; Razum, Görgen, & Diesfeld, 1997). Our research team included four settlement agency researchers (including administrators, program leaders, and a psychologist from three newcomer settlement agencies); three university faculty members (two from nursing and one from education, whose area of specialization was early childhood education); a post-doctoral fellow from a community–university partnership; and one doctoral student from a nursing faculty. Research staff included two PhD students (a research coordinator from a sociology department and a research assistant from a nursing faculty) and an undergraduate student from a nursing faculty. Some team members had personal experience as newcomer parents. Past experience in action research highlighted the importance of including administrators and a diversity of expertise on the team, as well as a need to acknowledge but minimize power differences across team members. The first research-team meeting was used to develop the research strategy, delegate proposal writing, and brainstorm potential funding sources.

The initial purpose of our research was twofold and was stated as objectives rather than research questions:

- To identify and describe some of the complex issues faced by ECD program staff, families, evaluators, and funders when conducting, interpreting, and making decisions based on

formal assessments of children from diverse ethno-cultural backgrounds.
- To design and initiate a process of identifying, implementing, and evaluating strategies to address such issues.

## Data collection and participants

The research design included audiotaped focus groups and parent interviews with verbatim translation, as well as research-team meetings at which detailed minutes were recorded. Not counting the initial planning meeting, six research-team meetings were held over one year, four focus groups were conducted, and seven parent interviews were completed. Convenience sampling through agency contacts was used to recruit focus-group and parent-interview participants. Ethical clearance was granted through the university review process, and consents were signed by most research participants. All parents who were interviewed signed the consent form. Solicitation of signed consents was overlooked when the focus-group interviews with frontline staff were conducted. Some, but not all, consents were collected later, and the university ethics committee was notified. Permission to continue the research was granted by the ethics committee as the information in the consent form had been communicated to participants before commencement of the focus-group process.

The first research-team meeting after the planning meeting was a recorded focus group that included seven ECD program administrators, many of whom were on the team, and served to document perceptions of the issues in detail and reveal research-team biases before planning and conducting the remaining focus groups and interviews. This discussion was followed by three focus groups with a total of 12 frontline staff from six ECD programs. Three ECD programs sampled in the research were in newcomer settlement agencies, and three programs provided services to the general population, including immigrant and refugee children. Standardized assessment tools used in the agencies sampled included the Nipissing (prescreening tool), Denver, DISC, OUNCE Scale, Child Development Inventory, Developmental Knowledge Scale, Kindergarten Inventory, and Healthy Babies, Healthy Children Assessment (Home Visitation) tool. Not all tools were used in each program. All focus groups were completed and findings were discussed by the research team before any parent interviews were done.

As with the focus groups, the research team collaborated in developing the interview guide for the parent interviews. Of the seven parent interviews, six were with mothers and one included both parents; thus, eight parents participated. Two families had children in Head

Start programs serving the general population, and five had children in ECD programs in three different settlement agencies. Interpreters were used for six interviews although all but one mother spoke English with varying degrees of fluency. Most families had been in Canada from one to six years, but in one family the parents had been in Canada for more than 10 years. Families came from Burundi, China, Iraq, Sudan, and Vietnam. Three families and one father transited through a second country (Egypt, Ethiopia, Malaysia, and Turkey) before settling in Canada. Some, but not all, of these families had spent time in refugee camps. Some of the children had been born in Canada, but others were born in source or transit countries. Concerns raised by program administrators and frontline workers, as revealed in research-team discussions and focus groups, were not always raised by the parents. Parents tended to view life in Canada positively and were not, with one exception, representative of the most vulnerable families served by the programs.

## Data analysis

Research analysis was ongoing as data was collected and findings were relayed back to the research team. Transcripts were read and summaries, of all ideas expressed within them were prepared by two research assistants independently, then checked for omissions by at least one researcher. These summaries were shared with the entire research team. Academic members of the team had access to the raw data, but agency researchers could access only the summaries, to protect the confidentiality of staff and families associated with their agencies. (Particular comments or phrasing may have identified participants to their agency administrators.) Using the summaries, themes were identified and discussed at research-team meetings as data collection progressed. Early in the study, it became obvious that the second research objective could not be met with current funding and that analysis of each child assessment tool, as originally planned, was not the most useful direction the research could pursue. Comparative analysis across data sources was completed, and discrepancies with what research-team members perceived as relevant before data collection were identified and discussed. As with data analysis, policy, practice, and research suggestions were generated in team meetings. Debates in research-team meetings were lively as interpretations of findings varied within the group and reflected our differing positions in relation to the research intent. Findings were not contentious in relation to what the data said, but meanings needed to be negotiated. Our diversities strengthened the final conclusions. Results with policy implications will be presented through consideration of focus-group data before introduction of parent data. Findings from both sets of data are compared and contrasted.

## Findings: What the agency staff said

Themes emerging from the focus groups with frontline staff were congruent with concerns raised in the research-team discussion and emphasized trust, the use of standardized tools, and program characteristics. What became evident early in data collection was a need to accommodate family needs as part of ECD assessment and programming.

### Trust

In some agencies, parents were the primary targets of intervention, while in others children were the focus. A central point made in all focus-group discussions was the importance of building trusting relationships with families to program effectiveness. Language considerations, cultural sensitivity, gender, relating with family, timing and use of standardized tools, use of information, and relationships with children were instrumental in achieving trust.

Language barriers were not easily bridged through interpreters—"but the person who interprets for you, they don't know what you are looking for, so that is difficult and not accurate, you think?"—and consents posed significant concerns: "He does, he listens to me and it's like ra-ra-ra, and he signs because he has trust with the worker, and that's all." Beyond issues of language, however, were concerns that some questions were culturally insensitive. Sometimes assumptions were made to avoid asking a question, thus potentially compromising the accuracy of assessments required to meet program requirements:

> I found it difficult to administer that for a couple of reasons and, one, I did have a multicultural broker in the program and she felt very uncomfortable asking some of those questions to the families because the family may interpret it as being insulting or just not appropriate at all. And I can understand that but it put me in a situation because I need to have that information and I can't just leave it ... I can't leave it blank! So there were a lot of things that I wasn't asking families and that the interpreter or the multi-cultural health broker is saying, "I can't ask this. Don't worry, that is not an issue with the family" and it might not have been but I just, I didn't know.

Gender was also raised as a potential barrier to trust, as "these gender role issues can be very difficult for workers that are female workers" or "I know that certainly as a male ... when I was working with mothers; that was very difficult. That was very awkward for the families. It was un ... atypical to have a man who wasn't part of the family being involved, and especially in their home." Engaging fathers was sometimes a challenge as well.

Relating to recent newcomer families was particularly difficult for staff who did not share the immigrant experience.

> And the one, I guess, that hasn't been mentioned, too, but I experienced just sitting around this table is that as much as I try to empathize, and I am ignorant of these issues, and concerns, I can try as hard as I can and I have not experienced and I am going to blunder through this, right. I am going to blunder through and try to be sensitive to some of these things but a lot of times my actions or my interactions with these parents are probably going to be ... just not appropriate, eh? ... And there is this huge sense of relief when they finally interact with another family or service provider who knows what they have been through. Because I could never be there so there is that ignorance piece, too.

This quotation speaks to the need to have workers who reflect the diversity within the clientele of the agency.

Soliciting consents was difficult. Agency workers stated that refugees in particular associated paperwork with negative experiences with authorities. Requiring that families sign consent forms at the beginning of involvement in a program was perceived as an impediment to development of a trusting relationship, and thus detrimental to the entire ECD process:

> Paper itself is something threatening because all the experiences they had with people coming and doing paperwork, somebody disappearing, somebody going to jail, all that kind of stuff, so the simple thing that you come in with a consent and want that signed is like closing the door on you and I, and again you know by now a lot of the workers have established reputation in the communities that we work but in the beginning, it was a huge barrier!

The concern with timing of consents extended to concern about the timing and pace of standardized testing: for example, "the assessments have been a real struggle because sometimes ... they are not ready. You don't have a relationship with the family and you are supposed to be doing these assessments" or "Even with the children you need a couple of weeks to get a relationship."

Parents need to trust that information will not be used to their child's detriment and yet a concern may need to be identified to meet criteria for participation in a program:

> I think there's this muddling and this disconnect with service providers having an understanding of what they're using those assessments for and funders for what they're using, so that I think that sometimes we go for the sake of gathering information and then in fact the big danger is we fire it off to the people who are going to be the guys to interpret it, and it can determine whether our program's going to continue. Like there are some big issues here, I think ... In good faith we would label a child as having a severe communication disorder on that child with a huge amount of faith that it's not going to be misinterpreted after that child leaves our program.

Trust then provides a context within which parents feel comfortable providing accurate information, even information they consider sensitive. Financial information and questions about contact with family members who may be in difficult circumstances in the home country were of most concern to agency staff. With a trusting relationship, the use of standardized tools becomes easier.

> I think good listening works very well. With the participants coming to the group ... Either they are accustomed to that kind of parenting program or they have heard about it, or because their peers are doing it, sometimes it is okay to give them a form ... with the one-on-one, when I go visit families, I don't pull out a form. I just sit there and talk and be a very good listener and usually after a visit or two, some of the information would have come out and they actually feel more comfortable volunteering the information to you, versus, you know, putting out a form and ... I still do that but almost right at the very end when all the information has already been gathered ...

This focus-group participant went on to state that she tends to complete the assessment form in front of parents even if she could do it by memory. This demonstrates an ethical sense that it is a parent's right to know that there will be a written record. She also states that sometimes she knows things because she is part of a family's community, but the parent does not share the information "so there may be a gap of actually what you might have known, versus what they might have told you." She was not asked what she records in such situations.

Finally, several frontline workers shared their perceptions that development of a positive relationship with the children was an important key to development of a trusting relationship with parents. What was evident in the focus-group data was the futility of considering the merits of any standardized tool to assess ECD in newcomer children without taking the time to create a trusting relationship as part of the assessment process.

## Appropriate use of standardized assessment tools

Along with trust, concern about appropriate use of standardized assessment tools, particularly quantitative tools, emerged as a key theme in the focus groups with frontline workers. These tools were used to assess specific children and collectively, through mapping the progress of the group of enrolled children, to evaluate programs. The problem was that the tools were unable to capture fully the nuances of what was really achieved. Specifically, child development could not readily be separated from parenting practices or from family stress, but funders were interested only in child-development baselines and progress. This was more of an issue for settlement agency programs than government ECD programs as parental expectations and overall settlement agency mandates were broader in scope. While parental participation was included in both types of programs, government Head Start programs had a child focus, and settlement agency programs had an overall family focus but received funding for a child-focused ECD program and needed to meet specific child-focused criteria. We will develop this tension further under the next theme; for this section, we will focus on the use of the tools themselves.

What seems clear from the focus groups is that the tools were seldom administered according to the protocols recommended. Alterations to accommodate cultural differences were common. Only one tool, the Nipissing, was viewed favourably by participants. The Nipissing, better classified as a prescreening tool as opposed to an ECD assessment tool, is administered through questions for the parents and not direct testing of the child. The administration process allowed interaction with parents that facilitated understanding of why milestones may not be achieved in the absence of any significant deficit in developmental potential intrinsic to the child. Examples from the focus-group transcripts illustrate cultural issues.

> One of the challenges or the interesting things that I wanted to bring up is just around expectations around child development and sometimes how that's connected to culture .... We haven't been able to find a tool that measures an effective way for most of the programs, that parent interaction .... We use, for example, the CDI [Child Development Inventory], that really doesn't tell you much about the quality of the relationship with, between the parent and child, only if the parent has an idea of ... Western ideas of child development.... Then, we tried to introduce the DISC, like what a mess! Because there are so many things in there that are just value statements that are very Western and, you know, we spent a lot of time talking about the word *ashamed* and we are like, Wow! That has a lot of different words for a lot of different people, right, and so always out of awareness that you really have to be sensitive and careful about some of those tools ... Kids just aren't exposed to the same things. Like with identifying pictures ... things that ESL kids have never seen before and so if you are asking them to identify it, and they can't, it doesn't mean that they're not understanding what you are saying. It's just they have never seen this object .... They just get a different way that they play with their kids or interact with their kids. They don't have exposure to scissors ... and so when you are screening them it may come up that they are delayed but really it is that they just haven't had the chance to experience those things.

Agency staff members were in favour of more qualitative assessments that capture stories rather than statistics.

> If you know that, you know, this is a family who comes from a country where the last ten years, you know, there was war, genocide, a lot of people killed, if then you go with your, whatever, you know, your Social Network Index, and you are not, you might be careful about

asking, you know, "Are your parents alive, and how often are you talking to them?" because you know that possibly this is going to open a whole thing. This is not just a simple question for this parent ...

Frontline staff also liked Individual Program Plans (IPPs), but funders disliked their lack of standardization. Staff wanted to see more focus on process and less on outcomes.

The best tools have meaning for families and for practice. Several excerpts speak to this issue: "really a lot of times we're doing these particular measures because they're going to speak to the outcomes that we're going to report"; "I would like to see a tool that, well, that really generates information, but as also be used as something to engage, engage the families into a learning process"; and "I think the best tools will be the families really see relevance to it; like, you know, the discussion before and also make meaning to the funder as well."

What focus-group participants seemed to be saying was that they needed more flexibility in setting assessment priorities, processes, and goals. They also needed more useful tools for practice and were frustrated by the criteria set by funders.

### Assessment and program characteristics

Mixed programs, those that included both newcomer and Canadian-born children and parents, and settlement agency programs differed in terms of challenges, primarily because of less culturally diverse staff and fewer internal linguistic resources in the mixed programs. One mixed program in the study had both Head Start and family-focused programs, while the other two were child-focused. The settlement agencies all had family-focused programs. Assessment tools posed particular difficulties for mixed programs, as mentioned below.

> We have to go by the parent's report to you. If they're not speaking well in their own language, then we'll call in, like we had a little girl this year assessed, just kind of like observation and then parents saying that they're not talking a lot, you know, in their own language.

> If we have concerns about a child who's ESL [English as a Second Language], we'll just make a referral to a speech and language pathologist because I have tried DISC-ing ESL kids and with their speech, we found that the results just aren't accurate ... and usually we'll have a multicultural health worker who'll come in.

The child-focused programs seem to have fewer issues around consents: "well, primarily because it is child focused. I don't find there's a lot of resistance, 'cause a lot of them want their kids in the program and they want to learn, they're so excited." In a family-focused agency, one participant said,

> I don't usually start right at the beginning even though people say: "You need to sign the consent." I just get an impression right at the beginning, not until six months or something. You kind of know the family they know that all say "you are my friend" and they are more willing to do, even if they don't quite understand everything.

While common issues were identified across focus groups, there were differences of opinion about the usefulness of existing assessment tools and the solicitation of consents.

## Findings: What the parents said

As in the focus groups, parent interviews revealed themes related to language, cultural sensitivity of the assessment items, concerns about the information gathered, the use of standardized assessment forms, and the application of consent forms. Views of such themes, however, were often different from those of agency staff and managers. Parents did not talk about gender differences between the worker and parent, concerns that the worker could relate to their experience, the timing of standardized tests, or the development of relationships between workers and children. They did share some personal issues and their thoughts about program participation and evaluation, but these comments were practice rather than policy relevant and are not included here. Common themes identified by the parents are presented below.

### Language

With respect to language, parents were concerned about retention of their heritage language, pressure to learn English to parent their children effectively, the social limitations of not speaking English, and the opportunities through their child's participation in an ECD program for the parents to enhance their communication skills in English. For example, one parent said, "And I think that's most people's dreams, like to maintain Vietnamese at home." Another parent suggested that more heritage-language resources should be available. In response to a question about the importance that the parents speak English, one of the parents replied that in relation to the teacher,

> I should be [able to] talk to them. Yeah. And should, I would like to know more my son, how to him do at school without me, so I often call his teacher and run to the school, talk to them.

### Cultural sensitivity

Parents shared less concern about cultural sensitivity and assessment item sensitivity than focus-group participants. In relation to family and child assessment practices, responses included "yes, it feel great" and "it's awesome" (regarding the Nipissing). One parent, while not upset by the testing per se, did express concerns about potential labelling of a child.

> There were not questions that I felt uncomfortable or not feeling good because I was very open minded. I didn't mind them asking questions because my purpose was to help them to fully understand my son's situation. However, with my husband, he wasn't really good about those questions and the tests because he felt that they were asking these questions as if the son was having subnormal intelligence. For me I would much rather, you know, tell them more just to increase their understanding of my son. Perhaps he has a psychological issue that I didn't know or perhaps, I didn't you know, parent him appropriately, so it could be my parenting methods. So no, I did not feel upset at all. For my husband there were moments when he felt, he had a bad feeling, but however, I try to talk to him a little while he was more accepting to the assessment.

Only one parent expressed concern with questions related to income and to relationships with extended family members back home. As the interpreter reported:

> Yeah, she said like about spending money or like are you talking to your parent ... because that calling Vietnam.... So, when you mention that they going to cry automatically. So I try to stay away from that. If some of them have money they can afford to call Vietnam; some don't, that is emotional ... And then I pay attention lately if I mention about parent or Vietnam when they don't have money. Then after that question they go home and the husband and wife will have a conflict, because they need money to send home.

This quotation is interesting as it is an example of the interpreter reporting what the parent said then adding more information that did not appear to come from this parent but rather from the interpreter's collective experience. This happened frequently when parents were interviewed.

### Use of consent forms

Only one parent shared a concern about the potential use of information. With regard to consent forms, just one parent shared any concern; she also raised the concern during the consent process for the research interview. The mother thought that the researcher was trying to take her children from her, particularly as a small honorarium was offered. This was the most vulnerable parent interviewed, and the interpreter said,

> She is telling you that, 'cause everybody in here they never have good stuff. They never ask about those stuff and you came from far away. She just heard about university and she never see university and you give her money too. She thought that with the money you just buy her children with it.

This mother appeared to be in crisis. The interview was curtailed. The agency was aware of the issue and already seeking help for this woman.

## What we learned

Once we had all of the findings, the research team met to discuss implications and policy recommendations. The complex process of newcomer ECD assessment and programming, always a component of our objectives, emerged from our data as central to quality programming, with assessment-tool appropriateness not the top priority at that time. Such tool development is now underway in our community (Gokiert et al., 2010), but other issues raised in the research were addressed first. Our findings therefore reinforce the concerns raised in the literature on cultural relevance of standardized assessment tools (Epstein, Schweinhart, Parecki-DeBruin, & Robin, 2004; Fuller et al., 2009; Greenfield, 1997; O'Connor, 2011; Suske & Swanson, 1997; Willgerodt, 2003; Williams & Williams, 1987), cultural differences in parenting practices that may affect ECD assessment (Dreher & Hayes, 1993; Lewis, 2000; Pachter & Dworkin, 1997; Rogoff, Mosier, Mistry, & Goncu, 1993), and the need for family-focused ECD programming (Bornstein & Cote, 2004; Community–University Partnership for the Study of Children, Youth, and Families, 2006; Dotsch, 1999; Kummerer, Lopez-Reyna, & Hughes, 2007; Navabi, 2011; Vesely & Ginsberg, 2011). Our findings, however, also provide guidance for changes to policy and needs for further research.

Some of our findings from parent interviews were not a good fit with the perceptions of ECD program managers and frontline staff. Parents were less concerned about consents, cultural sensitivity in questioning, and test-item sensitivity than ECD program staff, and none of them mentioned the gender of the frontline worker as an issue. From the research-team discussion, we came to the understanding that both sets of data could be equally valid. If so, what did this mean? What seems to explain the discrepancies most satisfactorily is an important insight for all research with vulnerable populations. Participant recruitment generally means working through agencies on the front lines. Protection of families and individuals in crisis tends to exclude them from participation in research in two ways. Such persons are unlikely to volunteer for participation, and agency staff members are unlikely to approach their most vulnerable clients as potential research informants, yet such clients are the most in need of services. Policy-makers like to base funding decisions on research, but data that accurately reflects frontline realities may not always be available. The mixed methods of focus groups and family interviews facilitated more in-depth exploration of issues from multiple perspectives. The multidisciplinary community/academic research team allowed a more nuanced interpretation of findings.

A limitation of the research may be the use of agency staff for interpretation in the parent interviews. Lack of funding mandated this data-collection decision, but families may have been reluctant to speak openly, and interpreters did at times insert their own observations into the interview process. Alternatively, we may have better data because of the trust participants already had in the interpreters. What became obvious early in our research was the complexity of ECD programming for newcomer populations.

## Translating research into policy

In the initial report submitted to the granting agency and community stakeholders, policy, practice, and research suggestions, rather than recommendations, were made, partly because of the lack of congruency between parent and worker/manager data. Seven policy suggestions were generated. While these policy suggestions are framed in the Canadian context, they have relevance for other immigrant-receiving countries. As we were engaged in action research, our policy suggestions are part of our findings as the research team engaged in discussion and interpretation of data as a data-generating strategy in itself.

### Suggestions for policy related to newcomer ECD programming

- *Families should be provided with supports that address their primary concerns and that demonstrate respect.* Community development and teaching/learning literature (Knowles, Holton, & Swanson, 2005; Huang & Wang, 2005) emphasizes the importance of starting where the learner is and building interventions from perceived needs. Newcomer parents may be struggling to meet basic needs for the family and struggling in an alien environment. Support for meeting such needs may be necessary to establish trust and stability before the ECD needs of their children can be given priority.
- *Policy- and decision-makers should be more accepting of process-oriented information-gathering instruments and procedures when funding of programming for vulnerable populations is considered. The funding (or continued funding) of programs for young immigrant children should not depend solely on the results of standardized tests.* Given the complexity of each family's life circumstances, measuring the success of a program based on these results prevents the agencies from addressing the family's needs in a complex way and thus does not contribute to the development of the child.

In addition, unlike child-centred programs, which typically have clearer objectives and simpler means for accomplishing them, family-centred programs are often more open ended, in both what they do and how they do it. Thus, training staff and using a prescribed set of tools are much more difficult.

- *Policy- and decision-makers should acknowledge that agencies with programs facilitating settlement issues of parents and parenting in a new culture are legitimate applicants for ECD funding.* As parental lack of integration into society and stress related to migration may affect early childhood development, agencies with a holistic, family approach to programming are best situated to address the complex issues newcomers with young children face. Child-centred programs typically seem to have clearer objectives and simpler means for accomplishing them. Family-centred programs are often more open ended, both in what they do and how they do it. Agencies should have secured funds for early childhood development programs.

- *Immigrant-serving agencies, particularly those involved in providing early childhood development programs, should have secured funding for cultural consultative services and/or collaborative care with other agencies providing services to a more diverse clientele.* Attention must be paid to communication barriers, with particular attention to agencies providing services to both immigrant/refugee and Canadian-born families.

- *Templates and protocols for conducting alternative assessments should be developed in close collaboration with the immigrant-serving agencies, particularly those which are involved in early childhood development programming.* This approach would allow for cultural variations.

- *The development of culturally appropriate assessment tools and staff training should be part of a comprehensive effort at achieving cultural competence for organizations to be able to serve and work with children and families from culturally diverse backgrounds.* The increasing diversity of Canadian society presents a compelling need for organizations to develop culturally competent systems of care that translate knowledge about the context, priorities, and needs of culturally diverse families into appropriate resources, services, and supports. Culturally appropriate assessment tools become a significant element in the development and provision of a culturally competent system of care.

- *Programs should have a clear mandate, meaning that they are clear about their purpose and how they operate.* This clarity is essential for appropriate and fair program approval, evaluation, and decision-making about ongoing funding.

Once we had analyzed the data, developed policy suggestions, and written the final report, the research team met with provincial government policy-makers, who had also been involved in funding the research, to share the findings. While there was trepidation over the shift from the original two objectives to a more in-depth focus on the first objective, the report was well received. There was willingness to engage in discussion of more relevant criteria for ECD assessment practices and outcome evaluation for newcomer children and families. This agreement to engage in more culturally aware, family-focused ECD programming for newcomer families is an excellent fit with current recommendations (Bernhard, 2012).

## Discussion

Assessment of ECD in newcomer children is complex and ideally should serve multiple purposes. In working with children, we constantly make judgements about their development. We do this both formally and informally, and we make decisions based on these judgements. More formal assessments are done on children to determine eligibility (selection) for programming, identify developmental difficulties (diagnostic), determine individual child strengths and weaknesses (individual program planning), track developmental change (progress), and test treatment effects (program evaluation). Policy-makers, who tend to be government or other funders, want such evidence. Assessing children, however, can serve other functions. Secondary functions important to intervention programs include training staff about the developmental process, drawing staff attention to behaviours and skills that are deemed important, and facilitating discussion about individual children among staff, professionals, and parents. Our research arose out of concerns of program administrators and frontline staff that funding policies mandated assessment practices and tools that were inappropriate in their work with newcomer children and families. While the policy-makers were sympathetic, they still required evidence to justify investments in programs.

There are many tools available for assessing children. Each tool is developed for a specific purpose and has its own unique profile of costs and benefits. Choosing the most appropriate (i.e., valid, useful, inexpensive, short) assessment tool is a difficult procedure because it requires a careful analysis of who is being assessed and why. Validity is not a generic property of a tool; rather, it is a judgement of the degree to which evidence, both empirical and theoretical, supports decisions based on test scores (Messick, 1989). Each intended use of a test must therefore be validated. The process of validation involves accumulating evidence to provide a sound scientific basis for the proposed score interpretations (American Educational Research Association, American Psychological Association, National Council on Measurement [AERA, APA/NCME], 1999). These thoughts are not recent. Our data convinced the policy-makers that both the assessment processes and the tools being used (or required) lacked validity. It became obvious as data collection with frontline staff progressed that the tools were not being administered in a standardized way and that variation and flexibility in practice violated tool-administration protocols. That this was occurring was not a major concern for funders because they recognized the practical reasons for the alterations. Our research findings provided justification for ongoing funding of ECD programs, particularly those in nongovernmental, family-focused settlement agencies, while solutions related to enhanced newcomer ECD assessment tools and practices were sought.

Publicly funded programs face increasing pressure to assess young children formally. These pressures are both top down and bottom up. Top-down pressures are a consequence of the need for governments and other social investors to justify their investment. Bottom-up pressure is the consequence of program administrators, professional staff, and others wanting to apply best practices, which include determining need and monitoring progress. Both top-down and bottom-up processes should occur simultaneously and to the extent possible inform each other (Trocmé, 2003). Whether from a clinical, research, or management perspective, there is great benefit in applying clarity and structure to assessment practices.

Much literature in nursing and other practice fields advocates supporting client strengths as empowering and thus more likely to lead to successful outcomes, but program requirements often lead to emphasis on standardized, evidence-based practices based on populations easily accessed for research. The diversity in most societies, particularly those with large immigrant populations, may make such practices ineffective and, in some cases, harmful (Bernhard, 2012). As frontline professionals, we are taught to partner with clients, be they individuals, families, or groups, in mutually setting goals and devising the activities needed to achieve them. That is our professional mandate. As frontline professionals, professional consultants, and administrators, we must become skilled in communicating our knowledge and suggestions in the policy arena. It is not a question of them and us. We are together in this process of developing programs that meet clients' needs.

## Suggestions for research related to newcomer ECD assessment and programming

We have three suggestions for further research related specifically to ECD assessment and programming.

- Working groups composed of ECD specialists, researchers, and frontline workers with ECD family and child assessment experience with immigrant and refugee families need to ascertain essential critical-assessment items, choose and/or develop appropriate tools, test them, and communicate results to funders/policy-makers, as well as publish in the research literature.
- Current tools need to be examined item by item in terms of usefulness of the item and for cultural appropriateness, cultural sensitivity, or cultural ambiguity of the wording. Two groups of tools would be optimal, with one group focused on child assessment and the other on family assessment.
- *Further research that focuses specifically on family-focused programs in newcomer populations is needed.* This research must explore how to evaluate the extent to which the interventions of family-focused programs produce meaningful outcomes for newcomer children. That is, can the process of increasing family functioning that these programs claim they do be documented in a systematic way? Can we demonstrate that programs that create or enhance healthy family functioning are making significant contributions to newcomer healthy child development?

Research related to the first two suggestions is currently underway in our community, as is a longitudinal study related to the third suggestion that, while not newcomer focused, has captured a newcomer sample within the larger database. There is a tension that merits further research between the *family as context* approach, as is most common in the ECD literature (Educational, Audiovisual and Culture Executive Agency, European Commission, 2009; Hernandez, Denton, & Macartney, 2008; Leseman, 2007; Shewbridge, Kim, Wurzburg, & Hostens, 2010; Taguma, Shewbridge, Huttova, & Hoffman, 2009), and the *family as focus* approach described as a possible model by Karoly and Gonzalez (2011), recommended strongly by Bernhard (2012), and advocated by our research. The remaining research suggestions emerging from our study relate to the merits of participatory, action, and community-based research methods, particularly for vulnerable populations; the need for more ethno-culturally specific research in recent high-needs newcomer populations; and thoughts about how ethical research with particularly vulnerable families could be approached. These suggestions are more relevant to practice than to policy, so we have addressed them elsewhere.

## Final thoughts

Action research is time and human-resource intensive. It is, however, inherently collaborative and oriented toward change. One issue that merits more exploration is moving from the research process, including integration of findings into practice, to scholarly dissemination in peer-reviewed literature. Research-team members in community-based research have differing priorities and measures of success when engaging in such research. Publication may be delayed, as occurred in this situation. While not ideal, such delay also allowed follow-up information to be presented. Funding policies did evolve, subsequent research did occur, and innovation did happen. Such progress provides validation of the research process in its entirety and of the suggestions that we thought at the conclusion of this research endeavour were too soft to be called recommendations.

### REFERENCES

Abu-Laban, B., Derwing, T., Krahn, H., Muller, M., & Northcott, M. (1999). *The settlement experiences of refugees in Alberta*. Edmonton: Prairie Centre of Excellence for Research on Immigration and Integration.

American Educational Research Association, American Psychological Association, National Council on Measurement in Education [AERA, APA/NCME]. (1999). Standards for educational and psychological testing. Washington, DC: American Psychological Association.

Baum, F., MacDougall, C., & Smith, D. (2006, Oct). Participatory action research. *Journal of Epidemiology and Community Health, 60*(10), 854–857. http://dx.doi.org/10.1136/jech.2004.028662 Medline:16973531

Beiser, M. (2005, Mar–Apr). The health of immigrants and refugees in Canada. *Canadian Journal of Public Health, 96*(Suppl 2), S30–S44. Medline:16078554

Bernhard, J.K. (2012). *Stand together or fall apart: Professionals working with immigrant families*. Halifax: Fernwood.

Bornstein, M.H., & Cote, L.R. (2004, Nov). "Who is sitting across from me?" Immigrant mothers' knowledge of parenting and children's development. *Pediatrics, 114*(5), e557–e564. http://dx.doi.org/10.1542/peds.2004-0713 Medline:15520089

Bradley, R.H., & Corwyn, R.F. (2002). Socioeconomic status and child development. *Annual Review of Psychology, 53*(1), 371–399. http://dx.doi.org/10.1146/annurev.psych.53.100901.135233 Medline:11752490

Burgio, L.D. (2010). Disentangling the translational sciences: A social science perspective. *Research and Theory for Nursing Practice, 24*(1), 56–63. http://dx.doi.org/10.1891/1541-6577.24.1.56 Medline:20333912

Commission on the Social Determinants of Health. (2008). *Closing the gap in a generation: Health equity through action on the social determinants of health. Final report of the Commission on the Social Determinants of Health*. Geneva: WHO.

Community–University Partnership for the Study of Children, Youth, and Families. (2006). Cross-cultural lessons: Early childhood developmental screening and approaches to research and practice. Edmonton: Author. Retrieved June 1, 2012 from http://www.cup.ualberta.ca

de Santis, L. (1990, Jun). Fieldwork with undocumented aliens and other populations at risk. *Western Journal of Nursing Research, 12*(3), 359–372. http://dx.doi.org/10.1177/019394599001200308 Medline:2363291

Dotsch, J. (1999). Non-biased children's assessments. Toronto: The Atkinson Foundation. Retrieved August 16, 2012, from www.esbgc.org/files/SPN_Resource_Library_listing.doc

Dreher, M.C., & Hayes, J.S. (1993, Apr). Triangulation in cross-cultural research of child development in Jamaica. *Western Journal of Nursing Research, 15*(2), 216–229. http://dx.doi.org/10.1177/019394599301500206 Medline:7682374

Educational, Audiovisual and Culture Executive Agency, European Commission. (2009). Tackling social and cultural inequities through early childhood education and care in Europe. Retrieved December 4, 2012, from http://eacea.ec.europa.eu/about-eacea_en

Epstein, A.S., Schweinhart, L.J., Parecki-DeBruin, A., & Robin, K.B. (2004). *Preschool assessment: A guide to developing a balanced approach.* New Brunswick, NJ: National Institute of Early Education Research.

Fuller, B., Bridges, M., Bein, E., et al. (2009, Nov). The health and cognitive growth of Latino toddlers: At risk or immigrant paradox? *Maternal and Child Health Journal, 13*(6), 755–768. http://dx.doi.org/10.1007/s10995-009-0475-0 Medline:19554440

Gokiert, R., Chow, W., Parsa, B., et al. (2010). Early childhood screening. Edmonton: Community–University Partnership for the Study of Children, Youth, and Families. Retrieved June 1, 2012, from http://www.cup.ualberta.ca

Greenberg, J.P. & Khan, J.M. (2011). The influence of immigration on early childhood education and care enrollment. *Journal of Early Childhood Research, 9*(1), 20–35. http://dx.doi.org/10.1177/1476718X1036618.

Greenfield, P.M. (1997). You can't take it with you: Why ability assessments don't cross cultures. *American Psychologist, 52*(10), 1115–1124. http://dx.doi.org/10.1037/0003-066X.52.10.1115

Hernandez, D.J., Denton, N.A., & Macartney, S.E. (2008). Children in immigrant families: Looking to America's future. *Social Policy Report, 22*(3), 3–24.

Hills, M., Mullett, J., & Carroll, S. (2007, Feb–Mar). Community-based participatory action research: Transforming multidisciplinary practice in primary health care. *Pan American Journal of Public Health, 21*(2–3), 125–135. http://dx.doi.org/10.1590/S1020-49892007000200007 Medline:17565799

Huang, C.L., & Wang, H.H. (2005, Mar). Community health development: What is it? *International Nursing Review, 52*(1), 13–17. http://dx.doi.org/10.1111/j.1466-7657.2004.00259.x Medline:15725271

Karoly, L.A., & Gonzalez, G.C. (2011, Spring). Early care and education for children in immigrant families. *Future of Children, 21*(1), 71–101. http://dx.doi.org/10.1353/foc.2011.0005 Medline:21465856

Kelly, P.J. (2005, Jan–Feb). Practical suggestions for community interventions using participatory action research. *Public Health Nursing (Boston, Mass.), 22*(1), 65–73. http://dx.doi.org/10.1111/j.0737-1209.2005.22110.x Medline:15670327

Kindergarten skills lacking (2012, May 31). *Edmonton Journal.* p. A11.

Knowles, M.S., Holton, E.F., III, & Swanson, R.A. (2005). *The adult learner* (6th ed.). London, UK: Elsevier.

Kummerer, S.E., Lopez-Reyna, N.A., & Hughes, M.T. (2007, Aug). Mexican immigrant mothers' perceptions of their children's communication disabilities, emergent literacy development, and speech-language therapy program. *American Journal of Speech-Language Pathology, 16*(3), 271–282. http://dx.doi.org/10.1044/1058-0360(2007/031) Medline:17666552

Leseman, P. (2007). Early education for immigrant children. Migration Policy Institute. Retrieved December 4, 2012, from http://www.migrationpolicy.org/pubs/lesemaneducation091907.pdf

Lewis, M.L. (2000). The cultural context of infant mental health: The development niche of infant–caregiver relationships. In C.H. Zeanah (Ed.), *Handbook of infant mental health* (pp. 91–107). New York: Guilford Press.

Lupick, T. (2009, November 4). Local immigrants find barriers to early childhood development services. *Straight.com*. Retrieved from http://www.straight.com/news/local-immigrants-find-barriers-early-childhood-development-services

Maggi, S., Hertzman, C., Kohen, D., & D'Angiulli, A. (2004). Effects of neighbourhood socioeconomic characteristics and class composition on highly competent children. *Journal of Educational Research, 98*(2), 109–114. http://dx.doi.org/10.3200/JOER.98.2.109-114

Messick, S. (1989). *Educational measurement* (3rd ed.). New York: Macmillan.

Minkler, M. (2010, Apr 1). Linking science and policy through community-based participatory research to study and address health disparities. *American Journal of Public Health, 100*(S1 Suppl 1), S81–S87. http://dx.doi.org/10.2105/AJPH.2009.165720 Medline:20147694

Multicultural Health Brokers Co-op. (2004). *Mapping the life experiences of refugee and immigrant families*. Edmonton: Author.

Murgatroyd, C., & Spengler, D. (2011). Epigenetics of early child development. *Frontiers in Psychiatry, 2*, 1–15. http://dx.doi.org/10.3389/fpsyt.2011.00016 Medline:21647402

Navabi, M. (2011). "Promising practices" of early childhood education for immigrant and refugee children in British Columbia. Vancouver: Affiliation of Multicultural Societies and Service Agencies of BC. Retrieved August 16, 2012, from http://www.ecebc.ca

O'Connor, J. (2011). Applying Bourdieu's concepts of social and cultural capital and habitus to early years research. In T. Waller, J. Whitmarsh, & K. Clarke (Eds.), *Making sense of theory and practice in early childhood: The power of ideas* (pp. 115–127). Maidenhead, UK: Open University Press.

Oscós-Sánchez, M.A., Lesser, J., & Kelly, P. (2008). Cultural competence: A critical facilitator of success in community-based participatory action research. *Issues in Mental Health Nursing, 29*(2), 197–200. http://dx.doi.org/10.1080/01612840701792258 Medline:18293225

Pachter, L.M., & Dworkin, P.H. (1997, Nov). Maternal expectations about normal child development in 4 cultural groups. *Archives of Pediatrics & Adolescent Medicine, 151*(11), 1144–1150. http://dx.doi.org/10.1001/archpedi.1997.02170480074011 Medline:9369877

Ragsdell, G. (2009). Participatory action research: A winning strategy for KM. *Journal of Knowledge Management, 13*(6), 564–576. http://dx.doi.org/10.1108/13673270910997196

Razum, O., Görgen, R., & Diesfeld, H.J. (1997). "Action research" in health programmes. *World Health Forum, 18*(1), 54–55. Medline:9233067

Reutter, L., & Kushner, K.E. (2010, Sep). "Health equity through action on the social determinants of health": Taking up the challenge in nursing. *Nursing Inquiry, 17*(3), 269–280. http://dx.doi.org/10.1111/j.1440-1800.2010.00500.x Medline:20712665

Rogoff, B., Mosier, C., Mistry, J., & Goncu, C. (1993). Toddlers' guided participation with their caregivers in cultural activity (pp. 230–254). In E.A. Forman & N. Minick (Eds.), *Contexts for learning: Sociocultural dynamics in children's development* (2nd ed.). London, UK: Oxford University Press.

Sanagavarapu, P. (2010). What does cultural globalisation mean for parenting in immigrant families in the 21st century? *Australian Journal of Early Childhood, 10*(2), 36–42.

Shewbridge, C., Kim, M., Wurzburg, G., & Hostens, G. (2010). OECD reviews of migrant education: Netherlands. OECD. Retrieved December 4, 2012, from www.oecd.org/netherlands/44612239.pdf

Simich, L., & Jackson, B. (2010). What makes some immigrants healthy and others not? *Health Policy Research, 10,* 26–29.

Suske, K.S., & Swanson, M.W. (1997). Cross-cultural variability in early childhood development: Implications for success. *Physical & Occupational Therapy in Pediatrics, 17*(3), 87–96.

Taguma, M., Shewbridge, C., Huttova, J., & Hoffman, N. (2009). OECD reviews of migrant education: Norway. OECD. Retrieved December 4, 2012, from www.oecd.org/education/educationeconomyandsociety/migranteducation-home.htm

Trocmé, N. (2003). The importance of process in developing outcome measures. Keynote address: National Outcomes Symposium, Ottawa, February 20–21, 2003.

Vesely, C.K., & Ginsberg, M.R. (2011). Strategies and practices for working with immigrant families in early education programs. *Young Children, 66*(1), 84–89.

Willgerodt, M.A. (2003, Nov). Using focus groups to develop culturally relevant instruments. *Western Journal of Nursing Research, 25*(7), 798–814. http://dx.doi.org/10.1177/0193945903256708 Medline:14596180

Williams, P.D., & Williams, A.R. (1987, Mar). Denver Developmental Screening Test norms: A cross-cultural comparison. *Journal of Pediatric Psychology, 12*(1), 39–59. http://dx.doi.org/10.1093/jpepsy/12.1.39 Medline:3572676

# 7

# Cultural negotiations of sense of place through shared parent–child art-making in a preschool for immigrant children

*Anna Kirova, Patti Pente, and Christine Massing*

With the increased numbers of immigrants in the Western countries, the need to find meaningful ways to engage immigrant families in early childhood settings and to build bridges between teachers and parents has been a focus of several recent studies (e.g., Knopf & Swick, 2008; Vandenbroeck, Roets, & Snoeck, 2009). Persistent barriers to such involvement are well documented. They include the inability of parents to communicate in the official language of the host country (Turney & Kao, 2009), parental discomfort with the culture of the school (Isik-Ercan, 2010), conflicting goals of families and teachers (Lahman & Park, 2004), teachers' inability to move beyond their own culturally bound ideas about child rearing (Eberly, Joshi, & Konzai, 2007), and teachers' emphasis on some cultural groups or aspects of culture to the exclusion of others (Sohn & Wang, 2006).

To overcome these barriers, educators and researchers must rethink the current paradigm of parent involvement when they work with immigrant families and must engage in practices that honour newcomer parents' visual and oral traditions (Souto-Manning & Swick, 2006). While art is generally understood to provide alternative forms of both meaning-making and expression of meaning, very few studies identify strategies that use arts and creative processes as a way of meaningfully involving immigrant parents. An exception is a project in which disposable cameras were sent home with immigrant children to allow families and children to share photos with their teachers, thus providing teachers with a glimpse into the family's world (Strickland, Keat, & Marinak, 2010). However, sharing the home life in the host country—the life "here and now"—may not be what is most meaningful to the parents of the children. Many live in poverty (Beiser, 2005) or in circumstances that do not resemble the life the parents left behind and/or the places they still call home.

The research described here proposes a unique approach to engaging immigrant families, children, and their immigrant teachers in art-making as a means of entering a dialogue about their sense of place. In the tradition of some humanistic geographers (e.g., Hay, 1988), this approach recognizes the importance of the emotional realm of our human relationships with place and of the human ability to reflect and interpret such relationships through artistic representations. As an embodied experience (Bresler, 2004; Springgay, 2008; Stinson, 2004), art-making can expose tacit and possibly unrecognized values, so that in creating art and reflecting on it, there may be potential strategies for greater understanding within diversity of perspectives and experiences. In some instances, the connections to cultural traditions and identity that are created through the arts have been instrumental as political means of self-determination for minority cultures (Ballengee Morris et al., 2000). There is power in the arts to forge understanding of self and others; thus, art-making is an important strategy toward the successful negotiation of identity that most immigrants face when they move to a new home. Art is understood in this research as contributing much more than an expression of feelings, which is a common educational value attributed to the arts in Western culture (Eiserman, 2009). Art is also an important means of communicating cultural and personal identity, and/or political and religious values. In a culturally diverse population, where observation and sharing of cultural differences are vital for a robust, inclusive multicultural society, art-making can be significant. In relation to one's sense of place, such diversity speaks to how place is constructed: one's ability to know a place may revolve around distinctive odours, colours, textual and visual qualities in the environment, seasonal changes of temperature, or more indirect, abstract modes of experience that resist objectification (Tuan, 1974). These links between art and place suggest that there is potential for shared cultural exchange.

## Place as theoretical framework

The primary objective of this study was to explore how immigrant preschool teachers and their immigrant students and families investigate their bicultural identities through aesthetic explorations of sense of place. In the study, the exploration of participants' relation to place was informed by the view that "to become human is continually a matter of embodied placement and displacement and the attempt to arrive at or establish a new place, where we understand place as both physical site and locus of meanings and values" (Mugerauer, 1994, p. 156). Given that mobility defines contemporary geopolitical landscape (i.e., in 2010, 43.3 million people in the world were forcibly displaced: United Nations High Commissioner for Refugees, 2010), it is more difficult than ever to develop the strong bonds with a place that usually come through extended residential and ancestral connections to a particular locale. Even in the case of voluntary migration, developing a sense of belonging to a place is not easy: "Mobility may promote individual freedom and appreciation of one's nation, but it tends to erode the development of a strong **local** sense of place" (Hay, 1992, p. 101, bold in original). However, as a common experience among humans, "their need for a sense of 'place'—a feeling of living in an environment which has boundaries and identity" (Hay, 1992, p. 99) is preserved even in the experience of migration.

Relph's (1976) work on "sense of place" and "placelessness" and Tuan's (1974, 1977) work on positive affective ties to place described as "topophilia" are examples of the attention given to the concept of "place" and its role in one's identity since the 1970s. However, as Patterson and Williams (2005) point out, there is no conceptual clarity regarding the concept of place, due in part to the interdisciplinary work (e.g., geography, environmental psychology, social psychology, philosophy, phenomenology, among others) on place carried out from different epistemological traditions. In this article, we follow the distinction made by Tuan (1974, 1977) between "sense of place," described as one's awareness of a positive feeling for a place, and "rootedness," or a feeling of being at home. In our work with first-generation immigrants, we recognize that it is in the experience of migration that one comes to realize the full meaning of home as place. As Hay (1992) points out, "the multitude of connections to place may only become evident once one has left home and feels homesick" (p. 101). It would seem that the sense of place as home is felt strongly by migrants in relation to the place of their childhood and youth—a place where they have lived the longest and/or have established intimate and significant relationships. Bonds to place are significant in that place provides the context for other meaningful relationships to develop; as these relationships develop, place becomes meaningful itself. Ties to family and friends or to special places become heightened by travels and living elsewhere or by involvement in the local community.

In understanding how place and relationships are interconnected, we found Proshansky's (1978) concept of place-identity instructive. In his later work (Proshansky, Fabian, & Kaminoff, 1983), place-identity is described as the individual's incorporation of place into a larger concept of self as a "potpourri of memories, conceptions, interpretations, ideas, and related feelings about specific physical setting, as well as types of settings" (p. 60). Beginning in childhood, when the home is of primary importance for the child's rootedness, place-identity changes throughout a person's lifetime. The formation processes of identity are guided by different principles according to culture and within a culture, and also vary over time and across situations (Breakwell, 1986).

Breakwell's identity-process theory (1986; Twigger-Ross, Bonaiuto, & Breakwell, 2003) identifies places as important sources of identity: aspects of identity that are derived from places people belong to because of the meaning and significance places have to us. Along with personal memories, places carry social memories and shared histories (places are located in the socio-historical matrix of intergroup relationships). Of particular importance for our study was Breakwell's (1986) notion of ever-changing relationships and the renegotiation of meaning of places and their contribution to identity. Being in new and different places affects identity though processes of attenuation/accentuation, threat, and/or dislocation.

In a country in which multiculturalism has been an official government policy for 40 years, an understanding of diversity as a dynamic interchange of differences among people enhances the goals of multiculturalism. In this context, renegotiated meaning emerges in cultural encounters when we identify and discuss conflicts in values rather than relying on straight assimilation or consensus. Here is one area where the potential for art-making, with its open-ended nature within the milieu of visual culture (Walker, 2004), could be valuable as a strategy for cultural learning and negotiation of identity. Through engagement in collaborative art-making, parents may gain new perspectives on the significance of their connections to a place as "back home" as well as the "here and now" while they revisit and consolidate their feelings in relation to both. In the process of art-making, a space is created that allows an ongoing dialogue among parents, children, and teachers to begin—a dialogue filled with love and place-identity relations that might have been hindered by mobility and alienation.

## Research site and the participants

The study took place in a child-care centre serving newcomers to Canada who were enrolled in on-site English as an Additional Language classes. The study involved a series of four shared art-making workshops with two bicultural preschool teachers working with 11 immigrant parents (10 mothers and 1 father) and their children (ages three to five). Each workshop was 60 to 90 minutes in length and took place in the children's classroom in the child-care centre. Following the workshops, the researchers conducted open-ended interviews with teachers for 20 to 30 minutes and with parents for 15 to 20 minutes.

The study inquired how place memories inform cultural ideas of self and others in relation to that specific locale. In engaging with the provided opportunities, immigrant teachers and families needed to understand their own sense of identity in relation to place, teaching, and/or community through personal artistic explorations. The notions of cultural hybridity, including aspects of cultural conflict and cohesion, were explored in light of a sense of place understood as a physical and psychological attachment that was involved in the formation of cultural identity. In this context, art was understood as a visual form of self-expression and communication as well as a cultural practice in which social values are embodied.

It is important to note that the participants in the study had a different relationship with a place they called home. As immigrants to Canada, the teachers and the parents who participated in the study had experienced deep connections to their homeland and the people in their lives in the homeland: their families, friends, and/or their community members. However, the young children who participated in the study experienced place in their families' homes within the host country where they were born and where they had lived with their parents all their lives. In a sense, parents are children's primary source of meaning of home as "place," partly because it is where they experience nurturing and intimate relationships that potentially contribute to lasting affection for home. These different relationships with the place that each participant referred to as "home" opened up possibilities for negotiating meanings of place.

## Methodology

This research used qualitative arts-based research with a focus on art-making as a hermeneutic process of reflection and sharing of experiences of place "back home" as well as cultural practices as they relate to place. During the workshops, immigrant preschool teachers, parents, and their children created aesthetic responses to the question "What does winter look like in your home country?" using a variety of materials including paint, clay, and fabric. The question reflected the notion articulated by Tuan (1977) that home feels more intimate in the winter, for winter can remind us of our physical and psychological vulnerability.

The study is based in creative artistic practice and combines arts-based and ethnographic methods. As a relatively new area of qualitative research, arts-based research is generally defined as a loose grouping of methods based on selected art forms, through which data is created and collected, analyzed, and/or represented within a creative register to understand the experiences of the participants and researchers (Irwin, 2004; Leavy, 2009; McNiff, 2008; Rolling, 2010). A form of praxis, characterized by a holistic approach in which theory and practice are merged, develops through the research process (Irwin, 2004; Leavy, 2009; Sinner et al., 2006). The creative aspects of arts-based research suggest that the researchers' and participants' voices thread throughout the work in the aesthetic and contextual explorations with regard to interpretation and representation (Pente, 2004).

The role of the researcher must be acknowledged carefully in all research, and with arts-based methods that invite participants who are not professional artists to make art, care must be taken to avoid what Desai (2002) warns is a pitfall of superficiality. To educational research she links a particular shift within contemporary community art practices toward ethnography. When the artist acts as ethnographer, the danger of a facile interpretation of a community's character and a misuse of the term *collaboration* exists, for in many instances the artistic authority in determining the nature of the work is not a shared process (Desai, 2002). While all researchers influence the outcomes of any research, the potential misrepresentation of participants through data creation and analysis must be acknowledged and reduced as much as possible through the development of relationships with the community participating in the research. This process takes time.

In this research, our connection with the preschool and its community developed over two years so that we had already built a strong relationship with the preschool staff through a pilot study, and we were aware of and sensitive to our roles as researchers and the participants' roles as teachers, students, and parents.

### Data creation, collection, and analysis

The arts-based activities in this project include the participants' creations of art about winter in their respective countries and the researchers' creative decisions within photographic and written documentation of the event. Data presented here was created and collected during two 90-minute shared art-making workshops followed by interviews with the teachers and the parents who had agreed to participate in the study and signed consent forms. Photographs of artistic creations and of the art-making workshops were transferred to an iPad for participants to view during these interviews. These photos served as visual stimuli (Spindler, 2008), intended to evoke recollections of the workshop itself and of the memories of "back home" as depicted in the aesthetic creations. The interviews were audiotaped and transcribed verbatim.

As participant-observers, we videotaped and took still photographs of the participants during the workshops, where the selection and framing of the photographs were a form of the researchers' aesthetic response to the research environment. We also gathered material artifacts in the form of works of art created by the participants (these were later returned) and took field notes. Inasmuch as was possible, the focus of our observations was on the processes employed by participants to recreate their notions of place through the exploration of materials. This focus was evident in the aesthetic choices we made when photographing the participants, with emphasis on tight frames of parent and child working with materials, and the attention we paid to the actions of the participants' hands while they were engaged in art-making.

## Uncoverings

Three themes illustrating the participants' connections to place emerged from the interview and observational and visual data: place as ties to a special site, place as people ties to family and community, and place as ties to traditions.

### Place as ties to a special site

Place is where one's life unfolds. When asked to remember what "back home" was like in winter, some of our participants remembered places that had unique meaning for them. More specifically, some embodied aspects of the physical sites held deep significance—the colours, the view from a particular spot, or the sky above it. These were not necessarily connected to a particular season, however.

> Daniela and Javier have selected the paint table. They are seated side by side with their bodies opened up toward the table and materials. Daniela's body is angled very slightly toward her father and she rests her left arm on her father's right leg. Both direct their gaze toward their respective artworks, holding paintbrushes in their right hands to paint the pictures in front of them. Daniela's gaze shifts to her father's work, then back to her own. He reaches forward with her right hand and places his brush in the paint tray and Daniela mirrors his actions. No words pass between them. In the end, their pictures are nearly identical, depicting a volcano near Javier's home town. (Observational notes, November 8, 2010)

**Figure 7.1** Painting volcanoes. Photo credit: Patti Pente.

### Javier (parent interview)

**Researcher:** What was that that you were painting? What was in your mind? The image? Because we started, you remember, thinking about winter in your country.

**Javier:** *Yes, this is like, like a night, yeah night. This is a moon, trees, and this is the trees of the (indistinguishable).*

**Researcher:** Of the moonlight.

**Javier:** *Oh, I remember the mountain, the mountain with the sun.*

**Researcher:** Sunshine. There's the night scene starting, beginning. So, was there a particular mountain where you were living?

**Javier:** *Yes, from my home I saw a volcano and a mountain.*

**Researcher:** Volcano? In El Salvador? Was it active?

**Javier:** *No, before it was working but now no.*

**Researcher:** Good thing.

**Javier:** *Some mountain with the sky.*

**Researcher:** Yeah, that one. And she [Daniela] did the same thing.

**Researcher:** In terms of colours, when you remember El Salvador and Edmonton, do you see those same kinds of colours here?

**Javier:** *Sometimes the sky is different—it's like a red, right. In El Salvador the sky is blue with the ... (Interview, December 13, 2010)*

## Commentary

In his art, Javier made a connection to the geography of "home," specifically the volcano on the top of a mountain that was a prominent feature in the town in which he grew up. However, the colours of the sky over the mountain seemed to dominate his memories, and he chose to talk about the colours rather than the physical features of the landscape. What was most interesting in this art-making experience was that his daughter, Daniela, who had never seen the mountains and the volcano, participated fully in his experience of recalling and recreating his memories of home by painting side by side with her father (not indicated in the exchange above). Both father and daughter were absorbed in the painting, each painting his or her own picture. While Javier had lived next to the mountain with the volcano on top and had a picture of the place in his mind (Interview, December 13, 2010), Daniela seemed to rely on her father's memory of his childhood home that he recreated on the piece of paper to draw her own picture. Frequent glances toward her father's painting kept her on track and, in the end, the two pictures were almost identical. The shared joy of silently painting next to each other was apparent to the rest of us who were observing the activity from a distance. The dialogue between the father and his daughter was carried on through the medium in which he chose to recreate his memories of home—in colourful images rather than in words.

When Javier was asked about the workshop, the nature of the experience seemed to resonate with his own artistic expertise as a musician. Art reminded him of music in the creative opportunities that each form offered him. He made the connection between music and his own family—his brothers—back home and the experiences they shared making music together. Just as he has created art alongside his daughter in this workshop, he used to create music alongside his brothers back home in the church. During the interview, for example, Javier stated: "I sing song because I play guitar … My brothers, they are too. They play the guitar and sing" (Interview, December 13, 2010). When asked about his performances, he explained further: "Because in the Catholic community, you know, we make some groups so that is why I sing some Catholic songs" (Interview, December 13, 2010). It seems that not only the experience itself (the act of creation), but the feeling of being part of the experience alongside a member of his family evoked in Javier a memory of home. Even though few words passed between the father and the daughter, the art workshop seems to have created a space where they could reconstruct these experiences from "back home" together.

## Carolina (teacher interview)

**Researcher:** Now, I notice you made the mountain? Was there a particular place you had in mind when you were making that?

**Carolina:** *Yeah, this place is supposed to be downtown Bogota. Downtown but we have all our buildings and everything and the background is the mountain. The east mountains.*

**Researcher:** Ohhh. Great.

**Carolina:** *It's so beautiful because it has like, it's our like train, all the mountains in the back of the city and the little church on top is called Monserrate. It's a very, very, very touristic place—religious and touristic place because you can go and you take the train and you go visit and it's a beautiful view of the city. A very touristic place, yeah. (Interview, December 7, 2010)*

## Commentary

Using paint as a medium, Carolina recreated a special site from which the entire city where she lived could be viewed—a church on the top of a mountain. Looking at the city from "a bird's-eye view" gave an "impression of the city" rather than a detailed three-dimensional map of it. Carolina highlighted the important aspects of the memory—the openness of the view, the closeness of the mountains to the city, and the scale of the buildings compared to the magnificent mountain (Interview, December 7, 2010).

## Alifa (parent interview)

**Researcher:** You made that? Any place like a plain or a river or a mountain, or …?

**Alifa:** *A river.*

**Researcher:** A river. Yeah, you had a river where you lived?

**Alifa:** *Not a big river, a small river because river the [name] river, [name] river. River the too long.*

**Researcher:** A long river?

**Alifa:** *yeah.*

**Researcher:** So were you playing as a child?

**Alifa:** *In wintertime.*

**Researcher:** In winter. Why winter and not summer?

**Alifa:** *Wintertime or summer. Summer lots and lots of water in Eritrea. (Interview, December 6, 2010)*

## Commentary

Alifa's recollection of her childhood where she had played by the river throughout all seasons was conveyed in her art. Her experience in the workshop allowed her to connect to a specific physical location in her home country and share it with her child. She depicted that place in her art, bringing place as childhood memories of the river by her home into the preschool space.

## Place as people ties to family and community

In relation to the second theme, some of our participants' connections to place were less locale based and more socially based—their connection to people from their immediate family and social community was evoked in response to the question we asked.

### Banwai (teacher interview)

**Researcher:** Now the things that you made, can you talk a little bit about the things you made?

**Banwai:** *Um, I made like, I made a village scene which I believe that back home, people back home in the villages, they have all those materials like the mode of cooking, they cook on firewoods, they cook on firewoods and pounding rice so it is that scene as I made it, it made me to think of our villages and our peoples back home when they see such an image. Canada because they call in the Western world, ibo, that's whites' country, white*

**Figure 7.2** Painting my village. Photo: Patti Pente.

*people, their country. This is such thing we say. They [Canadians] will ask question: 'Is this really from the place where you are coming from?' 'Yes' [Banwei responds]. 'So these people have these kinds of thing?' [Canadians ask]. I say, 'Yes.' Now I'm thinking of back home and then I think it's really nice.*

**Banwai:** *I painted the same, like a village scene. People working and like here and make me to remember like back home.*

**Researcher:** In Sierra Leone.

**Banwai:** *Yes, we have mountains. They call it mountain "Lion Mountain" which was the history Sierra Leone and you will see people working and trees, green trees and like palm trees and other things. (Interview, December 8, 2010)*

## Commentary

For Banwai, "back home" was the village where people gathered together to work. Her most vivid memory of the feeling of being "at home" was where the people, the women and children, gathered around the fire to cook, laugh, and share their food as well as their personal lives. Unlike the Western world, where everyone lives "behind the walls" of their homes, in her village, life, food, joy, and sorrow were public events to be shared with others in the village. Her art conveyed the nostalgia for these times with their close ties to community members.

## Sara (parent interview)

**Researcher:** And so one of the things we would like you to remember is a place in your country and through your art you said it brought you back to your country?

**Sara:** *When I was making the work, I was reminded of my grandmother and my uncle because we live all the family, enjoy the food or fire ...*

**Researcher:** Oh, you made some fire, or candles, or ...

**Sara:** *Candles and sometimes fire, fire, I don't know. Here when September, in September, I don't know how do you say ...*

**Researcher:** Do you make it? Do you ...

**Sara:** *No, no. We didn't make.*

**Researcher:** Oh.

**Sara:** *With fire and you light ...*

**Researcher:** Firecrackers?

**Sara:** *No, fire ... We put fire in the back.*

**Researcher:** Oh, I know what you mean.

**Sara:** *English is not my first language so I can't remember the name of it, but I know what you mean, yeah, so you remember.*

**Researcher:** So you have like a stick and you fire it and it sprinkles …

**Sara:** *Yes … (Interview, December 6, 2010)*

### Commentary

As Sara commented while making art, the memories of time spent with family came back to her. Like Banwai's description of her painting, Sara recalled sharing food with her family. The memories of the happy times when she was lighting firecrackers with her family were also vivid in her mind even though she did not easily find the words to express this feeling in English.

**Researcher:** Do you remember when we did the workshop we asked you to remember a place?

**Sara:** *Yes, yes. I was thinking about tamales. That why I paint in green, a line in green. That's banana leaves.*

**Researcher:** Oh, I see! So you … let's see if we can find your art. Is this yours? The green?

**Sara:** *It's green, but …*

**Researcher:** No?

**Sara:** *The lines, green and purple.*

**Figure 7.3** The colours of home. Photo: Patti Pente.

**Researcher:** So you were thinking about a specific place then when you were painting? The green. A place in your country?

**Sara:** *Yes, the ... beach.*

**Researcher:** The beach, mmm-hmmm.

**Sara:** *I was thinking sky, the blue of the sky.*

**Researcher:** Beautiful sky. (Interview, December 6, 2010)

### Commentary

Sara painted a green line that she said represented the banana leaves used to wrap tamales. It seemed as though different images had merged in her memory of home: blue for the blue sky and green for the banana leaves. What was important here, however, was not to "match" the colour to the actual object/image that she was remembering, but to appreciate the possibilities of exploring and recreating her memories through the use of colour as an impression rather than a concrete, realistic picture of the beach she returned to in her memory when she was asked to recall what the winter was like in her home country. Undoubtedly, the colours, not the details of the beach, with its sand, water, or rocks, were the most important aspects in her memory. The choice of medium—paint—to communicate her memory also spoke to the importance of colours to trigger specific memories.

## Place as ties to traditions

Participants spoke about their connections between traditions and place. Traditions and rituals, most of which are cultural, guide every new generation in its ways of becoming part of place not only as a dwelling but also as an ancestral land: a place where others in that community and family have generational, historical ties. Yet traditions and rituals do not belong to the land—we carry them with us, wherever we go, passing them on to our children who may never see the land where the traditions were born. Because of this, traditions change as immigrants "encounter" a new "place" and community, thus forging new, hybrid traditions.

Sara, an immigrant from El Salvador, and her daughter Sarita have joined in the shared art-making workshop. Sara was engaged in wrapping brightly coloured embroidery thread around a tree branch, a past tradition in her home country at Christmastime, while Sarita was preparing her materials by choosing skeins of thread from a basket in front of her:

> Sarita withdraws her right hand from the basket, clutching a pink skein in her hand. Her gaze moves downward, following the skein

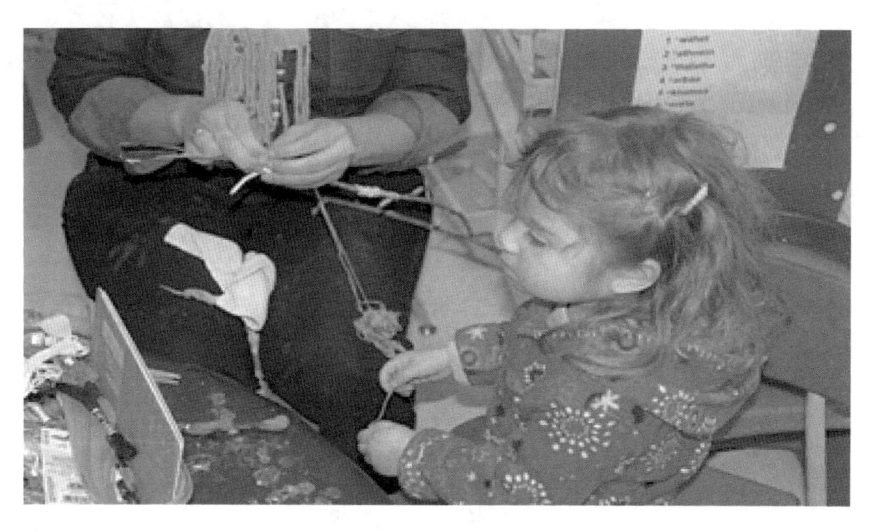

**Figure 7.4** Decorating branches for Christmas with coloured thread. Photo: Christine Massing.

as she brings it closer to her, then upward at the basket, then back down. Sara moves her head in the same manner, making a *sagittal* head beat down, up, then down again. As she wraps thread around the branch, she makes a series of slight rotational head beats, her gaze fixed upon her work. Simultaneously, Sarita grasps three skeins of thread in her hands and makes small rotational head movements as she gazes at them. (Video data, November 10, 2010)

### Sara (parent interview)

**Researcher:** You made a tree? You decorated a branch? Is this something that you make in your country?

**Sara:** *Well, in our country we don't use, we don't use the ... Christmas tree. Different.*

**Researcher:** Oh yes.

**Sara:** *Now [in Canada], I am.*

**Researcher:** Yes.

**Sara:** *But before more families had only the branch.*

**Researcher:** The branches.

**Sara:** *Yes, with some decoration because we make ... in my country it's difficult. We make different, sometimes we bakes with egg.*

**Researcher:** Eggs?

**Sara:** *And shells. Yes, eggshells and fabric.*

**Researcher:** And you decorated the branches for Christmas? And so this is what you made with your branches? Beautiful, wonderful. So, anything that you would like to tell us about a place in Canada that you found that you love?

...

**Researcher:** So you remember Christmas particularly. Winter for you is Christmas or more or less when you think about it?

**Sara:** *Yeah, in my country it's summer.*

**Researcher:** Yes, it's summer, but when you think of winter what comes to mind because this is what you …?

**Sara:** *Winter?*

**Researcher:** Yeah, yeah, can you tell …

**Sara:** *I remember Christmas too because when I was living in my country, like my aunt send us some card with pictures of the snow.*

**Researcher:** (laughs) From here, from Canada?

**Sara:** *Then I remember that. (Interview, December 6, 2010)*

### Commentary

Sara's comments on her experience of winter "back home," where the weather is warm all year round, highlighted the strong differences from the experiences of Canadian-born citizens for whom winter is typically cold. This difference was revealed in the connection she made between Christmas, a widely celebrated winter holiday in Canada, and her memory of "winter" in her home country. She recalled going to the beach at Christmas and using branches to represent a Christmas tree. She carried this memory of Christmas back home into the workshop by wrapping branches with colourful wool (as well as by painting the "beach"). While going to the beach brought her back to a beloved place of her past, decorating the branches that were provided as workshop materials served as a catalyst, reminding her of her cultural tradition of celebrating Christmas. She made specific connections among special people in her life, food, and traditions. She moved from these events and people who were specific to her life to broader cultural traditions such as decorating a branch rather than a tree and throwing firecrackers in bonfires.

The connection Sara made between winter/Christmas in Canada and her home country becomes clearer when she describes how her aunt used to send cards from Canada that had pictures of snow. That seemed to have helped her create the connection between winter and Christmas and her home country, even though Christmas in her country is in the middle of summer. Celebrating Christmas seems to represent, to some extent, a commonality between Canada and her home country. It exists in both places. Sara was very articulate about the ways in which it was different, however. First, she spoke of the climatic differences between the two countries during Christmastime, that during winter the Canadian weather is snowy, but in her country Christmas happens in summer. She also mentioned the strong differences in the ways that the physical location affects people: in Canada people are likely to be indoors, while in her country the celebrations are outdoors, where they set off fireworks and go to the beach. Second, the traditions are different; for example, in Canada people use a Christmas tree and in her home country people might use a wrapped tree branch instead of having a Christmas tree. This was a vivid memory from her childhood.

In terms of sharing a cultural tradition with her daughter, the workshop materials allowed for a shared participation in a cultural tradition that was no longer part of the family Christmas celebration as they "now have a tree" instead of decorated branches (see Figure 7.4) The practice of cultural craft-making provided open space for negotiation of cultural traditions and setting boundaries of cultural identities.

## Materials as connections to place

The "uncoverings" we have presented here demonstrate the depth of experience in which the parents, their children, and teachers engaged during the workshops. Some of the materials, or the tactile sensations associated with using the materials, evoked memories of particular people, places, and traditions in the parents' and teachers' home countries. Banwai, one of the teachers, elaborates on the connection between materials and place:

> I believe that seeing the concrete materials will remind them [the parents] about back home and most of our countr[ies], most of our countr[ies] have these same materials. It will remind them about back home and they will be happy for their children to learn something that they can see from here and compare the same [thing] back home. They will not forget the memory of their country. (Interview, December 8, 2010)

The participants in the workshops also showed a strong tendency to use the materials to depict the real world they remembered being around them at "home." Thus, materials are always intrinsically interconnected with the experience of art-making and cannot be separated from affective responses. It is important to acknowledge that in a research context, through the selection of materials, researchers influence and shape the experiences the participants have, the product/art (if there is one), and thus the memories and connections the participants make to their past and present. For example, one of the participants, Mei, noted that in her home country, "The materials are not like here" (Interview, December 6, 2010). Her experience in the workshop was focused on learning how to use unfamiliar materials and "playing" rather than working with her daughter. Thus, the nature and quantity of the materials provided in this workshop could have potentially limited the participants' responses.

The type of materials available to participants in a workshop as vehicles for exploration needs to be considered if early childhood educators are to use art-making in engaging parents and children in experiences that open possibilities of defining, negotiating, and redefining cultural practices, values, expectations, and identities. Therefore, the choices must be expanded even further when inviting parents to use the materials with their children with the aim of exploring cultural practices, traditions and beliefs, and values.

## Discussion

In immigrant families "intergenerational gaps in perceptions and experience frequently yield feelings of nostalgia" (Rumbaut & Portes, 2001, p. 149) in parents. As some children self-identify more strongly as members of the dominant society through their peer relationships in school, and not as members of the ethno-cultural community to which their parents belong, parents' longing for the country left behind increases (Adams & Kirova, 2007). Lack of opportunities for parents to bring to the school space some of their family history and their own childhood experiences from "back home" alienates parents even further from their children's experiences in school and contributes to children's further separation from their families and ethnic communities. Although literature on parent involvement emphasizes the importance of getting to know the families and the multiple worlds they inhabit (e.g., Souto-Manning & Swick, 2006), culture is typically brought into schools in superficial ways (Crozier & Davies, 2007).

The parents involved in this study, however, were able to use art media and techniques to portray meaningful elements from their home contexts. As the data revealed, the process of shared art-making allowed for similarities among parents' recollection of their meaningful relationships with the parents' home place to emerge. First, parents spoke passionately about the special place "back home." Both in their art and in their words, their love for the place was evident.

As they spoke of the colours of the sky, the mountains, the sand, the majestic view, or the small river passing though the village, we could see that they were almost physically transported "there." As Hay (1992) points out, "nature is part of us through the air we breathe, the food we eat, and the water we drink" (p.104) and thus cannot be separated from our sense of place we call "home." Second, although the ancestral connection to the place was stronger in some of the parents' memories than in others', many portrayed their community, events, or everyday lives in the place—lives that had been shared for many generations. It was the sense of connectedness to others in significant places through their art traditions, as well as their memories of their own experiences of being with others in these places, that was conveyed by their art and in their descriptions of the art they made. Lastly, the feeling of longing for the "good times" back home dominated the memories of the parents. While the better life in the host country is what immigrants seek when they immigrate, the struggles many people encounter once they arrive, as well as the loss of extended families, friends, and community, are some of the reasons the participants were overwhelmed by a desire to go back home when they spoke of their experiences in relation to the art they made. This longing, paired with their understanding that their children would probably never form such loving, meaningful relationships with their parents' home, is what makes experiences like the workshops we provided for them and their children a very rare and cherished opportunity to talk about "back home" outside of their homes in the host country. This talk became an important educational experience for their children. In the process of art-making, parents constructed memories of home, which they were able to share with their children. Recalling such memories may have been augmented through the creation of the visuals and discussions that then focused on the artwork, echoing Barlow, Jolley, and Hallam's (2011) findings that children's memories of events are enhanced through drawing. As Hay (1992) puts it, "Our whole being, involving relations of meaning between ourselves, community, place, and nature could thus be renewed once we look within, rekindle our ties without, and join these in spiritual union" (p. 104). Traditions from one's homeland can serve as cultural resources for the children as they navigate life in their new home (Espinoza-Herold, 2007).

By engaging in a shared art-making experience with immigrant parents and their children, bicultural teachers were able to learn more about the special places, people, and traditions in the parents' homelands. Carolina, a teacher, further elucidates this idea:

They [the mothers] were talking about this—I think it was about the Christmas—and that, so we're having a conversation and talking about traditional dishes back in our countries and talking about, yeah, sharing the topic. (Interview, December 7, 2010)

Teachers gained insights into families' cultures and lives, enhancing their understandings of areas of difference (Eberly, Joshi, & Konzai, 2007). However, just as the shared art-making transported parents to their home countries, teachers similarly reflected on memories of special places and traditions back home. Thus, the workshop allowed parents and teachers to connect with each other as they recognized commonalities in their experiences and identified differences. Schools often hold the balance of power in teacher and parent relationships, marginalizing immigrant parents' perspectives and cultural capital (Bernhard, 2010) by emphasizing the specific professional knowledge teachers hold (Alasuutari, 2010). Although the centre where the study took place was primarily staffed by bicultural teachers, dominant early childhood education (ECE) discourses influence their ways of being with parents. As Adair (2009) emphasizes, immigrant teachers "have little space to use their own personal immigrant experience to influence their pedagogy and still be considered professional" (p. 170). Yet this was not the case during the workshop; neither teachers nor parents held expertise in using the materials, and they were not expected to achieve any particular goals. By bonding during the workshop, parents and teachers could use the experience as a basis for future conversations (see also Strickland, Keat, & Marinak, 2010).

Art workshops seemed to blur the boundaries between the public sphere and people's private lives, much as Vandenbroeck, Roets, and Snoeck (2009) found in their study of immigrant mothers. Both parents and teachers constructed hybrid identities as they moved between public and intimate spaces, as well as between "back home" and Canada (Vandenbroeck, Roets, & Snoeck, 2009). Carreón, Drake, and Barton (2005) explored the ways in which immigrant parents authored spaces for engagement in schools. The findings in this study supported the notion that teachers, children, and parents can *co-author* spaces for mutual engagement through shared experience, creating openings for more authentic partnerships. From our interviews with both parents and teachers, multiple perspectives on engagement were elicited, and parents became an integral part of this public space through being active participants in its creation.

### ACKNOWLEDGEMENTS

*The authors acknowledge Social Science and Humanities Research Council of Canada (SSHRC) for the financial support of this study. We also thank the child-care staff, the parents, and the children for their participation in the study and the insights they offered in our understanding of the role of place in one's sense of self. Without the collective efforts of all involved, the study described in this chapter would have not been possible.*

## REFERENCES

Adair, J.K. (2009). *Teaching child of immigrants: A multi-sited ethnographic study of preschool teachers in five U.S. cities* (Unpublished doctoral dissertation). Arizona State University, Phoenix (UMI No. 3360743).

Adams, L.D., & Kirova, A. (2007). Introduction: Global migration and the education of children. In L.D. Adams & A. Kirova (Eds.), *Global migration and education: Schools, children, and families* (pp. 1–12). Mahwah, NJ: Lawrence Erlbaum Associates.

Alasuutari, M. (2010). Striving at partnership: Parent–practitioner relationships in Finnish early educators' talk. *European Early Childhood Education Research Journal, 18*(2), 149–161. http://dx.doi.org/10.1080/13502931003784545

Ballengee Morris, C., Mirin, K., & Rizzi, C. (2000). Decolonialization, art education, and one Guarani nation of Brazil. *Studies in Art Education, 41*(2), 100–113. http://dx.doi.org/10.2307/1320657

Barlow, C., Jolley, R.P., & Hallam, J.L. (2011). Drawings as memory aids: Optimizing the drawing method to facilitate young children's recall. *Applied Cognitive Psychology, 25*(3), 480–487. http://dx.doi.org/10.1002/acp.1716

Beiser, M. (2005, Mar–Apr). The health of immigrants and refugees in Canada. *Canadian Journal of Public Health, 96*(2 Suppl 2), S30–S44. Medline:16078554

Bernhard, J. (2010). From theory to practice: Engaging immigrant parents in their children's education. *Alberta Journal of Educational Research, 56*(3), 319–334.

Breakwell, G.M. (1986). *Coping with threatened identity*. London, UK: Methuen.

Bresler, L. (2004). Prelude. In L. Bresler (Ed.), *Knowing bodies, moving minds: Towards embodied teaching and learning* (pp. 7–11). Dordrecht, Netherlands: Kluwer Academic Publishers.

Carreón, G.P., Drake, C., & Barton, A.C. (2005). The importance of presence: Immigrant parents' school engagement experiences. *American Educational Research Journal, 42*(3), 465–498. http://dx.doi.org/10.3102/00028312042003465

Crozier, G., & Davies, J. (2007). Hard to reach parents or hard to reach schools? A discussion of home-school relations, with particular reference to Bangladeshi and Pakistani parents. *British Educational Research Journal, 33*(3), 295–313. http://dx.doi.org/10.1080/01411920701243578

Desai, D. (2002). The ethnographic move in contemporary art: What does it mean for art education? *Studies in Art Education, 43*(4), 307–323. http://dx.doi.org/10.2307/1320980

Eberly, J., Joshi, A., & Konzai, J. (2007). Communicating with families across cultures: An investigation of teacher perceptions and practices. *School Community Journal, 17*(2), 7–26.

Eiserman, J. (2009). They can still act Chinese and be Canadian at the same time: Reflections on multiculturalism and the Alberta art curriculum. *Canadian Review of Art Education, 36*, 62–82.

Espinoza-Herold, M. (2007). Stepping beyond *sí se puede: Dichos* as a cultural resources in mother–daughter interaction in a Latino family. *Anthropology & Education Quarterly, 38*(3), 260–277. http://dx.doi.org/10.1525/aeq.2007.38.3.260

Hay, R. (1988). Toward a theory of sense of place. *Trumpeter, 5*(4), 159–164.

Hay, R. (1992). An appraisal of our meaningful relationship in place. *Trumpeter, 9*(3), 98–105.

Irwin, R. (2004). Introduction. In R. Irwin & A. De Cosson (Eds.), *A/r/tography: Rendering self through arts-based living inquiry* (pp. 27–38). Vancouver, BC: Pacific Educational Press.

Isik-Ercan, Z. (2010). Looking at school from the house window: Learning from Turkish- American parents' experiences with early elementary education in the United States. *Early Childhood Education Journal, 38*(2), 133–142. http://dx.doi.org/10.1007/s10643-010-0399-8

Knopf, H.T., & Swick, K.J. (2008). Using our understanding of families to strengthen family involvement. *Childhood Education Journal, 35*(5), 419–427. http://dx.doi.org/10.1007/s10643-007-0198-z

Lahman, M.K.E., & Park, S. (2004). Understanding children from diverse cultures: Bridging perspectives of parents and teachers. *International Journal of Early Years Education, 12,* 131–142. http://dx.doi.org/10.1080/0966976042000225525

Leavy, P. (2009). *Method meets art: Arts-based research practice.* New York: Guilford Press.

McNiff, S. (2008). Art-based research. In J. Knowles (Ed.), *Handbook of the arts in qualitative research: Perspectives, methodologies, examples, and issues* (pp. 29–41). Thousand Oaks, CA: Sage. http://dx.doi.org/10.4135/9781452226545.n3

Mugerauer, R. (1994). *Interpretation on behalf of place Elmira: Environmental displacements and alternative responses.* New York: State University of New York Press.

Patterson, M.E., & Williams, D.R. (2005). Maintaining research traditions on place: Diversity of thought and scientific progress. *Journal of Environmental Psychology, 25*(4), 361–380. http://dx.doi.org/10.1016/j.jenvp.2005.10.001

Pente, P. (2004). Reflections on artist/researcher/teacher identities: A game of cards. In R. Irwin & A. De Cosson (Eds.), *A/r/tography: Rendering self through arts-based living inquiry* (pp. 91–102). Vancouver, BC: Pacific Educational Press.

Proshansky, H.M. (1978). The city and self-identity. *Environment and Behavior, 10*(2), 147–169. http://dx.doi.org/10.1177/0013916578102002

Proshansky, H.M., Fabian, A.K., & Kaminoff, R. (1983). Place-identity: Physical world socialization of the self. *Journal of Environmental Psychology, 3*(1), 57–83. http://dx.doi.org/10.1016/S0272-4944(83)80021-8

Relph, E.C. (1976). *Place and placelessness.* London, UK: Pion.

Rolling, J. (2010). A paradigm analysis of arts-based research and implications for education. *Studies in Art Education, 51*(2), 102–114.

Rumbaut, R.G., & Portes, A., (2001). *Ethnicities: Children of immigrants in America.* Berkeley: University of California Press.

Sinner, A., Leggo, C., Irwin, R., Gouzouasis, P., & Grauer, K. (2006). Arts-based education research dissertation: Reviewing the practices of new scholars. *Canadian Journal of Education, 29*(4), 1223–1270.

Sohn, S., & Wang, X.C. (2006). Immigrant parents' involvement in American schools: Perspectives from Korean mothers. *Early Childhood Education Journal, 34*(2), 125–132. http://dx.doi.org/10.1007/s10643-006-0070-6

Souto-Manning, M., & Swick, K.J. (2006). Teachers' beliefs about parent and family involvement: Rethinking our family involvement paradigm. *Early Childhood Education Journal, 34*(2), 187–193. http://dx.doi.org/10.1007/s10643-006-0063-5

Spindler, G. (2008). Using visual stimuli in ethnography. *Anthropology & Education Quarterly, 39*(2), 127–140. http://dx.doi.org/10.2307/25166657

Springgay, S. (2008). *Body knowledge and curriculum: Pedagogies of touch in youth and visual culture.* New York, NY: Lang.

Stinson, S. (2004). My body/myself: Lessons from dance education. In L. Bresler (Ed.), *Knowing bodies, moving minds: Towards embodied teaching and learning* (pp. 153–167). Dordrecht, Netherlands: Kluwer Academic Publishers. http://dx.doi.org/10.1007/978-1-4020-2023-0_10

Strickland, M.J., Keat, J., & Marinak, B.A. (2010). Connecting worlds: Using photo narrations to connect immigrant children, preschool teachers, and immigrant families. *School Community Journal, 20*(1), 81–102.

Tuan, Y.-F. (1974). *Topophilia: A study of environmental perception, attitudes, and values.* Englewood Cliffs, NJ: Prentice-Hall.

Tuan, Y.-F. (1977). *Space and place: The perspective of experience.* Minneapolis: University of Minnesota Press.

Turney, K., & Kao, G. (2009). Barriers to school involvement: Are immigrant parents disadvantaged? *Journal of Educational Research, 102*(4), 257–271. http://dx.doi.org/10.3200/JOER.102.4.257-271

Twigger-Ross, C.L., Bonaiuto, M., & Breakwell, G. (2003). Identity theories and environmental psychology. In M. Bonnes, T. Lee, & M. Bonaiuto (Eds.), *Psychological Theories for Environmental Issues* (pp. 203–233). Aldershot, England: Ashgate.

United Nations High Commissioner for Refugees (2010). *UNHCR global trends 2010.* Retrieved from http://www.unhcr.org/4dfa11499.html

Vandenbroeck, M., Roets, G., & Snoeck, A. (2009). Immigrant mothers crossing borders: Nomadic identities and multiple belongings in early childhood education. *European Early Childhood Education Research Journal, 17*(2), 203–216. http://dx.doi.org/10.1080/13502930902951452

Walker, S. (2004). Art-making in an age of visual culture: Vision and visuality. *Visual Arts Research, 30*(2), 23–37.

# 8

# African refugee women's songs and stories

## Possibilities for diversifying literacy practices in early childhood education

*Christine Massing*

Early Childhood Education (ECE) is a field believed to be very accessible to the growing numbers of immigrant/refugee women (Statistics Canada, 2011) as their first point of entry in the labour force in Canada (Service Canada, 2011). These women might reference the knowledge of children they have gained as mothers, aunts, siblings, or teachers in their home countries. In the Alberta context, they typically take a 58-hour course (online or face to face) or a 10-month certificate program to obtain the lowest level of certification, and some enter diploma or degree programs when they have the language skills (Government of Alberta, 2013). Both in their courses and in the field, they are required to follow the expectations made explicit in the dominant discourse of ECE (Bredekamp & Copple, 2009). This discourse derives its authority from the research of Western developmental psychologists and emphasizes that all children progress through universal stages of development regardless of the social, cultural, and personal circumstances of their lives (e.g., National Association for the Education of Young Children, 2009). Despite two decades of critique on the part of reconceptualist scholars (e.g., Cannella, 1997; Mallory & New, 1994; Dahlberg, Moss, & Pence, 2007) and the preponderance of research focused on the role of culture in development (Nsamenang, 2010; Rogoff, 1990, 1995, 2003), this discourse still governs the field.

Immigrant/refugee educators, parents, and children are perceived to be deficient as teachers and as learners in the dominant ECE discourse (Souto-Manning & Swick, 2006). This dominant discourse is strengthened and legitimized through well-established processes in the field of ECE such as accreditation and licensing. ECE certificate and diploma programs and professional development sessions in the field generally reproduce dominant ideologies, upholding the notion that the educator must be equipped with a specific skill and knowledge set—child development and developmentally appropriate practices—s/he can apply toward the goal of producing positive academic outcomes in young children (Lobman & Ryan, 2007; Moss, 2006). An educator's technical knowledge is prioritized at the expense of her/his practical, experiential, and cultural ways of knowing and being. Therefore, immigrant/refugee educators are required to work and interact with children in prescribed ways that are often in conflict with their own culturally constructed beliefs and values (Bernheimer, 2003; Gupta, 2006). The limited scholarship in this field suggests they either shed their own personal theories and cultural understandings to be seen as professional (see Gupta, 2006; Langford, 2007; Nuttall & Ortlipp, 2011) or resist the content altogether (Reyes, 2006). This framework silences the cultural knowledges immigrant and refugee women bring to the field (Adair, 2009), but these knowledges could support the transitions of growing numbers of immigrant/refugee children and families into early childhood settings or the Canadian school system (Statistics Canada, 2010).

Research in the area of literacy likewise positions immigrant/refugee educators, children, and families within a discourse of cultural and linguistic deficit (e.g., Stanovich, 1986). Notions about which literacy practices contribute to success in reading and writing are narrowly circumscribed; thus, immigrant/refugee families are presumed not to have the capacity to provide the "right kind" of literacy environments, resources, and experiences for their children (Dudley-Marling, 2009; Grieshaber, Shield, Luke, & Macdonald, 2012; Hsin, 2011; Marshall & Toohey, 2010; Reese & Gallimore, 2000; Rivera & Lavan, 2012; Soltero-González, 2009). Since songs and storybook reading are conventionally employed to teach language, vocabulary (in English), rhyming, sequencing, phonological awareness, and awareness of word and print (Tomlinson & Hyson, 2009) in ECE settings, immigrant/refugee educators' familial and cultural practices are marginalized or absent. Socio-cultural researchers have long problematized these traditional notions of literacy (Gee, 1996; Street, 2001), illuminating the rich and complex literacy practices of immigrant/refugee and minority-group families (e.g., Heath, 1983; Taylor and Dorsey-Gaines, 1988; Gregory, Long, & Volk, 2004). However, with some exceptions (Bigelow, 2010; Perry, 2009; Roy & Roxas,

2011), African immigrant/refugee literacies are still underexplored in research. In this chapter, we uncover some of the literacy *funds of knowledge* African refugee women working or studying in the field of ECE might bring to their work with immigrant/refugee children from similar backgrounds (González, Moll, & Amanti, 2005).

## Purpose and research questions

The data for this chapter was drawn from two related ethnographic studies. In the first, an exploratory pilot study taking place over the period of one year, data was collected during a series of professional development sessions I facilitated on communication and guidance in a multicultural child-care centre attached to an agency serving immigrant/refugee families in a mid-sized Canadian city. The purpose of the sessions was simultaneously to expose the women to dominant practices to help prepare them for their centre's upcoming accreditation review, and to elicit critique of these practices from their personal and cultural perspectives. Ten immigrant/refugee women, employed as early childhood educators in the centre, participated in this study. In the second study, I sought to gain an understanding of how 16 immigrant/refugee women experienced their studies in a one-year early childhood education certificate program in the same city. For this chapter, I focus exclusively on the 11 participants who are from Ethiopia, Eritrea, Somalia, or Sudan, are first-generation refugees, and are mothers (eight women are from the first study and three from the second). Two questions guided my inquiry in the larger studies:

- What understandings do immigrant/refugee women construct of the dominant discourse in ECE?
- What impact do these understandings have on their perceptions of themselves in relation to children as they negotiate their professional identities as early childhood educators?

In this chapter, I concentrate primarily on the women's recollections of the ways in which storytelling and songs were used in their families and cultures.

## Methods

Both studies employed a qualitative, ethnographic methodology as I sought to study the culture of the ECE community of practice and how it is experienced by women from diverse cultural backgrounds. As a participant-observer, I was situated in multiple, overlapping contexts of their learning and practice: the workplace and professional-development sessions in the first study and the college classrooms, common areas, library, computer lab, and external field placement sites (all child-care centres) in the second. I spent over a year with the participants in the first study, but quite intermittently depending on schedules and availability, and an average of three days a week (five hours a day) over a period of 10 months with the group in the second study. Data-collection methods included field notes, spatial mapping, artifact and document collection (especially class notes, handouts, textbooks and teaching materials, assignments, assessments, and field placement evaluations), photos, focus-group sessions (each participant took part in three or four 60- to 90-minute sessions), and semi-structured interviews (between two and six 45-minute interviews per participant) or contextualized conversations (Stage & Mattson, 2003). During the focus-group discussions, I used an adapted form of multivocal visual-cued ethnographic methods (Spindler, 2008; Tobin, Husueh, & Karasawa, 2009; Tobin, Wu, & Davidson, 1989). I showed the participants video clips from typical ECE teaching videos to elicit their cultural and personal perspectives and critiques of dominant practices. One of these clips depicted a teacher reading a book to a group of children, which led to discussions on literacy practices. I recorded and transcribed the focus-group discussions and interviews verbatim and then reviewed them line by line with the participants to see whether there was anything they wanted to add, change, or delete. I assigned codes to common viewpoints in transcriptions across the data sources, combined similarly coded data into categories, and clustered like categories to interpret the data (Angrosino, 2007).

## Theoretical and conceptual framework

My work here is theoretically grounded in a socio-cultural–historical framework. Street (2001) theorized that the autonomous model of literacy, congruent with the dominant discourse of ECE, presumes that literacy is a universal, technical skill that can be taught and is transferrable to other cognitive processes and contexts. In contrast, in the ideological model of literacy, literacy practices are both socially constructed as we act and interact with others, and inextricably linked to the cultural, historical, and social contexts in which they develop and are used (Street, 1993; Vygotsky, 1978). Vygotsky's (1978) concept of the zone of proximal development (ZPD) emphasizes the role of experts in guiding a learner, through interpersonal interaction, to achieve more than the learner could on her/his own. With respect to this study, experts (adults) guide children in understanding and using cultural tools (songs and stories), which can then be employed as mediational devices in learning; they might create other possibilities or introduce new limitations (Wertsch, 2007). In this manner, children gain access to culturally valued knowledges, skills, and understandings that transform their actions and behaviours in certain ways (Wertsch, 1991, 1998). Songs and stories, as cultural and historical products, reflect the values and beliefs of the culture and constantly evolve in use. For instance, the story draws in elements from the context as well as the values and beliefs of the storyteller to transform as it is told and retold; such transformation has specific implications in the context of immigration. However, as Smythe & Toohey (2009) maintain, children do not necessarily have equal access to the resources that are esteemed in the dominant culture, and cultural resources are not all deemed to hold equal value in a society or community. Therefore, literacy resources and practices that have evolved in the context of the dominant culture are privileged in schools and early childhood settings, while those originating in diverse cultural contexts are marginalized. Consistent with sociocultural–historical theory, Bakhtin's (1981, 1986) conceptualization of *voice(s)* connects the individual's mental functioning with communicative processes in the social context (Wertsch, 1998). Words, or utterances, never belong to an individual speaker, Bakhtin believed, because they emerge from a larger, collectively developed system of language. When an individual speaks, then, an utterance is always "half someone else's. It becomes one's own when the speaker populates it with his own intention, his accent…" (as cited in Wertsch, 1998, p. 77). So an utterance represents the intermingling of the individual's own voice with the voices of others in the socio-cultural context. *Heteroglossia* denotes the form that governs the meaning in any utterance. Songs and stories, for example, emerge from a context and a tradition and not just from the individual who shares them. Within that specific socio-cultural context, the words have more power; their meanings may be altered or diminished when they are detached from their original context and re-introduced in another (Bakhtin, 1981). Finally, *dialogicality* implies the social nature of all language: two utterances meet and individuals both contextualize the utterance and orient themselves to it (Wertsch, 1991). Hall, Vitanova, and Marchenkova (2005) describe dialogue as the moment when the historical and the present converge in an utterance. Within the social context, an utterance is imbued with meanings bestowed on it by the group or by tradition, but people (re)interpret manners of speaking in deeply individual ways as well.

Conceptually, this research is also informed by *funds of knowledge*, defined as the "historically accumulated and culturally developed bodies of knowledge and skills essential for household or individual functioning and well-being" (Moll, Amanti, Neff, & González, 1992, p. 133). Since literacy is envisioned as situated within, and emerging from, particular socio-cultural and historical contexts, it is crucial to uncover the knowledges, experiences, and practices of immigrant/refugee families. Familial funds of knowledge, as embodied in their practices "back home" and here, become resources (Wright, 2001) or cultural tools that, once identified, can be used to support teaching and learning in school and ECE settings. This concept has often been used to frame studies of immigrant/refugee children and their families (e.g., Iddings, 2009; Smythe & Toohey, 2009); however, the focus in this study is on the educators (and future educators) themselves, who come from the same cultural backgrounds as the children with whom they work and exemplify the use of such cultural practices as singing and oral storytelling.

## Findings

The songs and stories shared in these sessions originated from various sources. Some could be characterized as personal stories invented by a family member and shared with the children. Other songs and stories were passed down from generation to generation, as Helen expressed: "When I was young my mom she was singing some kind of song ... like how they do it when she was young. Her dad taught her and she was singing it for us..." (Interview, February 12, 2012). Still others were borrowed from other cultures, perhaps the remnants of colonization. For instance, a group of women sang "Frère Jacques" to me in Amharic and mentioned hearing stories such as "Little Red Riding Hood," "The Little Red Hen" (Focus group, October 23, 2012), and "Cinderella" (Bijou, interview, May 31, 2013). I have merged the themes for songs and stories for ease of explanation and because in many cases they are used for similar purposes. In addition, most of the women contended that they and their family members sing stories aloud; thus, the two are often intertwined. As Sara, originally from Eritrea, explained, "My mom didn't go to school. She just knows that story. She listen to it, remember it and she sing it to me, to tell me, she's singing. Some people read a story" (Interview, February 21, 2012).

I develop three main themes here: the use of songs and stories to teach cultural values, to guide children's behaviour, and to convey encouragement or the adult's hopes for the child. Although I present the commonalities, there was also a difference between songs and stories, as songs were associated with enjoyment and pleasure in the participants' memories.

## Teaching cultural values

A dominant theme running through the discussions was the importance of teaching cultural and familial values, especially respect. Respect was overwhelmingly viewed to be the deeper value underlying proper behaviour. The women felt strongly that the family must instruct children how to respect their elders as a foundation for teaching the correct ways of behaving. As Akeda, an Eritrean grandmother, said, "they have to learn at home, not outside" (Focus-group discussion, October 13, 2011). Amina, from Somalia, explained several of the conversational and behavioural norms for demonstrating respect, which applied across all the women's cultures: "When the child tell you something, he can look at the adult, but if the adult is angry or they get mad or something like that, the child give the respect, he look down" (Focus-group discussion, October 20, 2011).

Stories in particular often contained messages enforcing respect for one's elders, as Helen remembered from her childhood in Eritrea:

> respect for people who are older and, you know, for example older people they cannot carry something, they cannot work or you know, whatever, you have to help them. So we need to help them, they (the parents) teach us. They told us the story (to teach us). (Helen, interview, February 17, 2012)

Amina confirmed that since they did not have books back home, elders' stories were both a source of information and a means of enforcing respectful listening: "Back home we listened to the older people, what they said ..." (Focus-group discussion, October 17, 2013). Bijou, from Sudan, recalled one example of a story her mother told them to teach respect:

> Another story she used to tell me was about a grandma, but she could be an evil grandma... She loves all her grandchildren, but often she gives them something and they get sick and she's the only one who can heal them, took them to the hospital and nothing would work. Only her, she can heal those children by singing her magical saying ... I used to tell my mom 'I don't want to go to my grandma's house.' And my grandma come and give us some stuff and I don't want to eat it! The story was to teach you to respect your grandmother otherwise she will be[come] evil. (Interview, May 31, 2013)

Fatima, a refugee woman from Somalia, told her own five sons stories about how her mother modelled respect for others regardless of the circumstances of their lives. For instance, Fatima's mother used to invite homeless people to eat lunch with them, and the children would express disgust at having a "dirty" person in their home. She told them a story about how she fed a homeless family for a period and then, when their fortunes changed, the family gave her honey and butter from their farm. She described the moral of the story as follows:

She said "we are same (as) this person. We came from (the) same, God made us both. He give us, he doesn't give him to show how we help each other ..." That's what she did. Yeah, because she always tell us "God, he has power to give everybody everything, but why (does) he give some people some and he didn't give the other one (any)? He's going to see how we help that person." And (it's) still in my mind. I tell my boys too "if you help the poor, God give you more. If you didn't help them maybe he can put you his place." (Interview, May 14, 2013)

While it was not common in their parents' generation to ask questions of the storyteller as a means of showing respect, several women mentioned that this cultural practice was changing rather than static. For instance, Simret recalled that, when her grandmother told them bedtime stories back home in Ethiopia, "maybe we might ask her lots of questions but when she was a child she was not asking any questions, but we asked questions and we had fun" (Focus-group discussion, October 23, 2012).

## Guiding children's behaviour

The participants shared that in their cultures, songs and storytelling were a means of teaching children how to behave and of reminding them what to do and not to do. This teaching was prioritized in the early years as children were expected to know how to act by the age of seven. As Sara put it, they "just come like adult ... they know everything" (Focus-group discussion, October 13, 2012). Katrina added: "From seven and up they are old enough to understand. From seven they go to school already and they know what's wrong and what's right" (October 13, 2012). Amina recalled how grandmothers and grandfathers told stories about "scary things" to frighten the children into coming home early: "Always we were going outside to play but when it's night time ... we came back home" (Focus-group discussion, October 17, 2013; see Heath, 1983, p. 188 for a similar example). Some of the Eritrean and Ethiopian women remembered a popular song, used by family members and teachers alike, intended to teach children healthy habits. Simret translated the words of the song into English: "Last night when I slept, I dreamed about my science class ... I washed my hands, I had my breakfast and this reminded me of my science class" (Focus-group discussion, October 17, 2013). The children themselves sometimes adopted this practice, using song to scold recalcitrant peers. Helen explained: "There is a song, sometimes when you do something wrong, some groups they sing about what you do—the bad things ... they sing a song 'you are a bad person and you are doing this thing and this thing ...'" (Interview, February 17, 2012).

## Conveying encouragement or hopes for a child

Growing up in war-torn Eritrea, Sara gathered strength from her mother's personal stories, which she described as "something like encouragement." As she explained, "My dad passed away when I was young. She [Sara's mother] told me stories, 'You can grow up, you can do everything.'" Sara escaped the interminable strife in her homeland, lived in a refugee camp for 11 years, and then was able to come to Canada. Carrying these stories with her throughout her journey, Sara drew on them for help with the transitions as she struggled to cope with single motherhood herself: "Now I am strong. When I came here I didn't feel scared. I didn't feel afraid" (Interview, January 12, 2012).

Similarly, Simret and Muna asserted, and the Eritrean women concurred, that "honey and milk" was a prevalent theme in songs, signifying goodness and sweetness in one's life. Childhood, Muna further clarified, was a special time, as symbolized by honey and milk. Parents and grandparents reminded children to take pleasure in the present in this popular song (translated by Muna):

> *Oh children, oh children!*
> *Let's play as much as we can*
> *Once childhood passes, it doesn't come again*
> *My childhood, my childhood*
> *My honey and milk. (Focus-group discussion, October 23, 2012)*

The idea of honey and milk was invoked not only to exhort children to enjoy themselves but to give them hopes for the future. Closely tied to the teaching of behaviour, one song promises children a good future if they accomplish certain tasks now. Singing to me in Amharic, Simret translated the following song into English:

> "Honey and milk is, like, you will have something very good in your life. You'll have something nice so that now you have to get up in the morning, go to school instead of waiting for your parents. You can do it by yourself." So this is like encouragement. (Focus-group discussion, October 23, 2013)

Helen shared that her father told personal stories about his own life to convey his hopes for her future (see also Roy & Roxas, 2011). Her father, one of 12 children from a farming family, did not have the opportunity to go to school because his help was needed at home. "So, always he was telling me stories, 'you need to learn. I didn't learn so I feel like I don't know anything. So be straight for your education ... you have to go hard, hard'" (Interview, February 17, 2012). Being "straight" was a path that he felt included eschewing an early marriage in favour of further education. These stories deeply affected Helen, who described how she moved to Ethiopia to continue her education and then, after settling in Canada, studied English and Early Childhood Education at a local college (Interview, February 17, 2012). Asmaa's mother likewise told her children a story with a moral to encourage them to get an education:

> She talk[ed] about man and his son. They were farmers, they live on a farm far from the city ... They have a neighbour ... He also has a farm ... And the man that had a son, he woke up early every day, and his son doesn't want to go to work with his dad. And he says, "Come, we need to work, we need to put seeds, we need to grow food. Wintertime we want to eat something." ... He made everything, he put seeds, he put water. And the other man, every morning he come and he say, "Today I want to make this side and tomorrow I will make that side." He didn't make anything. He talks only. He goes his home and he sleeps. This man [with the] son, his farm grows everything ... wintertime this man has food and that other man didn't have anything. Only he talks, he didn't act. If you come to school every day, you read something, you learn something, but if you come here and say, "Today I read this page and tomorrow that page and I will finish that" but then you didn't read anything ... If you read, you read, you read, you finish and you go to university, you go everywhere. My mother she was telling me this ... She say, "I never go to school, but I need you to go to school and to learn everything, to learn, to write Koran, everything." So she told stories to encourage us. (Interview, May 14, 2013)

While Asmaa was unable to complete her studies back home, she too enrolled in an ECE program at a Canadian college.

Finally, name songs were important in some of the participants' cultures. Achi detailed how in Sudanese families name songs were often sung by grandmothers or mothers to the children and accentuated the characteristics of the child and the adults' hopes for her or him in the future (Interview, January 16, 2012). In the Eritrean tradition, name songs are then sung to the child on important occasions: "We do a song. There is meaning in each name ... and sometimes they tell them what is the meaning of the name from the Bible so they know, they understand what it mean" (Helen, interview, February 17, 2012).

## Discussion

The concept of transcultural capital considers how migrants might activate and use their funds of knowledge, skills, and networks from "back home" in their new places of residence, thus transforming disadvantage into benefits for themselves, their families, and their communities (Triandafyllidou, 2009; as cited in Hope, 2011). Hope (2011) suggested that refugees may be well situated in terms of connecting their transnational capital to literacy learning in the new context. Supporting the findings of Monzó and Rueda (2003) and Adair

(2009, 2011), this study reveals some of the instructional and cultural funds of knowledge immigrant/refugee educators bring with them to Canada that could be operationalized in their work with immigrant/refugee children. These women may offer a unique, dual-focused view of cultural and familial literacies as cultural insiders and as educators who are well positioned to gain insights into dominant values and beliefs. In this sense, they could act as cultural brokers, interpreters, and resources both for newcomer families and for their Canadian-born colleagues.

Since many of the women's own parents were "illiterate" (as defined by the autonomous model of literacy), stories were often memorized, transmitted orally from previous generations, or invented, based on personal life experiences and circumstances of the family member, rather than read from books. As Ahmed elaborated, oral stories in the Somali context are representative of the cultural values that are to be transmitted to children "and the experiential wisdom inherent in them ensured the survival of tradition in the minds of the young" (as cited in Bigelow, 2010, p. 37). Thus these stories contained rich insights into the values, behaviours, and knowledges of the family and the culture (Brown, 2011), insights the women were also trying to pass along to their own children (see also Taylor, Bernhard, Garg, & Cummins, 2008). Integrating these songs and stories into early childhood settings, however, is often problematic.

Each of the participants has been educated into the dominant discourse of ECE, through her enrollment in certificate programs, where storybook reading and singing English songs are prioritized as the literacy practices "worth knowing" in the Canadian context. In Bakhtinian terms, they constitute the *authoritative discourse* infused with historically derived, scientific power (Bakhtin, 1981). These books and songs are written texts, rather than oral texts, serving to bolster their perceived weight of authority (Ong, 2001). During my fieldwork in the 10-month ECE certificate program, for example, I observed that my participants spent an average of 20 minutes a day learning to sing songs in English and had several storybook reading assignments each month. In this manner, the instructors prepared them for working in the field. Participants in the workplace site were similarly exhorted to embrace dominant practices to pass the accreditation review. Yet Simret argues, and other educators agree, that the overemphasis on reading in North American schools and child-care settings leads to the exclusion of the literacies of many immigrant/refugee parents and educators: "I see it here with teachers. You have to read the book every night. But maybe the family, they don't have the experience with reading, but they have another way of telling stories" (Focus-group discussion, October 23, 2012). Herein lies the conflict for immigrant/refugee women working in the field of ECE.

Immigrants and refugees often experience tensions around such juxtapositions as maintaining home and cultural literacy practices while participating fully in dominant practices, or wanting their children to be successful in school while affirming connections to their families and communities (Bloome, Katz, Solsken, Willett, & Wilson-Keenan, 2000). In my fieldwork, I observed the early childhood educators in the workplace and the ECE students on their field placements in child-care centres. My observations of the participants in the workplace or on field placement revealed that stories and songs from one's home culture were rarely shared with the children, in English or the home language, even if the children came from the same country as the participant. Acutely aware of literacy "best practices" in schools and child-care settings, the participants helped children gain access to the "culture of power," to use Delpit's (1995) words, by reading story books to them (see also Gee, 1996; Heath, 1983). The ECE students, especially, entertained children in field placement sites with the simplistic, silly, and often irrelevant rhyming songs they memorized in college. The educators very occasionally shared their own songs imbued with deeper meanings and intentions, though stories were always read from books. Therefore, dominant practices almost always prevailed over cultural ones. Consistent with Bahktin's theorization of *voice*, the words in these cultural songs and stories are deeply rooted in the socio-cultural context in which they were collectively developed and voiced; they lose not only meaning but power when they are transferred to the Canadian context. As a result, these educators often struggle to overcome their voicelessness by adopting the language and words—the songs and stories—that are closely connected to the new context. Bakhtin (1981) contended that discourse must be *internally persuasive* to us, "tightly interwoven with one's own word," creating new meanings for the individual (p. 345). For the individual, there is discord between the discourses, or voices, that are wrestling for supremacy (Platt, 2005). Reconciling the two necessitates authoring new voices, connecting the contexts of back home and here (Vitanova, 2005), which is challenging in view of the pervasive authority of dominant literacy practices.

When the knowledges and practices of "differently literate" families are subjugated to dominant literacy discourses, the discontinuity between home and school/ECE setting can have devastating effects on the immigrant/refugee child's personal and cultural identity construction (Dudley-Marling, 2009; Reese & Gallimore, 2000). If educators are able to activate cultural tools to mediate children's understandings and bridge these literacy practices, then the children are better supported in their transitions, and parents can be "present in their absence" (Vandenbroeck et al., 2009). This notion of presence resonated with the educators who lamented that, in Helen's words, "they [the children] stay here with us most of the time" (Focus-group discussion, October 13, 2012). Furthermore, when educators are fully able to mobilize their transcultural capital, immigrant/refugee children's literacy learning "benefits from the blending of pre-migration histories with future possibilities" (Hope, 2011, p. 91). Gregory, Long, and Volk (2004) proposed that *prolepsis* (see Cole, 1996) functions as "the cultural mechanism that brings the end into the beginning" (p. 183). The educators' memories of the past are carried into literacy events (Heath, 1983) with children in the present, assisting them in building cultural resources for the future (Espinoza-Herold, 2007). Therefore, it is essential to expand our understandings of literacy to legitimize cultural values and practices, or cultural models (Gee, 1996), that are normally excluded from institutional settings, and position them as "best practices" in a linguistically inclusive pedagogy (Taylor, Bernhard, Garg, & Cummins, 2008).

## ACKNOWLEDGEMENTS

*This research was supported by the Social Sciences and Humanities Research Council of Canada.*

## REFERENCES

Adair, J.K. (2009). *Teaching children of immigrants: A multi-sited ethnographic study of preschool teachers in five U.S. cities* (Unpublished doctoral dissertation). Arizona State University, Phoenix (UMI No. 3360743).

Adair, J.K. (2011). Confirming chanclas: What early childhood teacher educators can learn from immigrant preschool teachers. *Journal of Early Childhood Teacher Education, 32*, 55–71. http://dx.doi.org/10.1080/10901027.2010.547652

Angrosino, M. (2007). *Doing ethnographic and observational research.* Los Angeles, CA: Sage.

Bakhtin, M.M. (1981). Discourse in the novel. In C. Emerson & M. Holquist (Eds.), *The dialogic imagination: Four essays by M.M. Bakhtin* (pp. 259–422). (C. Emerson, & M. Holquist, Trans.). Austin, TX: University of Texas Press.

Bakhtin, M.M. (1986). The problem of speech genres (V.W. McGee, Trans.). In C. Emerson & M. Holquist (Eds.), *Speech genres and other late essays* (pp. 60–102). Austin, TX: University of Texas Press.

Bernheimer, S. (2003). *New possibilities for early childhood education: Stories from our non-traditional students.* New York, NY: Peter Lang.

Bigelow, M.H. (2010). Orality and literacy within the Somali diaspora. *Language Learning: A Journal of Research in Language Studies, 60*(1), 25–57.

Bloome, D., Katz, L., Solsken, J., Willett, J., & Wilson-Keenan, J. (2000). Interpellations of family/community and classroom literacy practices. *Journal of Educational Research, 93*(3), 155–163. http://dx.doi.org/10.1080/00220670009598704

Bredekamp, S., & Copple, C. (2009). *Developmentally appropriate practice in early childhood programs*. Washington, DC: National Association for the Education of Young Children.

Brown, S. (2011). Becoming literate: Looking across curricular structures at situated identities. *Early Childhood Education Journal, 39*(4), 257–265. http://dx.doi.org/10.1007/s10643-011-0468-7

Cannella, G. (1997). *Deconstructing early childhood education: Social justice & revolution*. New York, NY: Peter Lang.

Cole, M. (1996). *Cultural psychology: A once and future discipline*. Cambridge, MA: Harvard University Press.

Dahlberg, G., Moss, P., & Pence, A. (2007). *Beyond quality in early childhood education and care: Languages of evaluation* (2nd ed.). New York, NY: Routledge.

Delpit, L. (1995). *Other people's children: Cultural conflict in the classroom*. New York, NY: New Press.

Dudley-Marling, C. (2009). Home-school literacy connections: The perceptions of African American and immigrant ESL families in two urban communities. *Teachers College Record, 111*(7), 1713–1752.

Espinoza-Herold, M. (2007). Stepping beyond *sí se puede*: Dichos as a cultural resource in mother–daughter interaction in a Latino family. *Anthropology & Education Quarterly, 38*(3), 260–277. http://dx.doi.org/10.1525/aeq.2007.38.3.260

Gee, J. (1996). *Social linguistics and literacies*. London, UK: Taylor Francis.

González, N., Moll, L.C., & Amanti, C. (2005). Introduction: Theorizing practices. In N. González, L.C. Moll, & C. Amanti (Eds.), *Funds of knowledge: Theorizing practices in households, communities and classrooms* (pp. 1–24). Mahwah, NJ: Lawrence Erlbaum Associates.

Government of Alberta (2013). *Child care staff certification guide*. Retrieved from http://humanservices.alberta.ca/documents/child-care-staff-certification-guide.pdf

Gregory, E., Long, S., & Volk, D. (2004). *Many pathways to literacy: Learning with siblings, grandparents, peers, and communities*. London, UK: Routledge.

Grieshaber, S., Shield, P., Luke, A., & Macdonald, S. (2012). Family literacy practices and home literacy resources: An Australian pilot study. *Journal of Early Childhood Literacy, 12*(2), 113–138. http://dx.doi.org/10.1177/1468798411416888

Gupta, A. (2006). Early experiences and personal funds of knowledge and beliefs of immigrant and minority teacher candidates dialog with theories of child development in a teacher education program. *Journal of Early Childhood Teacher Education, 27*(1), 3–18. http://dx.doi.org/10.1080/10901020500534224

Hall, J.K., Vitanova, G., & Marchenkova, L. (2005). Introduction: Dialogue with Bakhtin on second and foreign language learning. In J.K. Hall, G. Vitanova, & L. Marchenkova (Eds.), *Dialogue with Bakhtin on second and foreign language learning: New perspectives* (pp. 1–10). Mahwah, NJ: Lawrence Erlbaum Associates.

Heath, S.B. (1983). *Ways with words: Language, life, and work in communities and classrooms*. New York, NY: Cambridge University Press.

Hope, J. (2011). New insights into family learning for refugees: Bonding, bridging and building transcultural capital. *Literacy, 45*(2), 91–97. http://dx.doi.org/10.1111/j.1741-4369.2011.00581.x

Hsin, C.-T. (2011). Active agents: The new-immigrant mothers' figured worlds of home literacy practices for young children in Taiwan. *Asia-Pacific Education Researcher, 20*(1), 17–34.

Iddings, A.C.D.S. (2009). Bridging home and school literacy practices: Empowering families of recent immigrant children. *Theory into Practice, 48*(4), 304–311. http://dx.doi.org/10.1080/00405840903192904

Langford, R. (2007). Who is a good early childhood educator? A critical study of differences within a universal professional identity in early childhood education preparation programs. *Journal of Early Childhood Teacher Education, 28*(4), 333–352. http://dx.doi.org/10.1080/10901020701686609

Lobman, C., & Ryan, S. (2007). Differing discourses on early childhood teacher development. *Journal of Early Childhood Teacher Education, 28*(4), 367–380. http://dx.doi.org/10.1080/10901020701686633

Mallory, B., & New, R. (1994). *Diversity and developmentally appropriate practices: Challenges for early childhood education.* New York, NY: Teachers College Press.

Marshall, E., & Toohey, K. (2010). Representing family: Community funds of knowledge, bilingualism, and multimodality. *Harvard Educational Review, 80*(2), 221–241.

Moll, L.C., Amanti, C., Neff, D., & González, N. (1992). Funds of knowledge for teaching: Using a qualitative approach to connect homes and classrooms. *Theory Into Practice, 31*(2), 133–141.

Monzó, L.D., & Rueda, R. (2003). Shaping education through diverse funds of knowledge: A look at one Latin paraeducator's lived experiences, beliefs, and teaching practice. *Anthropology & Education Quarterly, 34*(1), 72–95. http://dx.doi.org/10.1525/aeq.2003.34.1.72

Moss, P. (2006). Structures, understandings and discourses: Possibilities for re-envisioning the early childhood worker. *Contemporary Issues in Early Childhood, 7*(1), 30–41. http://dx.doi.org/10.2304/ciec.2006.7.1.30

National Association for the Education of Young Children (NAEYC). (2009). *Developmentally appropriate practice in early childhood programs serving children from birth through age 8: A position statement of the National Association for the Education of Young Children.* Retrieved from http://www.naeyc.org/files/naeyc/file/positions/position%20statement%20Web.pdf

Nsamenang, A.B. (2010). Issues in and challenges to professionalism in Africa's cultural settings. *Contemporary Issues in Early Childhood, 11*(1), 20–28. http://dx.doi.org/10.2304/ciec.2010.11.1.20

Nuttall, J., & Ortlipp, M. (2011). Supervision and assessment of the early childhood practicum: Experiences of pre-service teachers who speak English as a second language and their supervising teachers. *Australasian Journal of Early Childhood, 36*(2), 87–94.

Ong, W.J. (2001). *Orality and literacy: The technologizing of the word.* London, UK: Routledge Taylor and Francis Group.

Perry, K.H. (2009). Genres, contexts, and literacy practices: Literacy brokering among Sudanese refugee families. *Reading Research Quarterly, 44*(3), 256–276. http://dx.doi.org/10.1598/RRQ.44.3.2

Platt, E. (2005). "Uh, oh no Hapana": Intersubjectivity, meaning and the self. In J.K. Hall, G. Vitanova, & L. Marchenkova (Eds.), *Dialogue with Bakhtin on second and foreign language learning: New perspectives* (pp. 119–147). Mahwah, NJ: Lawrence Erlbaum Associates.

Reese, L., & Gallimore, R. (2000). Immigrant Latinos' cultural model of literacy development: An evolving perspective on home–school discontinuities. *American Journal of Education, 108*(2), 103–134. http://dx.doi.org/10.1086/444236

Reyes, L.-V. (2006). Creating an inclusive early childhood professional development system in New Mexico, U.S.A. *Contemporary Issues in Early Childhood Education, 7*(3), 292–301. http://dx.doi.org/10.2304/ciec.2006.7.3.292

Rivera, L., & Lavan, N. (2012). Family literacy practices and parental involvement of Latin American immigrant mothers. *Journal of Latinos and Education, 11*(4), 247–259. http://dx.doi.org/10.1080/15348431.2012.715500

Rogoff, B. (1990). *Apprenticeship in thinking: Cognitive development in social context.* New York, NY: Oxford University Press.

Rogoff, B. (1995). Observing sociocultural activity on three planes: Participatory appropriation, guided participation, and apprenticeship. In J. Wertsch, P. del Rio, & A. Alvarez (Eds.), *Sociocultural studies of mind* (pp. 139–164). Cambridge, UK: Cambridge University Press. http://dx.doi.org/10.1017/CBO9781139174299.008

Rogoff, B. (2003). *The cultural nature of human development*. New York, NY: Oxford University Press.

Roy, L.A., & Roxas, K.C. (2011). Whose deficit is this anyhow? Exploring counter-stories of Somali Bantu refugees' experiences in 'doing school'. *Harvard Educational Review, 81*(3), 521–541.

Service Canada (2011). Early childhood educators and assistants. Retrieved from http://www.servicecanada.gc.ca/eng/qc/job_futures/statistics/4214.shtml

Smythe, S., & Toohey, K. (2009). Bringing home and community to school: What can schools do with it? In A. Kostogriz, J. Miller, & M. Gearon (Eds.), *Linguistically and culturally diverse classrooms: New dilemmas for teachers* (pp. 271–290). Bristol, UK: Multilingual Matters.

Soltero-González, L. (2009). Preschool Latino immigrant children: Using the home language as a resource for literacy learning. *Theory Into Practice, 48*, 283–289. http://dx.doi.org/10.1080/00405840903192771

Souto-Manning, M., & Swick, K.J. (2006). Teachers' beliefs about parent and family involvement: Rethinking our family involvement paradigm. *Early Childhood Education Journal, 34*(2), 187–193. http://dx.doi.org/10.1007/s10643-006-0063-5

Spindler, G. (2008). Using visual stimuli in ethnography. *Anthropology & Education Quarterly, 39*(2), 127–140. http://dx.doi.org/10.1111/j.1548-1492.2008.00012.x

Stage, C.W., & Mattson, M. (2003). Ethnographic interviewing as contextualized conversation. In R.P. Clair (Ed.), *Expressions of ethnography: Novel approaches to qualitative methods* (pp. 97–106). Albany, NY: State University of New York Press.

Stanovich, K.E. (1986). Matthew effects in reading: Some consequences of individual differences in the acquisition of literacy. *Reading Research Quarterly, 21*(4), 360–407. http://dx.doi.org/10.1598/RRQ.21.4.1

Statistics Canada. (2010). *Projections of the diversity of the Canadian population, 2006 to 2031*. Ottawa, ON: Ministry of Industry.

Statistics Canada (2011). *Canada year book 2011*. Retrieved from http://www.statcan.gc.ca/pub/11-402-x/2011000/pdf/ethnic-ethnique-eng.pdf

Street, B. (1993). Introduction. In B. Street (Ed.), *Cross-cultural approaches to literacy* (pp. 1–21). New York, NY: Cambridge University Press.

Street, B. (2001). Introduction. In B. Street (Ed.), *Literacy and development: ethnographic perspectives* (pp. 1–18). New York, NY: Routledge. http://dx.doi.org/10.4324/9780203468418

Taylor, D., & Dorsey-Gaines, C. (1988). *Growing up literate: Learning from inner-city families*. Portsmouth, NH: Heinemann.

Taylor, L.K., Bernhard, J.K., Garg, S., & Cummins, J. (2008). Affirming plural belonging: Building on students' family-based cultural and linguistic capital through multiliteracies pedagogy. *Journal of Early Childhood Literacy, 8*(3), 269–294. http://dx.doi.org/10.1177/1468798408096481

Tobin, J., Husueh, Y., & Karasawa, M. (2009). *Preschools in three cultures revisited*. Chicago, IL: University of Chicago Press. http://dx.doi.org/10.7208/chicago/9780226805054.001.0001

Tobin, J., Wu, J., & Davidson, D. (1989). *Preschools in three cultures*. New Haven, CT: Yale University Press.

Tomlinson, H.B., & Hyson, M. (2009). Developmentally appropriate practices in the preschool years. In S. Bredekamp & C. Copple (Eds.), *Developmentally appropriate practice in early childhood programs serving children from birth through age 8* (pp. 111–148). Washington, DC: NAEYC.

Vandenbroeck, M., Roets, G., & Snoeck, A. (2009). Immigrant mothers crossing borders: Nomadic identities and multiple belongings in early childhood education. *European Early Childhood Education Research Journal, 17*(2), 203–216. http://dx.doi.org/10.1080/13502930902951452

Vitanova, G. (2005). Authoring the self in a non-native language: A dialogic approach to agency and subjectivity. In J.K. Hall, G. Vitanova, & L. Marchenkova (Eds.), *Dialogue with Bakhtin on second and foreign language learning: New perspectives* (pp. 149–170). Mahwah, NJ: Lawrence Erlbaum Associates.

Vygotsky, L. (1978). *Mind and society: The development of higher mental processes.* Cambridge, MA: Harvard University Press.

Wertsch, J. (1991). *Voices of the mind: A sociocultural approach to mediated action.* Cambridge, MA: Harvard University Press.

Wertsch, J.V. (1998). *Mind as action.* New York: Oxford University Press.

Wertsch, J.V. (2007). Mediation. In H. Daniels, M. Cole, & J.V. Wertsch (Eds.), *The Cambridge companion to Vygotsky* (pp. 178–192). New York, NY: Cambridge University Press. http://dx.doi.org/10.1017/CCOL0521831040.008

Wright, M. (2001). More than just chanting: Multilingual literacies, ideology, and teaching methodologies in rural Eritrea. In B. Street (Ed.), *Literacy and development: Ethnographic perspectives* (pp. 61–77). New York, NY: Routledge.

# 9

# Refugee families with preschool children

## *Looking back*

*Darcey M. Dachyshyn*

While the data reported in this chapter is rooted in research undertaken with refugee families located in Canada (Dachyshyn, 2008b), I will also include experiences and research from other locations that now inform my understandings of the complexities involved in refugee resettlement. I do not intend to provide a detailed look at this original research, which can be found elsewhere (Dachyshyn 2007, 2008a, 2008b; Dachyshyn & Kirova, 2008); rather, the gaze I wish to bring is one of reflecting back from my current vantage point. I trust this perspective will open up opportunities for dialogue and discussion about the multi-faceted nature of resettlement.

I also wish to broaden the discussion to include not only refugees but also other newcomers who are involved in adjusting to a new location, be it Canada or elsewhere. The term *newcomer* is used in government and non-government policy and programs in reference to foreign-born persons intending to reside in Canada for an extended period, such as immigrants, Convention refugees, and refugee claimants (Best Start Resource Centre, 2010; Government of Canada, 2013a; Wayland, 2006). I use the term *newcomer* more broadly and suggest that, for example, temporary foreign workers, international students, and diplomatic workers, although residing in a foreign country for a limited time, are also newcomers to their present location. Taken as such, the term *newcomer* makes room for someone living and working abroad on a fixed contract basis, such as I am.

## The present vantage point

I have been a newcomer three times since 2008, first to the United States, then to Aotearoa (New Zealand), and now to Tanzania. *Expatriate* is the term most commonly used for someone like me in my current position, although I resist applying that word to myself. I do not feel *ex-* to anything and most certainly not ex-Canadian. I pride myself on being a citizen of one of the few countries in the world that accepts United Nations Convention refugees, persons who, because of fear of persecution, are not safe living in their home country (UNHCR, 1996). Canada is one of nine main countries (the others being the United States, Australia, Sweden, Norway, Finland, New Zealand, Denmark, and the Netherlands) annually to receive some of the estimated 10.4 million refugees of concern to the United Nations High Commissioner for Refugees (UNHCR 2013a, 2013b). I also pride myself on being from the first country to adopt multiculturalism policy, which since 1971 affirms, values, and encourages plurality of linguistic, cultural, ethnic, and religious identity among all those residing in Canada (Government of Canada, 2013b). For these and many more reasons I will always be proudly Canadian.

The larger reason I resist the term *expatriate,* though, is undoubtedly as a cushion against the inequities and injustices I see perpetuated upon indigenous Tanzanians by the expatriate community, of which I am a part. Where I am situated, we live on the best land in the best accommodation, and we can afford to hire domestic help, drivers, gardeners, and security staff, all while most Tanzanians scrape by with next to nothing. We say we are here to help, but our helping sees us ensconced in a more than comfortable lifestyle, one that is made possible only through the creation of a class of people upon whose backs we stand to reach our elevated position—and, I am embarrassed to say, a lifestyle that I would be very reluctant to give up.

At first glance this discussion of my present vantage point might not seem relevant to the topic of Canadian newcomer resettlement. However, my understanding of life and my theoretical orientation to my work as an early childhood educator are firmly rooted in sociocultural–historical theories of human learning, which tell us we are who we are because of where we come from (Rogoff, 2003; Vygotsky, 1978, 1986). Therefore, it is important for the reader to know the route that has brought me to the present view I bring to this topic.

All our life experiences have gone into making us who we are. What I learned then, in originally conducting this research, has profoundly shaped me. What I have experienced since has also influenced me. I believe that looking back and seeing with different eyes will bring new insights that will further our understanding of newcomer resettlement, especially in education contexts.

## Background and methodology to the study

The original study identified the settlement issues encountered by refugee families with preschool children living in Edmonton (Dachyshyn, 2008b). Seven focus groups and seven one-on-one interviews were conducted with refugee parents primarily from Africa (namely Burundi, Democratic Republic of Congo, Djibouti, Eritrea, Rwanda, Somalia, and South Sudan) as well as Afghanistan, Cambodia, and Kurdistan. The 63 parents involved collectively represented 89 preschool children and 141 children over six years of age. Parents from these communities were involved in the research because these were the ethno-cultural communities being most actively supported by cultural brokers working for the settlement agency that served as the research site.

The term *cultural broker* is used in reference to individuals who share the same linguistic and cultural background as the research participants, but who also have competency in English and so functioned as interpreters for me. These individuals, who routinely serve as links or liaisons between their community members and those from outside their cultural group, were essential in offering the linguistic and emotional support necessary for participants to understand the nature of the research and to feel comfortable participating in it. The cultural brokers also brought tremendous insight to me because of their position of sharing similar life experiences as the participants while at the same time having already worked through some of the settlement issues the research participants discussed, and so contributed to the data analysis.

The research results map the lived experiences of refugee families with preschool children during resettlement. The term *mapping* is commonly used in the context of ethnographic research. Though not strictly ethnographic, this research describes, analyzes, and interprets a "culture-sharing group's shared patterns of behaviour, beliefs, and language that develop over time" (Creswell, 2005, p. 436). In this case, the time frame for each participant varied. Some were very new to Canada and so were in the early stages of the resettlement experience, while others brought a more reflective outlook on the way things had once been for them.

To help ensure relevance of the research findings to the communities served, on three occasions I brought transcribed data, from focus groups and interviews, for analysis to working groups consisting of cultural brokers, settlement workers, and other researchers exploring newcomer issues. Data was first broadly categorized into four frames of reference: life experiences before the crisis that sent participants into refugee status, life during the time of crisis, life now in their present location, and their hopes for the future. Although I treated the material about past experiences and hopes for the future as significant contextual knowledge, the main data I analyzed relates to how participants experience life in the present. Through this process, several key settlement issues became evident as common across all ethno-cultural groups.

## Looking back on the settlement issues

The research indicated that refugee families with preschool children were dealing with eight interrelated settlement issues:

a) Decreased socio-economic status
b) Lack of community and family support
c) Unfamiliar child-rearing practices
d) Changing roles and responsibilities of family members
e) Dealing with racism and discrimination
f) Coping with mental health issues
g) Maintaining home language and culture
h) Adapting to the Canadian education system.

What I wish to offer here is my reflections looking back on what I learned from hearing the stories of individuals who participated in focus groups and interviews, and to add what I have learned since through my various experiences after leaving Edmonton at the completion of that research.

### Decreased socio-economic status

When I first began working with newcomers I was terribly naïve. Here I was living in a country built on immigration, one that continues to accept about a quarter of a million new people to its shores every year, and yet I knew nothing about the lived reality of being a newcomer. With respect to refugees, like so many others, I had accepted the stereotype of camp refugees who come from nothing and are provided with everything when they reach Canada. One participant, who at the time was attending English language classes, shared the following with me:

> People at school say, "Oh you people are immigrants you are lucky you get free money." However, this money is nothing, and if you are absent one day, they cut the money. If my baby is sick, I have to go to

the hospital, and I miss one day they cut the money. If my husband finds a part-time job and they know this, they will cut the money. We are just stuck in one place. (Participant from South Sudan)

What I did not know is that when UN Convention refugees are destined for Canada, they are expected to pay for the cost of the medical examinations performed as part of the process of being accepted as refugees to Canada, as well as for the cost of the flights that will bring them to safety. If they are unable to pay for these expenses at the time of the selection process, they are issued a loan and are expected to begin repaying that loan shortly after arriving in Canada (Government of Canada, 2011). I was incensed and embarrassed when I learned this. I wondered how a humanitarian gesture could bring with it economic debt. One participant explained things this way:

> When you are told that you are going to go to Canada, everything is done for you free, your medical, they check you, everything is done free. No one thinks that one day I will have to pay that back. When we came here, they said ok, we did this for you and this for you and this for you, including the flight to Edmonton, you have to pay this money back from the first day you began the immigration process. (Participant from South Sudan)

You will notice that the topic under consideration here is *decreased* socio-economic status. It is important to realize that refugees, like all newcomers, vary a great deal in the circumstances of their lives before arriving in Canada. According to Statistics Canada, nearly 28,000 refugees, who include just over 4,000 dependants, were accepted by Citizenship and Immigration Canada in 2011 (CIC, 2011). Of this number, slightly less than 7,500 were UN Convention refugees; the remaining 16,000-plus refugees were either privately sponsored refugees or asylum seekers (people claiming refugee status upon arrival at Canada's borders). While it is true that UN Convention refugees are among the most vulnerable of the world's population, many of whom have had protracted stays in refugee camps, there must be room in our thinking to imagine refugees who are from the educated and business classes of their societies. These will be people who did not leave behind a terrible life for a better life with respect to economic status; on the contrary, out of no choice of their own they are subject to a lifestyle of poverty or near poverty because it was not safe for them to remain in their home country. These are people with incredible funds of knowledge to offer Canada, but instead they are often marginalized. One woman explained: "If I were back home, my husband would be working as an engineer. Here he has tried and he cannot get any kind of jobs up to the standard of his professional job. He is just depressed" (Participant from Somali).

This reality is present to me here in Dar es Salaam. It is the Tanzanian-born South Asian population that, over several generations, has come to acquire large holdings within the business class of this society. If, as happened under the leadership of Julius Nyerere, Tanzania's first president following independence from Britain, the country chose again to nationalize businesses, banks, industries, and land, many highly skilled and highly educated people would lose all they had worked hard to attain and find themselves in a position of needing sanctuary elsewhere. Should such an event befall Tanzania—should these families find themselves navigating the education systems in Canada—they would most certainly not be the stereotypical refugee family coming from lengthy stays in refugee camps and having little by way of knowledge and employment skills relevant to the Canadian context.

I believe it is important when we intersect with newcomers, especially those who are refugees, that we learn their stories. Sometimes we do not want to hear these stories because we make assumptions about horrors of war, starvation, and dire circumstances. While of course such experiences will be the case for many, on the other hand we might hear stories of middle-class life left behind out of no choice of one's own: stories that might in fact mirror our own, except that we happen to have been born in one of the safest and freest countries on earth (Institute for Economics and Peace, 2012).

### Lack of community and family support

Reflecting back, based on what I have experienced since leaving Canada, I find the lack of community and family support during the process of resettlement a most interesting and perplexing issue. Certainly the message received from newcomers to Canada during my research is that people feel isolated and alone in their new location. One participant expressed that she felt she was *in a prison*, isolated at home with several small children. Another participant offered this information: "Here you are isolated and lonely, and it is very difficult for newcomers to integrate. They expect the same closeness with their neighbour just like it is in Africa, but this is not the case" (Participant from Burundi). The importance of extended family is stressed in the following comments:

> If you have your family you can pretty much go through any problem, it is much easier. Here you are with your partner and there is no other person. The guidance that you would need from other members of your family like your mom is not here. (Participant from Eritrea)

> The next day after my baby was born; I was back in the kitchen. I had no choice. I felt bad, sad, and lonely. There is nobody here. I think if I

> was back home my sister, my aunty, my mom, everyone would be there, but now here we do not have a choice. (Participant from Sudan)
>
> The little one [daughter] misses her grandmother. Whenever she sees an older woman, she calls her "grandma." I sometimes feel bad, because my children do not really know their grandparents. (Participant from Sudan)

While in no way equating my own experience with that of a refugee, I understand the feelings that come with relocation. Even though in my moves to the US and to Aotearoa I was joining countries dominated by white English-speaking citizens such as myself, I still often felt alien (Dachyshyn, 2012; Steinbock, 1995). In my work in Aotearoa especially, I found myself most closely aligning with other newcomers rather than to those born in Aotearoa.

Now in Tanzania, as a white, English-speaking person, I am physically in the minority, although in terms of power and privilege, because of my economic status, I am of the dominant culture. Whom do I align myself with here, with whom do I feel akin, and with whom do I feel alien? I feel in a very odd position. Many newcomers to Canada will also feel in an odd position. In their home country they may have enjoyed an elevated status, only to find themselves now unemployed or underemployed. They may at one time have been among the dominant and privileged of their society, but now their identity is defined primarily as someone who cannot speak English or French well.

While being a newcomer can be a time of feeling isolated and alone, feeling bereft of family and community support, I do question the nature of the lamented community and family support that was left behind in the home setting. My own experience has been that, in a crisis, families and communities rally to support one another, as we experienced while living in Christchurch, New Zealand, during the earthquake events of 2010–11, and very recently here in Dar es Salaam when a building under construction collapsed, trapping and killing both workers and unsuspecting bystanders. In those times of crisis, people rallied and pulled together. However, my experience is that no matter on which continent, especially if we live in urban settings, our day-to-day lives are dominated by the busyness of the capitalist, corporate, consumerist way of life, and competition—rather than cooperation and compassion—is the norm. In an online course forum with in-service early childhood practitioners here in Dar es Salaam, during a discussion about cultural shifts and how family relationships are changing such that parents spend very little time with their children, one student posted:

> This is due to unavoidable circumstances that push or trigger the rapid changes in socio-cultural, economic and political aspects that are taking place in the world. This is happening because the world is

dynamic and not static, and East Africa is not in a vacuum. This situation started in western countries a long time ago, but with time now it is happening in developing countries particularly in urban areas. Therefore even in rural areas it will be the same in just a matter of time. (Dar es Salaam course participant)

It is my view that people everywhere are losing ties to those living right next to them. As we encounter newcomers in our classrooms and communities, perhaps we can view such encounters as opportunities for welcoming engagement that we all could benefit from.

## Unfamiliar child-rearing practices

In the research I conducted, when participants spoke of child-rearing practices, the issue at hand was really discipline. Many newcomers felt their hands were tied, as the ways common *back home* for dealing with inevitable child-rearing challenges were seen in Canada as harsh and left them subject to suspicion and fear of sanctioning by child welfare authorities. Parents reported:

> If you speak loudly, calling your children, there is suspicion outside the door there, which makes us very uncomfortable even when we are in our own homes. (Participant from Somalia)

> Here it is harder to discipline the children. Back home, we can discipline the children by spanking them but here we cannot do that. (Participant from Cambodia)

As Canadian-born citizens we forget that previously we too had more options open to us regarding discipline. Corporal punishment, shaming, ostracism, isolation, and teasing used to be common practices among most cultures until very recently (Prochner & Hwang, 2008; Quinn, 2005). Now, in Western culture, praise and natural consequences are the main means by which we guide our children's behaviour, especially in preschool and school settings. In one of the focus groups, this statement was met with incredulous laughter by the other parents: "The recommendation here in Canada is the only way to discipline your child is to be a friend with your child" (Participant from Djibouti). This same participant went on to say:

> What is hard for immigrants regarding children is that children here have bad behaviour. If you do not act as your children want, they will tell you to go away or call the police. In Africa, we teach our children respect and moral values. It can always happen that a child does not listen, but this is rare, and his dad or any member of the tribe or close relative will punish him.

Do not get me wrong; I am very much against cruel and harsh punishment. The issue for me lies in the fact that we have in our culture *slowly* moved toward our present position. For many newcomers, in the time it takes for their flight to bring them to Canada, they need to work out other approaches to child-rearing, and in most cases without even being aware of this need.

I believe unequivocally that raising children can be a challenging endeavour and one that no single culture has developed perfect strategies for. I suggest that what we need is not parenting classes, where the dominant-culture expert teaches newcomers how to deal with their children, but rather parenting dialogue. Perhaps schools and early care and learning settings can be seen as places to provide opportunities for honest and open sharing about the challenges, the successful strategies, and the hopeful outlook of those who have already surpassed whatever challenges the other might presently be encountering with their children.

## Changing roles and responsibilities of family members

In my work with Canadian newcomers, I often heard about two scenarios. One, the wife or female partner in a family is the first one to attain paid employment, and the husband or male partner is the one left at home unemployed. This is a scenario fraught with difficulties. Two, the older children in the family, who in their home country would be taking responsibility for the care and support of the younger siblings, take on an air of independence in Canada that challenges the normative roles and responsibilities within the home. One participant summarized the situation in this way:

> In our culture, the man is in charge of bringing money to the family, he has to go to work, and most of the wives stay at home doing household tasks. Things are changing a little, but not too much. For education, homework, many times the children do it alone or an older family member or neighbour will help. (Participant from Burundi)

I wonder whether both of these scenarios are not so unlike our own situation, with the difference being we have had at least a generation to adapt to these ways of being, whereas for the newcomer family, as with discipline, in the time it takes for them to fly to Canada, they have had to adjust to this new way of life.

What I wish to do is raise awareness about the need for cultures, nations, communities, families, and individuals to work out on their own how these concepts manifest in contextually relevant ways. Agreed, people are now living in Canada, where gender equity and children's rights are paramount. We must acknowledge, however, that newcomers arrive with deeply held values, beliefs, and practices that fit the socio-cultural–historical context from which they arise. What I am calling for is time and opportunity for intercultural dialogue and communication about contextually relevant healthy living in the 21st century. Perhaps in our encounters with newcomers, we may find values, beliefs, and practices to adopt that complement our own.

## Dealing with racism and discrimination

Racism and discrimination are hugely complex issues, with multiple facets of manifestation and multiple theories of understanding (Aboud, 1988; Bannerji, 2000; Dei & Lordan, 2013; Van Ausdale & Feagin, 2001); but unquestionably, when newcomers in Edmonton spoke to me of racism and discrimination, it was not so much in relation to themselves but rather to their children. That is not to say newcomer adults in Canada are not subjected to racism and discrimination, but rather that they feel as adults they are better equipped to deal with this issue than their children are. Parents expressed heartache and anger knowing the hurtful comments and actions their children are subjected to, not only from other children but also from adults, including teachers. One mother provides these experiences about her daughter:

> At school, the teacher does not give her attention or give her answers sometimes. When she asks questions she does not get answers, she does not get any attention. Now it is already recorded in her mind that there is discrimination. And one day my daughter and another child were playing and they both fell down. The teacher just pulled up the other child, and did not even see my daughter, and when she came home, she was crying. She said, "They did not even see me and just picked up the other child." (Participant from Eritrea)

It was the Somali community that shared experiences of receiving the most blatant forms of racially motivated hatred and discrimination. Here are some examples:

> My daughter was told by one of the children at school, your mom is ugly and she is always dressing up like Halloween.
>
> At school, the teachers are suspicious of our children. They think maybe their hair is not combed or not proper because they have it covered. They are suspicious. I do not like it.
>
> I do not want to say that word that they call people, nigger. I do not like to hear that. The other children call our children that. (Participants from Somalia)

Socio-cultural–historical learning theory attests that children immersed in a systemically racist world cannot help but absorb racist views (Van Ausdale & Feagin, 2001). If this is the case, then I feel it is of paramount importance that preschool and school classrooms provide an alternative to the dominant culture. Schools and early care and learning settings must be safe places where children can experience plurality and the value of diversity (Bernhard, 2012; Derman-Sparks & Ramsey, 2011; Friendly, 2010). I want to believe that such settings are able to provide children from multiple backgrounds places to unlearn or challenge racism, and that they have the potential to set the world on a new course. The places and spaces where children gather need first and foremost to be places for children to be who they really are and to think deeply about issues of justice and equity in our world. Although we have not progressed to the point of truly valuing diversity, as adults we should not stand in the way of the next generation taking themselves to the point of true plurality and interculturalism.

## Coping with mental health issues

Mental health issues such as depression, suicide, substance-use disorders, and post-traumatic stress disorder (PTSD) affect both newcomer parents and their children, thereby adding an extra burden to settlement in the new location (Crowley, 2009; Hansson, Tuck, Lurie, & McKenzie, 2012; Henley & Robinson, 2011; Paterson & Hmwe, 2012). One participant said this of her daughter:

> I feel so bad for her, because she saw everything. She saw how they treated us. She had a good start, and then all of a sudden her life is on the run. She does not like police at all. Even here, in Canada she is scared when she sees them, because, the police were chasing us everywhere. She saw us when we were scared of them and talking about them. (Participant from Eritrea)

Another participant said the following about emotional states:

> Right now, we do not know where exactly our family members are, we do not know whether they are alive or have been killed. At times when that comes back to mind, it brings sorrow and pain. (Participant from the Democratic Republic of Congo)

Depression is a real concern for refugees as well as for other newcomers who choose Canada for a better life and then find their circumstances not as promising as they had anticipated, or who feel tremendous grief and loss at leaving people and places they love behind in the home country. My own experience was one of having left Canada full of hope and anticipation of a great life and a great job. Then, in first moving to the US, I found the work situation was not what I had anticipated. Later, in moving to Aotearoa, I was met by destructive earthquake activity soon after my arrival. Needless to say, PTSD as a result of the earthquake experience and depression that resulted from the inevitable decision to leave the place that my son called "Perfect, except for the earthquakes" are experiences I would rather have done without. At the time of such difficulties it is easy to lose hope. Sillito (2009) suggests that in simply *hearing* what newcomers have to say and listening to the stories they have to share, we can bring them hope (p. 189).

In hindsight, of course, we learn that many times negative events bring us to new and better places. For me, the short-lived newcomer experiences in the US and Aotearoa paved the way to a life in *paradise* in Dar es Salaam. Living in a place one feels is paradise has its complications, however. I am very aware that my presence here is subject to my being able to retain the proper visa; more significantly, it is subject to the good will of the Tanzanian people. By that I mean, in being here, I have become starkly aware of how civil unrest can erupt due to the economic disparities and social injustices that exist and, should that happen, how quickly my welcome here in paradise would come to an end. Many of the newcomers to Canada are in similar situations: their leaving of their home country is tinged with a range of feelings and experiences, and their entry to Canada is fraught with complexities. As we welcome newcomers to our country, our classrooms, our communities, and our lives, we welcome people who often have very mixed feelings. This participant accentuates these mixed feelings:

> My son says if there is fighting or violence in Africa, "I do not want to go there," but I say, "No." I do not want him to grow up thinking our country is bad. I try to tell him that there is not only war in Sudan, that there can also be good things there. (Participant from South Sudan)

Another participant expresses her conflicting feelings like this:

> I wish to go back, but I do not know if my children can go. They want to, but I do not know if they would be able to stay there because their life is different, but for me it makes no difference because I know the life there from before and I know I can live there. (Participant from South Sudan)

## Maintaining home language and culture

To review the literature regarding the importance of retaining home language and culture, the benefits of bilingualism, and the significant impact of multiliteracies is beyond the scope of this chapter (see Castro, Ayankoya, & Kasprzak, 2011; Chumak-Horbatsch, 2013; Murphy, 2011; Tabors, 2008, for sources related specifically to early childhood). The focus here will rather be on the various perspectives brought to this issue by the research participants and my reflections on recent experiences that relate to this topic.

Many newcomer families acknowledge the importance of their children being connected to both their home culture and language and the dominant culture and language, as is reflected in the words of this participant:

> We are happy about our friends in our community. We are very connected in our Kurdish community, but we do not want to keep our children only with children in our community because it will keep them from learning the language. For us it is better for our children to be with other Canadian children to learn the language. They would benefit from this friendship. (Participant from Kurdistan)

Another participant explained the nature of her own children's bilingualism:

> My children, if they see a Somali person they speak Somali. If they see you, they speak English. They know; right away, they can find out which language you speak. They speak Somali, and they speak English. (Participant from Somalia)

At the same time, however, other families and cultural groups have not so successfully maintained their home language and culture with their children, as attested to by these comments:

> I want to teach my children Khmer, but it is very hard, they do not want to learn it, they want to learn English. At school, they are only speaking English.

> My children speak only English. If I speak to them in Khmer, they will speak to me in English.

> When my daughter first started school she did not speak much English, but now she wants to only speak English. I really want her to keep speaking Khmer otherwise I cannot talk with her. (Participants from Cambodia)

While the academic research may be in favour of home-language retention, and the desire of parents might be strong, the outcome is not always what is hoped for or expected. The pressure to equip oneself and one's children in the dominant language in hopes of aiding the integration process can feel very strong. I recall asking a group of adult newcomers what they thought would be the most helpful to them in the process of resettlement, and the resounding answer was "More English!"

Wherever one goes today in education circles, language, and what language(s) children should learn, is a focus of attention. In Canada, of course, we are officially bilingual within a multicultural context, and a great deal of time and money is given over to heritage languages. While the US has officially taken a different approach, in reality millions of Americans are Spanish/English bilingual. During my time in Aotearoa, the revitalization of *te reo Māori* (Māori language) was and still is a focus of much attention. Now here in Tanzania the issue of Kiswahili being the language of instruction in pre-primary and primary education, and English the language of instruction for secondary and post-secondary education, is much discussed.

In my position of privilege as an English speaker, I know I can travel to most places in the world and be understood. Possessing a language other than English would be a bonus to me, but it is indeed not essential. Certainly there are arguments being made that languages such as Mandarin Chinese, Spanish, and Hindi are soon to be, if not already, spoken by greater numbers of people than English (Lewis, Simons, & Fennig, 2013). The reality is, however, that English dominates the realms of commerce, technology, and entertainment, and for the majority of the world population that do speak languages other than English, becoming fluent in English is a necessity to enter the global economy (Crystal, 2003; Guilherme, 2007; Hyland, 2009; Northrup, 2013; Nunan, 2003).

I asked my class of 37 master's in education students from Tanzania, Kenya, and Uganda whether we should just give in and let English dominate, and their answer was a firm "No!" Often we talk together in class about how maintaining their home language and culture can be possible in the face of post-colonialism and the externally imposed policies that have come with the push to meet the second UN Millennium Development Goal of Universal Primary Education by 2015 and the additional push for quality Education for All (Millennium Development Goals, n.d.), policies that in practice see *quality* and English language as synonymous (Assie-Lumumba, 2012).

This discussion might seem far removed from the Canadian context, but it is not so when we are working with newcomers. The reality is that many newcomers arrive in Canada from these contexts, contexts that are deeply troubled by notions of maintaining their home language and culture even within their own countries. Multilingualism, multiliteracy, and interculturalism are notions worth advocating for. It might be that, in some cases, leaving one's home country and settling in pluralistic Canada brings hope for maintaining one's identity in the face of globalization while at the same time attaining English competence. If there is to be any hope of resisting Euro-American monoculturalism, then places where newcomers gather need to be places that support and encourage the use and growth of home languages and cultural values, beliefs, and practices—while at the same time ensuring there are opportunities to learn the dominant language (Dachyshyn & Kirova, 2011).

### Adapting to the Canadian education system

Without a doubt, the newcomers I spoke with expressed their number-one concern is that their children have a good life, and central to having a good life is education.

> I want a greater sense of learning for my young children, because I do not want my children to be like I am right now, I want a better life for them, better learning, better education, more support from school, when they go to school in the future; an open-minded school system. (Participant from Kurdistan)

As with all the settlement issues I have discussed, newcomers come to educational settings with varied backgrounds. Some, who have come as Convention refugees, may have huge gaps in their education progress due to prolonged stays in camps. Many other newcomers will come from school systems based on conforming and teacher-centred models of teaching and learning. I recall taking a group of newcomer parents to my son's arts-based school where, upon arrival, we found groups of students clustered together in the hallways working on projects. Having come from a very structured form of schooling, these parents were shocked and could not see how children were possibly learning by such methods. For many newcomers, entering the Canadian education system means an often-difficult adaptation process.

Beyond academics, another issue newcomer parents raised is a perceived lack of moral education within Canadian schools, with one participant stating, "The only thing children get from education here is knowledge but not good behaviour or respect" (Participant from Rwanda). Furthermore, some perceive that schools do not understand the realities of newcomer parents' lives:

> The children are given assignments and the parents are expected to help even if they are not educated. They do not know English and they are asked to help children with their homework. Then if children do not do well in school the parents are blamed which is not their fault. Some parents also even if they are educated they do not have time because some of them are working and they have to go to English classes in the evenings, so they do not have time. (Participant from South Sudan)

The issue becomes one of deciding to what extent early learning centres and schools need to adapt to newcomers and how much newcomers need to adapt to these new settings and systems. Being the mother of a 15-year-old who has attended a variety of schools over the past five years, and who, despite many different forms of schooling, still remains a reluctant school attender, I know there are no simple answers or quick fixes to the nature of education, whether that be for newcomers or Canadian-born children and families. These are huge systemic issues that need grappling with, and addressing educational reform is beyond the scope of this paper. What I do suggest, however, is that in our work with newcomers with preschool-age children, we pay very close attention. It is from the simple, everyday ways in which parents and children interact that we can learn what really matters to families.

It is short-sighted to think that within Canada our systems of care and education are the best ways. If as a multicultural nation we truly wish to honour and value the diversity that is in our midst, then we must be open to learning from the many ways of being in the world that come to us. It would be to everyone's benefit to see encounters with newcomers as opportunities for deep learning. If early care and education settings were considered as intercultural spaces where multi-centric approaches to being and learning are sought and valued, I believe this interaction would enhance the lives of newcomers and the Canadian-born alike.

## Looking ahead

Canada as a nation provides a bold experimental meeting ground for working out the realities of an increasingly globalized world. In particular, early care and learning settings and schools provide ideal locations and opportunities for Canadian-born citizens and newcomers to live out notions of pluralism, valuing diversity, anti-bias, justice and equity, multi-centric curriculum, and interculturalism. That our young people will grow up to view diversity as the new normal is a goal worth working toward.

In my work with newcomers in Aotearoa, a context quite similar to Canada, one participant in my research offered this:

> As newcomers we have all been through hard times, but what I really think is don't let our youngsters go through the same history we've been through. We need to teach them acceptance, and to respect different people. We want to let them know that because we are all different we are filling the gap of being whole. (Uyghur immigrant)

I believe that as newcomers and those who are Canadian born come together in early childhood care and education settings, a unique opportunity exists to set children and families on a journey of acceptance and respect that, when lived out, brings unity and wholeness.

### REFERENCES

Aboud, F. (1988). *Children and prejudice*. Oxford: Basil Blackwell.

Assie-Lumumba, N. (2012). Cultural foundations of the idea and practice of the teaching profession in Africa: Indigenous roots, colonial intrusion, and postcolonial reality. *Educational Philosophy and Theory, 44*(2), 21–36. http://dx.doi.org/10.1111/j.1469-5812.2011.00793.x

Bannerji, H. (2000). *The dark side of the nation: Essays on multiculturalism, nationalism and gender*. Toronto, ON: Canadian Scholars' Press.

Bernhard, J. (2012). *Stand together or fall apart: Professionals working with immigrant families*. Halifax, NS: Fernwood.

Best Start Resource Centre. (2010). *Growing up in a new land: Strategies for service providers working with newcomers.* Toronto, ON: Author.

Castro, D.C., Ayankoya, B., & Kasprzak, C. (2011). *The new voices—Nuevas voces: Guide to cultural and linguistic diversity in early childhood.* Baltimore, MD: Brookes.

Citizenship and Immigration Canada. (2011). *Facts and figures 2011: Immigration overview.* Ottawa, ON: Author.

Chumak-Horbatsch, R. (2013). *Linguistically appropriate practice: A guide for working with young immigrant children.* Toronto: University of Toronto Press.

Creswell, J.W. (2005). *Educational research: Planning, conducting, and evaluating quantitative and qualitative research.* Upper Saddle River, NJ: Prentice Hall.

Crowley, C. (2009, Jun). The mental health needs of refugee children: A review of literature and implications for nurse practitioners. *Journal of the American Academy of Nurse Practitioners, 21*(6), 322–331. http://dx.doi.org/10.1111/j.1745-7599.2009.00413.x Medline:19527311

Crystal, D. (2003). *English as a global language* (2nd ed.). Cambridge: Cambridge University Press. http://dx.doi.org/10.1017/CBO9780511486999

Dachyshyn, D.M. (2007). Refugee families with preschool children: Adjustment to life in Canada. In L. Adam & A. Kirova (Eds.), *Global Migration and Education: Schools, Children, and Families* (pp. 251–262). Mahwah, NJ: Lawrence Erlbaum.

Dachyshyn, D.M. (2008a). Refugee family resettlement: Implications for early care and learning programs. *Early Childhood Education, 38*(1), 4–9.

Dachyshyn, D.M. (2008b). *Refugee families with preschool children: Transition to life in Canada.* Saarbrucken, Germany: VDM Verlag.

Dachyshyn, D. M. (2012). Children dwelling in the absence of home. *Indo-Pacific Journal of Phenomenology, 12*(Special Edition), 1–10.

Dachyshyn, D.M., & Kirova, A. (2008). Understanding childhoods in-between: Sudanese refugee children's transition from home to preschool. *Research in Comparative and International Education, 3*(3), 281–294. http://dx.doi.org/10.2304/rcie.2008.3.3.281

Dachyshyn, D.M., & Kirova, A. (2011). Classroom challenges in developing an intercultural early learning program for refugee children. *Alberta Journal of Educational Research, 57*(2), 219–232.

Dei, G.J.S. & Lordan, M. (Eds.). (2013). *Contemporary issues in the sociology of race and ethnicity: A critical reader.* New York: Peter Lang.

Derman-Sparks, L., & Ramsey, P.G. (2011). *What if all the kids are white? Anti-bias multicultural education with young children and families* (2nd ed.). New York: Teachers College Press.

Friendly, M. (2010). *Can early childhood education and care help keep Canada's promise of respect for diversity?* Toronto: Childcare Resource and Research Unit.

Government of Canada (2011). *Country chapters: UNHCR resettlement handbook.* Retrieved from http://www.refworld.org/pdfid/4ecb9bfd2.pdf

Government of Canada (2013a). *Government of Canada.* Retrieved from http://www.canada.gc.ca/home.html

Government of Canada (2013b). *Canadian multiculturalism: An inclusive citizenship.* Retrieved from http://www.cic.gc.ca/english/multiculturalism/citizenship.asp

Guilherme, M. (2007). English as a global language and education for cosmopolitan citizenship. *Language and Intercultural Communication, 7*(1), 72–90. http://dx.doi.org/10.2167/laic184.0

Hansson, E.K., Tuck, A., Lurie, S., & McKenzie, K. (2012, Feb). Rates of mental illness and suicidality in immigrant, refugee, ethnocultural, and racialized groups in Canada: A review of the literature. *Canadian Journal of Psychiatry, 57*(2), 111–121. Medline:22340151

Henley, J., & Robinson, J. (2011). Mental health issues among refugee children and adolescents. *Clinical Psychologist, 15*(2), 51–62. http://dx.doi.org/10.1111/j.1742-9552.2011.00024.x

Hyland, K. (2009). *Academic discourse: English in a global context.* London, UK: Continuum International Publishing Group.

Institute for Economics and Peace. (2012). *Global peace index.* Sydney: Author.

Lewis, M.P., Simons, G.F., & Fennig, C.D. (Eds.) (2013). *Ethnologue: Languages of the world* (17th ed.). Dallas, Texas: SIL International. Retrieved from http://www.ethnologue.com

Millennium development goals. (n.d.). Retrieved from http://www.un.org/millenniumgoals/

Murphy, E. (2011). *Welcoming linguistic diversity in early childhood classrooms: Learning from international schools.* Clevedon, UK: Multilingualism Matters.

Northrup, D. (2013). *How English became the global language.* New York: Palgrave MacMillan. http://dx.doi.org/10.1057/9781137303073

Nunan, D. (2003). The impact of English as a global language on educational policies and practices in the Asia-Pacific region. *TESOL Quarterly, 37*(4), 589–613. http://dx.doi.org/10.2307/3588214

Paterson, B., & Hmwe, H.K. (2012). Age at immigration to Canada and the occurrence of mood, anxiety, and substance use disorders. *Canadian Journal of Psychiatry, 57*(4), 210–217.

Prochner, L., & Hwang, Y. (2008). "Cry and you cry alone": Timeout in early childhood settings. *Childhood, 15*(4), 517–534. http://dx.doi.org/10.1177/0907568208097205

Quinn, N. (2005). Universals of child rearing. *Anthropological Theory, 5*(4), 477–516. http://dx.doi.org/10.1177/1463499605059233

Rogoff, B. (2003). *The cultural nature of human development.* New York: Oxford University Press.

Sillito, J. (2009). Learning about hope through hope: Reflections on the ESL experience. In A.M.A. Mattos (Ed.), *Narratives on teaching and teacher education: An international perspective* (pp. 177–190). New York: Palgrave Macmillan.

Steinbock, A.J. (1995). *Home and beyond: Generative phenomenology after Husserl.* Evanston, IL: Northwestern UP.

Tabors, P.O. (2008). *One child, two languages: A guide for early childhood educators of children learning English as a second language* (2nd ed.). Baltimore, MD: Brookes Publishing.

United Nations High Commissioner for Refugees. (1996). *Convention and protocol relating to the status of refugees.* Geneva: Author.

United Nations High Commissioner for Refugees (2013a). *Emerging resettlement countries.* http://www.unhcr.org/pages/4a2ced836.html

United Nations High Commissioner for Refugees (2013b). *Figures at a glance.* Retrieved from http://www.unhcr.org/pages/49c3646c11.html

Van Ausdale, D., & Feagin, J.R. (2001). *The first R: How children learn race and racism.* Lanham, MD: Rowman & Littlefield.

Vygotsky, L.S. (1978). *Mind in society: The development of higher psychological processes.* Cambridge, MA: Harvard University Press.

Vygotsky, L.S. (1986). *Thought and language.* Cambridge, MA: The MIT Press.

Wayland, S.V. (2006). *Unsettled: Legal and policy barriers for newcomers to Canada.* Ottawa, ON: Community Foundations of Canada and the Law Commission of Canada.

# 10

# Refugee students in Canadian schools

## *Educational issues and challenges*

*Samuel Tecle and Carl E. James*

Starting with the story of one of the authors, Samuel Tecle, our chapter explores how his parents' struggles for a country played a critical role in his growing up, as articulated through his parents' messages of cultural and national identity, their expectation that he excel in school, and their insistence that he identify with "his community." Building on Sam's experiences as a child of Eritrean parents who grew up in an urban, racially diverse, low-income neighbourhood, we discuss the complexities, tensions, and challenges of students and teachers as they engage in the educational process—a process in which students like Sam are caught between their experiences of Canadian schooling, which forces a "Canadian" identity, and the expectations of their parents, which require them to remain true to "their" country of origin and by extension their "ethnic culture." How do these students negotiate and manage their identities as "Canadians" in a multicultural, multi-ethnic schooling context, given the messages they receive from parents, "their community," the school, and the larger society? How might equitable and inclusive education for such refugee students and their parents be constructed? We endeavour to show the importance of educators engaging and working with a complex and discursive understanding of race, ethnicity, and culture in all educational contexts.

For decades, nightly news reports have brought Western audiences images of Africans suffering from malnutrition, pleading for food aid,[1] walking along barren lands in search of food or fleeing violence, complaining about brutality by political foes, and asking for Western governments' help in bringing stability to their countries. The images, to which Western audiences have become accustomed, are not only a product of famine resulting from environmental, social, and political forces, but also a consequence of the colonial legacy to which the people of the region have been subjected. The news coverage on our television screens showing East African men and women trying to escape a life of economic destitution, political instability, military rule, and ethnic strife might at one level convey a sense of hopelessness in the situation and a seeming impenetrableness of the social, economic, and political structures that have sustained the difficulties that people of the region have been enduring for years. But on another level—historical, political, economic, and religious factors notwithstanding—the movement of East Africans could be said to represent the determination and resilience of a people who remain convinced and optimistic about a better life.

Famine, land claims, wars, and calls for political self-determination (i.e., independence) have contributed to the conditions from which many East Africans seek to escape. Eritrea's 30-year (1961–1991) fight for independence, Oromia's continuing liberation struggle, South Sudan's long battles for independence and now disputes over land and resources, and Somalia's (and Somaliland's) ongoing political unrest—just for examples—all have roots in their histories of colonization, territorial occupation, political ideology, and militarized rule. It is from these circumstances that many East Africans and others have fled, hoping to gain some measure of ordered life, security, and stability in a country that, by United Nations Convention, offers "refuge" from "well-founded fear of prosecution for reason of race, religion, nationality, membership in a particular social group or political opinion" (James, 2010, p. 170). Consistent with and as a signatory to this Convention, Canada is one of the countries that offers accommodation to people "who fear persecution or whose removal from Canada would subject them to danger of torture, a risk to their life or a risk of cruel and unusual treatment or punishment" (Citizenship and Immigration Canada, 2010).

As a result, Canada has, over the years, become one of few countries receiving refugees from all over the world, contributing to the large proportion of refugee adults and their children—many of whom are born in Canada after the relocation has taken place—who now reside in the country. In fact, according to Citizen and Immigration Canada (2012), "Canada will resettle up to 14,500 refugees and other vulnerable persons a year" with plans to increase that number by 20% each year. While reasons for becoming a refugee, as well as experiences of being a refugee, have been well documented (Al-Ali,

Black, & Koser, 2001; DeVoretz, Pivnenko, & Beiser, 2004; Goldring & Landolt, 2013), the experiences of the children of these refugees have been less studied. In many cases, the children of refugee parents have experienced their parents' struggles "back home" and now in their "new home" (for those born in Canada, their *only* home) must effectively negotiate and navigate the cultural, social, and educational structures (and institutions) as the family adjusts, settles or resettles, and attempts to integrate into the society. Concomitantly, these generation-and-a-half and second-generation Canadians are expected to live up to, or meet, their parents' expectations and aspirations to succeed in schooling and education to become contributing members not only to their new society but also to their local, ethnic community and to the country their parents left.

In this chapter, we explore how Canada's commitment to accommodating and responding to the needs of refugees, immigrants, and ethnic and racial minorities (as set out in its multiculturalism policy and programs) is operationalized in its schooling system.[2] How do the children of refugee parents negotiate school in light of competing expectations—i.e., work hard in school to attain academic success (such as attending university) and at the same time maintain the culture of the parents' homeland and commit to the social and political goals of the country the parents left behind? What are teachers to make of the children's "refugee" experiences? How are these children's experiences different from those of immigrant students? What considerations should educators give students based on their "refugee" experiences—particularly as learned through students' socialization and the stories they hear from their parents—since some of these students were born in Canada?

We come to these questions with the knowledge and understanding that many students entering schools in Western societies today bring very little or no actual experience of conflict or famine in the nations from which their parents fled. The parents, who fled countries in conflict, sought not only asylum, protection, and shelter for their children, but a place for their children to grow up to appreciate the countries and the circumstances from which they have come. In some cases considered "freedom fighters" (in their fight for their "homeland" stability and/or independence that did not exist when they fled), many of these parents come to their new countries with unfinished business in terms of struggles for self-determination, independence, and an imagined idea of their *home* countries—a reality that neither they as parents nor their children have actually experienced.[3]

In a schooling system that purports to be inclusive of, and responsive to, students' needs, interests, expectations, and aspirations, educators are encouraged to give attention to students' experiences as informed by their ethnic, racial, immigrant, and refugee backgrounds. Many of these first-generation, generation-and-a-half, and second-generation Canadian students must cope not only with the typical generational challenges and the so-called immigrant drive of their parents, but also their parents' expectation that they identify with their country of origin and as such come to join them in political struggles. But how can these students succeed in the Canadian schooling system without acquiescing to a Canadian-identity ethos of latent assimilation embedded in a multicultural discourse of colour blindness, racelessness, European reference, meritocracy, and equality of opportunity?

We initiate our discussion of schooling in relation to the experiences of the children of refugee parents by referencing Sam's story. Before doing so, we will briefly discuss the theories that shape our argument.

## Theoretical influences

Many studies have demonstrated the ways in which racism and colonialism have influenced and informed both historical and contemporary Canadian society (Alfred, 2009; Mackey, 2002; Thobani, 2007). The ongoing legacies of colonialism, capitalism, and racism have an impact on individuals' experiences—particularly those of refugees. Anti-colonial theory is used to understand the influence of colonialism and the indelible mark it has had on geopolitical conflict, and to acknowledge persistent struggles of the members of the former colonies, which have resulted in forced migration (Dei & Asgharzadeh, 2001). In other words, colonialism has had a role to play in territorial conflicts, ethnic disagreements, displacement of people, and—as a consequence—the creation of refugees. Colonialism also plays a role in the push and pull factors that make resettlement possible and necessary.

Push factors are the circumstances that make a current country or territory undesirable for its residents. Many of the common push factors include religious or ethnic persecution, political instability, armed conflict, persistent famine, and widespread poverty. In tandem with push factors are pull factors, which make resettlement in a particular country desirable or attractive (Coehlo, 1994). For those fleeing sites of conflict, Canada presents stability and a safe haven. Canada has several physical and social features that are attractive to people looking for a calm, stable, and safe place for themselves and their children—the pull factors. For many Canadians and people from elsewhere, Canada is believed to be a country rich in possibilities, accepting of people from elsewhere, and operating with a multicultural discourse of cultural freedom, equal opportunity, meritocracy, and democracy (Foster, 2005; see also Bannerji, 2000; Caldwell, Leroux, & Leung, 2013; Haque, 2012; Henry & Tator, 2009).

The immigrant drive is a concept that is useful to our understanding of the motivation, expectations, and ambitions of refugee parents and in turn their children (Anisef & Axelrod, 2000). High expectations and aspirations are part of the immigrant drive; so too is the sacrifice that immigrants and refugees are willing to make to realize their ambitions. Parents are known to resettle to new places, sacrificing their own well-being and giving up familiar surroundings, not merely for themselves but for their children in the hope that their children will do well and not suffer hardships as they did. Push and pull factors help to frame why people move and settle in new places with a willingness to work hard and adjust to the demands of the host society to attain their goals.

Our analysis is also informed by Critical Race Theory (CRT), which makes explicit the ways in which race, racism, and inequity structure individuals' lives. CRT speaks to how racial identities are imposed, essentialized, and homogenized (Aylward, 2002; Delgado & Stefancic, 2012). It makes central the social construction of race in terms of its impact on individuals' subjectivities with reference to interest convergence, intersectionality, and counter-narratives, all of which alert us to the complex social structures that inherently support and reinforce racial othering. CRT encourages the use of personal experiences or narratives to ground the issues under discussion (Zamudio et al., 2011) while exposing how hegemonic structures operate to racialize, marginalize, and re/colonialize individuals and groups (Brown, 2003; Delgado & Stefancic, 2012). As such, CRT is useful to this discussion as it helps us to analyze the historical and contemporary ways in which schools have accommodated, responded to, and represented immigrant, refugee, and Black students. Lacking the financial resources—and by extension the social and cultural capital—that often come with familiarity with the institutions and structures of a society, refugee and immigrant parents come to rely on the schooling system to provide for them, and more importantly for their children, with the supports, opportunities, and education necessary for their success—that is, for their children to attain upward social mobility in their new society. Put another way, the new members of the society believe that education will enable them to move from their "entrance status" (Porter, 1965) to the successful life they seek in Canada.

## Reflections on a classroom experience: Sam

Mari Matsuda (2010) writes that "At the end of all our theorizing, there is someone's body, so I start there" (p. 350). She goes on to proffer that our "understanding of those places where race meets power, where people are hurt, where people survive, where people thrive" (p. 350) is enhanced by grounding any analysis through personal reference. Therefore, consistent with Matsuda's assertion, the following reflection is presented to illustrate the complex histories that bear heavily on refugee parents and their children.

I was born in Khartoum, Sudan, in 1983 and at around five years of age came with my parents to Canada as a refugee. We settled for one year in Vancouver before moving to the Jane and Finch neighbourhood in Toronto. Although "officially" Ethiopian at birth and for a decade following, I have always self-identified as Eritrean—the result of familial socialization, particularly stemming from parents who were political activists, or "freedom fighters," as they were referred to in the long struggle for Eritrea's independence and self-determination. For most of my early schooling life, and to this day, Eritrea was not officially recognized as an independent state, and to me this is part of my parents' unfinished business. In fact, it was not until May 28, 1993, that Eritrea officially won its sovereignty.

As I was growing up in Toronto, my parents, like other Eritrean parents, were adamant about and quite active in preserving and re/creating a sense of Eritrean community and consciousness (see Arnone, 2008; Bernal, 2006). They endeavoured to foster among their children an understanding of the struggles "back home" and a meaningful attachment to the history and trajectory that they and others like them endured before they came to Toronto. Although the population of Eritreans was small (and likely because of that), concerted efforts were made to maintain a sense of collectivity and cohesion among community members (Hepner, 2003). In trying to maintain strong cultural ties to all things Eritrean, parents and community members would organize cultural events and celebrations rooted in Eritrean culture, tradition, and history. Sport leagues, homework clubs, and language tutoring all populated by Eritrean youth were some of the ways that parents worked to socialize us into Eritrean cultural specificities. But there was also parents' persuasive focus on high achievement as measured by excellent grades and acceptance to post-secondary institutions. Very early in our lives, Eritrean children learned that we were expected to do well academically in school. The high aspirations of our parents might seem contradictory when we consider that they often did not attend Meet the Teacher or curriculum nights or participate in parent councils. However, much of the parents' absence from these activities was not merely because of lack of familiarity with the educational system, language differences, and shyness, but because of their work schedules and the difficulties associated with resettlement. Nevertheless, Eritrean parents often communicated their expectations of us by reminding us of the sacrifices they had made and were making to be in this country for us.

In my interactions with my peers in the community and at school, I would be consistently hurt when people asked where I was from—mostly because they always asked twice. When I responded by saying Eritrea, they would ask again: "Where?" And I would respond with, "Right beside Ethiopia," and that answer would always make them feel better. No one ever really thought of what it did to me, always having to name the country twice, and having to validate it. I remember always being upset when someone would mispronounce the name of my country, would ask me to repeat the name of the country or ask for clarification, or could not pronounce my last name correctly. There were times when people assumed I was Somali, Ethiopian, Cuban, and even Dominican. I was also thought to be from Trinidad or the West Indies, and there were times when I let people continue to believe whatever they thought—it was easier than having to explain yet again. The explanations got tiresome. They got heavy, and sometimes I just did not want to deal with them.

I attended middle school in a suburb of Toronto where the majority of students in my classes were White, middle class, and came from families who had been in Canada for generations. For many of my classmates, the difficulties associated with resettlement, acculturation, and assimilation were foreign. This was the schooling context at the time when in my grade 7 class, my teacher Mrs. Winter (a pseudonym) gave us an "Origins Project" assignment, which required us to research our "home country" and afterwards make a presentation to our class. We had to make a poster with our native country's name and its flag. We were expected to interview our parents and go to the library to gather needed information. We were also encouraged to bring in cultural artifacts that symbolized the uniqueness and richness of our culture, and if possible we were to bring in pictures, clothes, and other cultural items that would help the class visualize the country.

For the majority of my classmates, completing this assignment as it was laid out was not a problem. But for me, such was not the case. This assignment presented me with great apprehension, mainly because of my family history, which made the assignment particularly difficult. I met the teacher privately and told her of my concerns and of the political situation of our "home country" that made it difficult for me to complete the assignment. Furthermore, I told her of the urgent nature by which we fled our "homeland" and that I would be unable to bring the required cultural artifacts for the presentation. Not knowing Mrs. Winter well enough, I was nervous about sharing my family history and background too openly. However, I did ask to be excused from the assignment or that it be changed to accommodate my unique situation. Despite my pleas for concession, Mrs. Winter did not budge: she did not modify the assignment to accommodate my concerns but instructed me to ask my parents and to get information from "here and there."

As the day of the presentation neared, I grew more fearful of having to present on a country that none of my classmates could find in an atlas or on a map. The maps at school at that time did not yet include Eritrea. In fact, since we were required to use primary sources and Eritrea was a relatively new country, there were few or no primary sources at hand, so I could not reasonably meet the requirements of the assignment. On the day of the presentation, I recall trembling and sweating mainly because I was not happy about this project; actually, I was downright upset and resented it on all levels. I recall at the time feeling anxious and upset, nervous, and fearful of my classmates' perceptions of me as a "poor refugee" student—especially knowing that I had asked the teacher to take into consideration my special situation but was not heard. As I reflect now, years later, the emotions return—or perhaps they have never left.

I did not do a good job on the project or the presentation. I did not do my best because I resented the entire process. The project haunts me to this day because I know that my responses then reflected my discomfort with being put on display. I felt that my ongoing struggle to figure out what it meant to be Eritrean in Toronto, in a middle school with mainly White students and teachers, was being made into a show. What resulted from my poor efforts and resentment of the project was a presentation that was uninspiring and lacked substance. To say "I am Eritrean" is easy now, but it was not before. The difficulties of growing up in a place that is far from what a child is told is "home"—a "home" the child has never seen or been to—are perplexing. Being one of few Black males in my middle school made things even harder. Yet I cannot help but think that, despite the difficulty, the weight and burden of my responsibility required me to have done a better job on the project.

## Issues, challenges, and opportunities

Sam's story tells of the key role that parents' experiences, expectations, and aspirations play in his and others' social and educational lives. Specifically, parents' political life "back home," their continuing commitment to their country of birth, and their belief in what would make for a productive life in Canada, especially for their children, influence the high expectations and aspirations that parents have for their children. These expectations and aspirations are passed on in messages about having a good work ethic and the need for children to bring home excellent grades. Such messages contribute to what Sam terms his "responsibility" to do well educationally, for he received the message that education holds the key for his social and economic mobility and hence his full inclusion in Canadian society.

Understandably, while immigrants (or economic migrants) and refugees (or political migrants) share similar migration experiences and aspirational ethos, there are notable differences, as Sam illustrates, related to the unfinished business of his refugee parents (they left before independence was won). In fact, as Sam indicates, the term *freedom fighters* was used to refer to the activities of his parents' and other Eritreans' struggle for a country that did not exist. Despite Sam's parents' relocation and settlement in Canada, they maintained their desire for an independent Eritrean nation. The desire never waned, for the parents continued to engage with the struggle "back home" while endeavouring to raise their families in Canada. The idea of "back home" for refugee parents is likely to be conceptualized differently from that of other immigrants, for many of them often entertain the idea of returning "home"—hence their desire (if not insistence) to have the young people of their group maintain the culture of and commitment to a country they can only imagine.

As a major socializing institution, schools—specifically the teachers and others within the educational system—can expect to encounter the children of immigrant and refugee parents as they navigate both their imaginary "homeland" and their place in the society of Canada, the country in which they were born and about which they have "real" knowledge. As students, they are exposed to a schooling system that—multiculturalism policies and programs notwithstanding—above all socializes them into what it means to be Canadian—something that may be contrary to the messages of their immigrant and refugee parents. In fact, the children of immigrant parents, exposed to the messages of their families and their schools, face several challenges: common generational differences, adjustment to the norms, values, and customs of the society, and living with xenophobia, racism, and discrimination (Gosine & James, 2010). Furthermore, in a study conducted with immigrant mothers of young people 16 to 20 years old, as well as key informants in educational and business sectors, researchers concluded that this group of youth faced challenges related to acculturation, identity development, language barriers, discrimination, and access to education (Yee, Johns, Tam, & Paul-Apputhurai, 2003).

This prioritizing of education is largely related to the fact that their immigrant parents have regularly communicated to these young people the importance of schooling as a site of possibilities (Gosine & James, 2010). And, despite the challenges, refugee parents live with the hope that educational achievement based on merit will serve their children well and that, on the basis of their educational attainment, their children will be able to succeed and avoid the hardships they themselves encountered in their lives in Canada. Therefore, it seems fitting that teachers should capitalize on the notion that education is highly valued among immigrant and racial minority students and parents, and to this end work with educational expectations that make learning satisfying and relevant to students' needs, interests, and aspirations. Indeed, schools should not treat these students as what Shields and Requa (2010) call "deficient widgets," treatment that results in "narrowing not only their individual opportunities for success, but inhibiting the creation of a healthy democratic citizenry as well" (p. 36). Rather, educators must think of these students as Canadians ready, willing, and eager to make their contribution to their society.

How then do teachers deal with the differences that students like Sam bring into the classroom without essentializing that which makes them unique and different? And how do they construct curricula, lesson plans, pedagogical approaches, and assignments that take into account these differences? Certainly, the way in which Mrs. Winter dealt with Sam's request for an amendment to the "Origins Project" assignment was not helpful for Sam. Mrs. Winter's unwillingness to alter the assignment can be understood, in one way, as her attempt to be equitable—that is, to treat all students equally so that they have the same opportunity to achieve their grades. Surely, while the students might have had an equal opportunity—in that they were doing the same assignment—the assignment was not truly equitable since students like Sam do not have access to the resources and materials to represent or talk about their origins. The same treatment is not equal treatment. The logic of sameness negates, in this case, the realities of the refugee experience with which the student has had to live. It is therefore important for teachers to take into account the backgrounds and experiences of students, considering that today's classrooms are increasingly diverse, even if that diversity may not be obvious. Sam's experiences with the assignment can work to assist teachers in understanding the struggles that students may deal with as they confront the disparate, contradictory, and conflicting expectations and messages they receive from their parents, teachers, and society in general.

Tara Yosso's (2005) contribution to the education of racialized students is useful here. She offers that teachers should not think that racialized students' disengagement from school, poor academic performance, and educational outcomes are a result of their lack of cultural knowledge and skills, or cultural capital. Rather, students come to school well supported by what she refers to as "community cultural wealth" from family and the community, which provides an "array of cultural knowledge, skills, abilities, and contact ... that often go unrecognized and unacknowledged" (p. 69). According to Yosso, family and community provide racialized young people with the capital needed to nurture and support their aspirational, social, and navigation skills and abilities to negotiate successfully the structural issues they encounter in the society. This resource may help them to live in hope that they can achieve all that is expected of them. Rather than seeing difference as a deficit or liability, teachers should come to view differences as opportunities to welcome what the differences bring to the class. Immigrant students can open up new learning—especially about global or geopolitical issues—to be shared not only with their peers but also with teachers. Hence, a rich teaching and learning situation can use students' stories on their terms as opportunities to explore and to reorient the classroom into an open and inviting place for students from all backgrounds.

## Conclusion

Sam's experience is representative of many students' experiences in Western societies where the students who are considered different constantly find themselves in classrooms that do not open up curricular, pedagogical, and experimental opportunities for their learning. Many such students are caught in a conundrum where it is difficult to succeed in Canadian schooling environments. While all students must contend with the complexities, tensions, and challenges related to generational differences, parental expectations, and school culture and programs, for minority students—in particular refugee students—confronting these issues is particularly difficult. Therefore, these students need the understanding, support, and sensitivity of their teachers. Indeed, as the terrain of global geopolitics continues to shift, narratives like Sam's are likely to become more common rather than the exception. We need to think of the experiences of refugee students in diverse and complex ways. Further, teaching from a perspective of equity requires that teachers be at all times inclusive of the experiences, ideas, and contributions of *all* students in their classrooms and schools. Such inclusiveness means having class materials, curriculum, pedagogy, and references that represent and speak to the diversity, differences, and variations that exist among people locally, nationally, and internationally. It calls for helping students to imagine, as well as be knowledgeable about and conversant with, an interrelated world of people, ways of knowing, and socio-political forces and structures.

## NOTES

1. Mark Bowden, UN Humanitarian Coordinator of Somalia, pleading with those able to contribute some relief, said, "Every day of delay in assistance is literally a matter of life or death for children and their families in the famine-affected areas" (see United Nations Office for the Coordination of Humanitarian Affairs, 2011).
2. It is estimated that Canada "resettles 10,000 to 12,000 refugees through its government-assisted and privately sponsored refugee programs" (Public Safety Canada, 2011).
3. We refer here to migrants who have been involved in political activities in the countries they left before witnessing or realizing the hopes for changes in political, economical, and social conditions for which they advocated, agitated, or fought. A change in government or, as in the case of Eritrea and South Sudan, national sovereignty, is often the expectation.

## REFERENCES

Al-Ali, N., Black, R., & Koser, K. (2001). Refugees and transnationalism: The experience of Bosnians and Eritreans in Europe. *Journal of Ethnic and Migration Studies, 27*(4), 615–634.

Alfred, T. (2009). Colonialism and state dependency. *Journal of Aboriginal Health, 5,* 42–60. Retrieved from http://www.naho.ca/jah/english/jah05_02/V5_I2_Colonialism_02.pdf

Anisef, P., & Axelrod, P. (2000). *Opportunity and uncertainty: Life course experiences of the class of '73.* Toronto: University of Toronto Press.

Arnone, A. (2008). Journeys to exile: The constitution of Eritrean identity through narratives and experiences. *Journal of Ethnic and Migration Studies, 34*(2), 325–340. http://dx.doi.org/10.1080/13691830701823814

Aylward, C.A. (2002). *Critical race theory and praxis.* Toronto: Faculty of Law, University of Toronto.

Bannerji, H. (2000). *The dark side of the nation: Essays on multiculturalism, nationalism and gender.* Toronto: Canadian Scholars' Press.

Bernal, V. (2006). Diaspora, cyberspace and political imagination: The Eritrean diaspora online. *Global Networks, 6*(2), 161–179. http://dx.doi.org/10.1111/j.1471-0374.2006.00139.x

Brown, D.A. (2003). *Critical race theory: Cases, materials, and problems*. St. Paul, MN: Thomson/West.

Caldwell, L., Leroux, D., & Leung, C. (2013). *Critical inquiries: A reader in the study of Canada*. Halifax: Fernwood.

Canada Immigration International. (2010). *Canada Immigration International: Refugee claims in Canada*. Retrieved from http://www.immig.ca/refugees.html

Citizen and Immigration Canada. (2012). Refugees. *Citizen and Immigration Canada*. Retrieved April 15, 2012, from http://www.cic.gc.ca/english/refugees/

Coehlo, E. (1994). Social integration of immigrant and refugee children. In F. Genesee (Ed.), *Educating second language children: The whole child, the whole curriculum, the whole community* (pp. 301–328). New York: Cambridge University Press.

Dei, G.J.S., & Asgharzadeh, A. (2001). The power of social theory: The anti-colonial discursive framework. *Journal of Educational Thought, 35*(3), 297–323.

Delgado, R., & Stefancic, J. (2012). *Critical race theory: An introduction*. New York: New York University Press.

DeVoretz, D., Pivnenko, S., & Beiser, M. (2004). *The economic experiences of refugees in Canada*. Burnaby, BC: Vancouver Centre for Excellence.

Foster, C. (2005). *Where race does not matter: The new spirit of modernity*. Toronto: Penguin Canada.

Goldring, L., & Landolt, P. (2013). *Producing and negotiating non-citizenship: Precarious legal status in Canada*. Toronto: University of Toronto Press.

Gosine, K., & James, C.E. (2010). Racialized students resisting: Hindrance or asset to academic success? In B.J. Porfilio & P.R. Carr (Eds.), *Youth culture, education and resistance: Subverting the commercial ordering of life* (pp. 41–56). Rotterdam: Sense.

Haque, E. (2012). *Multiculturalism within a bilingual framework: Language, race, and belonging in Canada*. Toronto: University of Toronto Press.

Henry, F., & Tator, C. (2009). *The colour of democracy: Racism in Canadian society*. Toronto: Nelson Education.

Hepner, T.R. (2003). Religion, nationalism, and transnational civil society in the Eritrean diaspora. *Identities: Global Studies in Culture and Power, 10*(3), 269–293.

James, C.E. (2010). *Seeing ourselves: Exploring race, ethnicity and culture*. Toronto: Thompson Educational Publishing.

Mackey, E. (2002). *The house of difference: Cultural politics and national identity in Canada*. Toronto: University of Toronto Press.

Matsuda, M. (2010). Poem for Armenian Genocide Day and rules for postcolonials. *Journal of Asian American Studies, 13*(3), 359–369. http://dx.doi.org/10.1353/jaas.2010.0003

Porter, J.A. (1965). *The vertical mosaic: An analysis of social class and power in Canada*. Toronto: University of Toronto Press.

Public Safety Canada. (2011). Canada's generous program for refugee resettlement is undermined by human smugglers who abuse Canada's immigration system. Ottawa: Government of Canada. http://www.publicsafety.gc.ca/cnt/nws/nws-rlss/2010/20101021-6-eng.aspx

Shields, C., & Requa, D. (2010). Minoritized youth, cultural capital, and the (micro) policy context of schooling. In B.J. Porfolio & P.R. Carr (Eds.), *Youth Culture, Education and Resistance* (pp. 21–41). Rotterdam: Sense.

Thobani, S. (2007). *Exalted subjects: Studies in the making of race and nation in Canada*. Toronto: University of Toronto Press.

United Nations Office for the Coordination of Humanitarian Affairs (2011). Somalia: United Nations declares famine in two regions. *United Nations Office for the Coordination of Humanitarian Affairs*. Retrieved March 12, 2013 from http://www.unocha.org/top-stories/all-stories/somalia-united-nations-declares-famine-two-regions

Yee, J., Johns, C., Tam, S., & Paul-Apputhurai, N. (2003). Apprenticeship opportunities and barriers for immigrant youth in the Greater Toronto Area. (Policy Paper). No. 1. Toronto: Joint Centre of Excellence for Research on Immigration and Settlement.

Yosso, T.J. (2005). Whose culture has capital? A Critical Race Theory discussion of community cultural wealth. *Race, Ethnicity and Education, 8*(1), 69–91. http://dx.doi.org/10.1080/1361332052000341006

Zamudio, M., Russell, C., Rios, F.A., & Bridgeman, J.L. (2011). *Critical race theory matters: Education and ideology.* New York: Routledge.

# 11

# The value of language in refugee youths' construction of identity

*Neda Asadi*

## Defining identity

Identity is not static or one dimensional; rather, it begins in infancy, is a lifelong process with multiple and changing dimensions, and is considered a focal point of adolescence and adulthood (Pasupaathi, 2011). The current use of the term *identity* has two categories with linked meanings. The first is a sense of personal identity:

> An identity is some distinguishing characteristic (or characteristics) that a person takes a special pride in or views as socially consequential but more-or-less unchangeable; the second meaning of identity refers to a social category, a set of persons marked by a label and distinguished by rules deciding membership and (alleged) characteristic features or attributes. (Fearon, 1999, p. 4)

Therefore, understanding identity is a complicated process of understanding ourselves through our roles and obligations, our commitment to faith and ideology, and the views of others. The complicated process expands across time and space because it is grounded in the past and shapes and reshapes through time. As a result, identity development is an important factor in shaping our lives. Proper identity development requires cornerstones such as relationships with others, access to basic human resources, and security (Pasupaathi, 2011).

For refugee youth, identity development can become a much-contested matter because an important component of identity is the ability to define group memberships—the religious, national, and ethnic groups to which one belongs. For refugee youth, the link to their place of residence has been abruptly disturbed; in many instances, they have lost family members, their sense of security has been violated, and their identity has been existentially threatened (Dei & Rummens, 2010). Their identity development is further complicated by their developmental stages: not only have refugees not fully developed their identities, but forced migration has also necessitated that they become members of new collectives while still negotiating their personal identities (Pasupaathi, 2011).

Whereas individuals build their personal identity through their associations with various groups, their stances, and their actions, social identity is also "mediated by the interlocutors' understandings of how acts and stances are resources for structuring particular social identities" (Ochs, 1993, p. 289). Therefore, an individual's identity reflects what the larger society, through its understanding of that individual's position, perceives it to be. Refugee youth have to be able to receive and comprehend the projected identity from their host country, even though they might not be able to relate to the projected identity and its obligations. One such instance is belonging to a group of refugees. For refugees to be granted security and asylum, they need to identify themselves as refugees. This labelling of a collective has many negative connotations from both the larger society's and the individual's perspective (Kumsa, 2006). According to Bauman (as cited in Kumsa, 2006), for mainstream society, "refugees signal a loss of nation—they have lost theirs and here they come to threaten ours! Refugees are seen as enemies of the nation and as threatening strangers because they evoke such deep ontological uncertainty and existential insecurity" (p. 240). Paradoxically, we expect our newcomer youth to develop a positive sense of self by entering institutions such as educational facilities, which they have the right to access because of their categorization as refugees. This projection of identity is done without any consideration for how refugee youth identify themselves or the consequences of their interpretation of the projected identity of refugee. According to Kumsa, students' narratives of refugee based on the reactions of the larger society reveal feelings of being stupid, ignorant, poor, uncivilized, and misfits. Therefore, it is no surprise that students actively try to dissociate from their identification as refugees: "'No, I am not a Refugee!' Jalane cried out" (Kusma, 2006, p. 230). "I hate it with passion! ... We had a country, you know!" (Kusma, 2006, p. 244); "I never thought I'm gonna skip, quit school and stuff, but the way [the principal] was to me, he was never like that to other people, you know" (Dei & Rummens, 2010, p. 3).

Personal and social identities are essential components of youths' perceptions of themselves, of educators' and school peers' perceptions of refugees, and of how youths engage with schooling and produce knowledge (Dei & Rummens, 2010). Positive development of self is an essential factor in refugee youths' success that enables them to cultivate the psychosocial resilience to deal well with adversities and stressful situations and to shape their lives (Rutter, 1999). Consequently, youths' personal and social identities become critically important in their learning process. Refugee youths' positive self-development gives them resilience and self-esteem, key factors in their success in school; further, their personal and social identities give them lenses through which to view and respond to their surroundings. Youth respond to the curriculum, the hidden curriculum, and the null curriculum in ways connected to their particular societal contexts and social spaces: "Not recognizing this fact is to push into the margins the lived realities and life prospects of those who are not like us" (Dei & Rummens, 2010, p. 4). The existing literature has clearly demonstrated differential educational outcomes among Canadian-born and foreign-born children and youth. Research on the issues in minority-youth education has revealed that students themselves point to connections among identity, representations, schooling, and knowledge production and that the need to feel connected to school and its pedagogical practices is critical to their educational success (Dei & Rummens, 2010; Kanu, 2007).

Marginalized students' identities are not understood, their circumstances are not considered, and their voices are not heard. The Canadian educational system marginalizes some groups of students in a variety of ways: "Marginalization is a process, not a label—a process of social devaluation that serves to justify disproportional access to scarce societal resources" (Dei & Rummens, 2010, p. 2). Policymakers, educators, and peers include or exclude certain groups of students based on their identification. One way in which schooling marginalizes students is by creating a common understanding of identity, including groups who have successfully adapted or negotiated the hegemonized identity while excluding others. Therefore, schooling supports and creates the power structure through the construction of "we"—those with desired identities—and "they"—those who are different. According to Waters and LeBlanc (2005; as cited in Mosselson, 2011), "refugees are, by definition, people who are 'imagined' to be ... nonmembers" (p. 129). The curriculum used in Canadian schools has Eurocentric roots, and that curriculum in turn promotes certain common sets of values and culture (Johnston, 2008). One in five Canadian children under the age of 15 is a new immigrant or refugee; however, despite the continued immigration from nontraditional areas such as the Caribbean, Asia, and Africa since the 1960s, the curriculum still reflects the common image of Canada as documented in recent analyses of homogenizing nationalist discourses in the K–12 social studies curriculum in Alberta (Richardson, 2002). Therefore, it is not difficult to identify the reason for the two to three times higher ratio of dropouts among English-language learner students than among other students (Roessingh & Field, 2000).

The need for refugee youth to articulate a space to define and develop their identity is overshadowed by many competing demands as well as by the larger society's failure to recognize the need to allow youth in resettlement to create their new and reimagined identity based on their existing values. Because identity development and acceptance facilitate minority youths' positive development, it is essential that educational institutions foster representation and identification based on race, culture, language, religion, class, and gender to allow students to become engaged with curriculum based on their daily existence rather than devaluing their social identities or cultural collective knowledge. Programming that reflects social histories, identities, and experiences helps students to relate to their environment, feel welcome, and belong. An important factor in the development of social meaning is language. As Bourdieu (as cited in Norton & Toohey, 2004) noted, value ascribed to speech cannot be considered apart from the person who speaks, and the person who speaks cannot be considered apart from his or her social network. Every time we use language, we negotiate our sense of self against the larger society, across time and space.

## Language

According to Edward Sapir (1921), language "is a purely human and noninstinctive method of communicating ideas, emotions and desires by means of a system of voluntarily produced symbols" (para. 7). Structural linguist Ferdinand de Saussure (1966; as cited in Norton & Toohey, 2004) suggested that the meaning of language is found within the whole structure of language, because individuals are shaped by sociological, psychological, and linguistic structures over which they have no control. Poststructuralist philosophers such as Foucault (1970; as cited in Norton & Toohey, 2004) have agreed that language is shaped by governed systems; however, Foucault placed more emphasis on an individual's sense of agency and contribution to the formation of meaning (Norton & Toohey, 2004).

Therefore, from the poststructuralist point of view, language is not an object but a form of behaviour that needs to be understood contextually: "The realization of the pragmatics of language signals a shift from language to discourse" (Norton & Toohey, 2002, p. 118). Bakhtin (1984; as cited in Norton & Toohey, 2002) emphasized the social aspect of language because he believed that others participate in the discourse of language through the act of "appropriation" (p. 117) to assign purpose or ideas to their language. According to Bakhtin, "Words are not neutral" (p. 117) but have a specific predisposition and a value system that depends on the historical, current, and future positioning of the speaker and his/her interlocutors (Norton & Toohey, 2002).

Social constructivists believe in the centrality of language in the construction of identity through two major modes: language as grammar and language as discursive action. The grammatical mode allows individual speakers to insert themselves or others into the discourse of language, whereas in discursive action the speaker and the interlocutors can negotiate their positions (Budwig, n.d.). Psychologists have also used language as a mechanism to construct self. Developmental psychologists such as Brooks-Gunn (1979; as cited in Budwig, n.d.) used verbal labels and other language-dependent measures to conceptualize self-recognition and self-understanding (Budwig, n.d.). Further, psychologists such as Mead (1934), Whorf (1956), and Lock (1980; all as cited in Budwig, n.d.) contended that language is used in self-development as significant symbols and typological variations. Mead believed that self is developed not simply through interactions but through communication of "significant symbols" (p. 8): "[self] arises in the process of social experience and activity, that is, develops in the given individual as a result of his relations to that process as a whole and to other individuals within that process" (p. 8). The development of self through language as a typological variation refers to the speaker's use of grammatical stances to influence his or her sense of self. Finally, psychologists such as Mead (1934), Lock (1980), Schieffelin and Ochs (1986), and Miller, Potts, Fung, Hoogstra, and Mintz (1990), who focused on language socialization, suggest that language develops self through action; that is, children see themselves in relation to the way others see them and the world. Language allows individuals to locate themselves in the larger society to acquire, disseminate, and interpret knowledge (Budwig, n.d.).

Social identity affects the amount and nature of exposure to an additional language. For refugee youth learners, the challenges that they face in developing their identity in a new country, given society's marginalization reflected upon them, will concurrently have a negative effect on their English-language development. Identity is multiple and complex and can change depending on the context; the more strongly language learners can identify themselves with the mainstream population, the better their learning acquisition will be (Zelasko, 2000). The inability or difficulty of refugee youth to access an additional language in terms of both the syntax and the social meaning of the language or culture can further cause feelings of self-devaluation because the failure to communicate hinders the formation of relationships with peers and educators and is a major barrier to the educational endeavours of newcomers. Their lack of familiarity with the dominant culture can also lead to miscommunication between newcomers and the pre-existing residents of the country. For example, the parents of refugee youth might be unaware of school expectations with regard to parental involvement and parental outreach programming. The varying levels of language mastery of family members can also play a role in creating cultural dissonance for youth and intergenerational conflict within the family (Kanu, 2007; Rossiter & Rossiter, 2009). In addition, language barriers hinder newcomers' ability to navigate the host country to access resources or obtain good employment, which will in turn lead to low-paying employment and low family income. To compensate for low family income, many refugee youth might need part-time or, in some cases, full-time employment while they attend school (Van Ngo, 2009).

## Bilingual programs

Goethe, a German philosopher, once said, "the person who knows only one language does not truly know that language" (Verad, 2010, p. 1). Language used in schools features a highly specific form of English that includes ways of behaving—"how to be a student"—which comes with many years of prior knowledge and understanding of cultural expectations. Language acquisition is a complex process; in optimum circumstances it takes three to five years to develop oral-language proficiency and four to seven years to gain academic-English proficiency (Brodie-Tyrrell & Prescott, 2010; Cummins, 2001). In circumstances in which students have faced interrupted schooling and are in disadvantaged socio-economic circumstances, it takes up to 10 years to acquire academic proficiency (Brodie-Tyrrell & Prescott, 2010). Students must overcome huge challenges to succeed in educational institutions. As La Bianco (as cited in Brown, Miller, & Mitchell, 2006) states, "we cannot leave English as a Second Language students' right to participate fully in their education to osmotic processes and blind faith" (p. 3). By allowing children to bring their native languages to school, educational institutions create an environment in which English-language learners feel welcomed and their identities are valued. The feeling of belonging creates an atmosphere in which all students believe they can equally contribute and participate in activities, understand, and build knowledge. Research has shown that children who continue to learn in their native language develop superior linguistic skills and acquire the second language much faster because of their ability to transfer their prior knowledge of literacy skills to their second language (Cummins, 2001). By gaining a deeper understanding of their native language and how to use it effectively, students gain the ability to process language. They are able to compare and contrast the ways in which their two languages are arranged and used. Fluency in their native languages and mastery of a new language help newcomer youth to acquire knowledge, form relations, and participate in mainstream society; therefore, language is a key in locating their identity and unlocking their voice, and linguistic ability is a key in helping newcomer youth move from the periphery to the centre.

More than 150 research studies conducted during the past 35 years strongly concluded that the thinking of bilingual children can also be more flexible as a result of their ability to process information in two different languages (Cummins, 2001). From the point of view of children's development of concepts and thinking skills, the two languages are interdependent. Children's knowledge and skills transfer across languages from their native language to the mainstream language; and the concepts, knowledge, and language skills they learn in the mainstream language transfer to their native language (Cummins, 2001). Collier and Thomas (2004) reported that the introduction of bilingual programs for English-language learners enhanced the outcomes and even closed the achievement gap. In dual-language models, teachers use two languages to teach mainstream curricula and create a stimulating environment in which students are engaged in solving real problems without needing to interpret from one language to another. This environment helps students to progress academically more than one year every year, a positive step in closing the gap between refugee youth and other English as a Second Language learners and native English-speaking students. According to Collier and Thomas (2004), bilingual teaching achieves the best outcomes in a two-way learning environment where at least 30% of the students are native English-speaking students who learn with their bilingual peers in an integrated setting. This integrated setting also decreases the negative perceptions and segregation between various ethnic and mainstream populations.

Enriching languages also benefits the host country economically because multilingual human resources represent an immense capital.

With the increased demand for effective cross-cultural contact in the pursuit of economic competitiveness, language proficiency is an important asset for any country: "In the era of globalization, a multilingual and multicultural populace can be a precious resource for the host country as it will enable the country to more effectively compete socially and economically in the global stage" (Cummins, 2001, p. 2).

## Arguments against bilingual education

There are several prominent arguments against bilingual education, one of which is the observation that many people have succeeded without it. However, the proponents of this opinion do not consider the circumstances and the human and social capital in support of those who have succeeded (Krashen, 1997). Another argument policy-makers often use against bilingual education is that the public is opposed to it; however, McQuillan and Tse (as cited in Krashen, 1997) suggested that this impression results from the way the question is asked. They reviewed academic publications as well as articles in newspapers and magazines between 1984 and 1994 and reported that 87% of academic publications supported bilingual education; only 45% of newspaper and magazine opinion articles did so, however. McQuillan and Tse concluded that public opinion and support can differ greatly if bilingual education is more clearly defined in mainstream articles and editorials.

According to Cummins (2001) the harshest criticism against bilingual education comes from researchers who claim that it results in poor-quality learning; policy-makers tend to interpret this to mean that the "experts" disagree on the role of bilingual education. This interpretation maintains the existing social power relations and allows policy-makers to pay only lip service to the importance of pedagogical programs. Cummins (1999) analyzed and responded to the arguments against bilingualism of prominent scholars Porter (1990) and Rossell and Baker (1996) and acknowledged that their arguments have been influential in maintaining antipathy toward bilingualism. However, in an in-depth analysis, Cummins argued that these scholars directly or indirectly support intensive bilingual programs.

## Language policies

Language policies in Canada have been used to inspire unity and to control minority language groups in various ways, from deculturalization to acculturation into Western hegemonic ways. The power of language is evident in the naming of official languages. Ignoring Indigenous languages as official languages in Canada exemplifies that communities and their values can be made invisible through the power of language. The naming of official languages "not only sends powerful messages about the relative value and status of language but limits the languages deemed acceptable for instruction" (Gourd, 2007, p. 121). In ignoring Indigenous Canadian languages, Canadian immigration and language policies have been advantageous to language groups that have similar power and values.

## Educational policies and language

Educational policies generally reflect the state's values and stances on issues, and the expansion of education is usually associated with the expansion of social rights. Cummins (2001) explains that "to educate the whole child in a culturally and linguistically diverse context, it is necessary to nurture intellect and identity equally in ways that, of necessity, challenge coercive relations of power" (p. 6). Therefore, discussions on the design of educational policies should put language theory and research at the forefront. However, researchers on additional language acquisition are rarely consulted during the political discussion of policy design. The power holders' lack of attention to research combined with the needs of students creates inequalities among learners. According to Gourd (2007), to "nurture the intellect" (p. 125), policy-makers need to go beyond meeting the needs of the job market and consider the three components of language learners' education. The first component that has been long recognized is knowledge of the dominant language to be able to participate in the socio-economic society. The second component is newcomers' learning of content knowledge while mastering the English language to keep up with their peers and maintain a sense of self-worth. The knowledge that children gain through their first language helps to make the English they hear and read more comprehensible. The third component is the development of students' social consciousness. On recognition of the importance of language, policy-makers and educators need to develop curriculum and instruction that consider students' needs given their available cultural and linguistic resources. Recognition of the importance of language and the implementation of proper programming will not only enhance cognitive development and the development of a sense of self, but also respect and affirm children's and communities' identities. This outcome in turn can assist in creating acceptance of diversity and the rejection of negative attitudes such as racism and marginalization (Cummins, 2001).

## Refugee youth and educational policies

The United Nations High Commissioner for Human Rights (HCHR) dedicated World Refugee Day 2003 to refugee youth three years after it recognized June 20 as World Refugee Day. In putting the spotlight on refugee youth, the HCHR (as cited in ForcedMigration.org, 2011) explained:

> It is the special plight of these innocents that UNHCHR wishes to spotlight, by dedicating World Refugee Day 2003 to Refugee Youth, and thereby open the eyes of a worldwide audience to their needs. We also wish to accentuate the positive by celebrating their many strengths, their huge potential, and their capacity to help themselves and their communities. Our aim is to provide refugee youth with a heightened sense of value and self-worth. (para. 2)

Although the Office of the High Commissioner for Human Rights (2007) has recognized the plight of refugee youth, created awareness, and addressed the needs of refugee youth to help them to reach their full potential, this statement and many similar statements hinder the success of refugee youth. To ensure the proper development and growth of refugee youth, we must acknowledge them as complete human beings with full rights rather than as extensions of their parents or guardians with special challenges and needs.

Once refugee youth are viewed within their own category and developmental stages, and considering what the discourses on globalization and power relations, among many other factors, have taken away from them, society as a whole, rather than refugee youth, becomes problematic, because these youth, through no action of their own, have been robbed of all their rights, face the difficulty of having to leave behind all that they know, and have to adapt to a new culture. And more, they are expected not only to face the challenges but also to thrive. It is important to take into account that refugee youth are attempting to maintain their academic standing while negotiating competing identities to be accepted as part of the mainstream culture at the same time that they are striving to meet their immediate needs (e.g., their financial struggles) and achieve family reunification in an environment in which their knowledge and existence are devalued. The challenge to ensure the success of refugee youth needs to become society's challenge. The challenge for policy-makers is to change their discourse on policy analysis based on the discursive frameworks of trauma or humanitarian rhetoric, which leads only to poor support services. Instead, policy-makers must address the needs of refugee youth by developing policies based on the discourses of human rights and the politics of belonging (Pinson & Arnot, 2007). Psychological discourses that inform educational policies with regard to the issue of refugee youths' shortcomings in education further contribute to their marginalization. These psychological discourses are grounded in European epistemologies that strive to control differences and encourage participation in the social and cultural reproduction of a hegemonic society (O'Loughlin, 2002). In addition, psychological models universalize and normalize the refugee experience without taking into consideration the heterogeneity of the refugee population—their diverse ethnic and religious backgrounds (Mosselson, 2011). The challenge for educators and policy-makers is to shape the evolution of national identity in such a way that the rights of all citizens (including school children) are respected and the cultural, linguistic, and economic resources of the nation are maximized. The ability to maintain and thrive in one's native language in the midst of foreignness is a key element in the success of refugee youth in the educational setting. Enhancing education through linguistics and encouraging children to develop their identity and sense of agency both serves the national self-interest and respects the rights of children.

## REFERENCES

Brodie-Tyrrell, J., & Prescott, K. (2010). *Assessment for learning: An ESL perspective*. Retrieved from http://www.decd.sa.gov.au/literacy/files/links/Assessment_for_Learning_An.pdf

Brown, J., Miller, J., & Mitchell, J. (2006). Interrupted schooling and the acquisition of literacy: Experiences of Sudanese refugees in Victorian schools. *Australian Journal of Language and Literacy, 29*(2), 150–162. Retrieved from http://www.sora.akm.net.au/downloads/Interrupted_Schooling.pdf

Budwig, N. (n.d.). *Language and the construction of self: Developmental reflections*. Retrieved from http://www.massey.ac.nz/~alock/nancy/nancy2.htm

Centre for Studies on Inclusive Education. (2010). Supporting inclusion, challenging exclusion: The UN Convention on the Rights of the Child. Retrieved November 19, 2010, from http://www.csie.org.uk/inclusion/child-rights.shtml

Collier, V.P., & Thomas, P.W. (2004). The astounding effectiveness of dual language education for all. *NABE Journal of Research and Practice, 2*(1), 1–20.

Cummins, J. (1999). The ethics of doublethink: Language rights and bilingual education debate. *TESOL Journal, 8*(3), 13–17.

Cummins, J. (2001). *Bilingual children's mother tongue: Why is it important for education?* Retrieved from http://www.fiplv.org/Issues/CumminsENG.pdf

Dei, G., & Rummens, J.A. (2010). Including the excluded: De-marginalizing immigrant/refugee and racialized students. *Education Canada, 51*(5), 48–53. Retrieved from http://www.cea-ace.ca/education-canada/article/including-excluded-de-marginalizing-immigrantrefugee-and-racialized-student

Fearon, D.J. (1999). *What is identity (as we now use the word)?* Retrieved from http://www.stanford.edu/~jfearon/papers/iden1v2.pdf

ForcedMigration.org (2011). *Youth*. Retrieved from http://www.forcedmigration.org/research-resources/thematic/refugee-youth

Gourd, K.M. (2007). A critical examination of language policies and practices in Canada and the United States. In K. Joshee & L. Johnson (Eds.), *Multicultural education policies in Canada and the United States* (pp. 120–131). Vancouver, BC: UBC Press.

Johnston, I. (2008). Decolonizing Canadian literary education. In A.A. Abdi & G. Richardson (Eds.), *Decolonizing democratic education: Trans-disciplinary dialogues* (pp. 13–25). Rotterdam: Sense.

Kanu, Y. (2007). Educational pathways to successful social integration for African refugee students in Manitoba. *Our Diverse Cities, 2,* 114–119. Retrieved from http://canada.metropolis.net/publications/odc09_pdfs/YattaKanu_ODC09.pdf

Krashen, S. (1997). Why bilingual education? *ERIC Digest* [Online]. Retrieved from http://www.ericdigests.org/1997-3/bilingual.html

Kumsa, K.M. (2006). "No! I'm not a refugee!" The poetics of be-longing among young Oromos in Toronto. *Journal of Refugee Studies, 19*(2), 230–255. http://dx.doi.org/10.1093/jrs/fel001

Lock, A. (1980). *The guided reinvention of language.* London, UK: Academic Press.

Mead, G. (1934). *Mind, self, and society.* Chicago: Chicago University Press.

Miller, P., Potts, R., Fung, H., Hoogstra, L., & Mintz, J. (1990). Narrative practices and the social construction of self in childhood. *American Ethnologist, 17*(2), 292–311. http://dx.doi.org/10.1525/ae.1990.17.2.02a00060

Mosselson, J. (2011). Conflict, education, and identity: Resettled youth in the United States. *Conflict & Education, 1*(1). Retrieved from http://conflictandeducation.org/wp-content/uploads/2011/04/1-1-Mosselson.pdf

Norton, B., & Toohey, K. (2002). Identity and language learning. In R. Kaplan (Ed.) *Handbook of applied linguistics* (pp. 115–123). Oxford: Oxford University Press.

Norton, B., & Toohey, K. (Eds). (2004). *Critical pedagogies and language learning.* New York: Cambridge University Press.

O'Loughlin, M. (2002). Is a socially responsible and critical psychology of difference possible? *Race, Gender & Class, 9,* 175–192.

Ochs, E. (1993). Constructing social identity: A language socialization perspective. *Research on Language and Social Interaction, 26*(3), 287–306. http://dx.doi.org/10.1207/s15327973rlsi2603_3

Office of the High Commissioner for Human Rights (2007). *Convention on the rights of the child.* Retrieved from http://www.ohchr.org/en/professionalinterest/pages/crc.aspx

Pasupaathi, M. (2011, Oct 24). *Collective identity and everyday discrimination among Bosnian refugee youth.* Paper presented at the Conference on Migration, Rights, and Identities [Video file]. Retrieved from www.youtube.com/watch?v=c6FNo3Vz4Hw

Pinson, H., & Arnot, M. (2007). Sociology of education and the wasteland of refugee education research. *British Journal of Sociology of Education, 28*(3), 399–407. http://dx.doi.org/10.1080/01425690701253612

Porter, R.P. (1990). *Forked tongue: The politics of bilingual education.* New York: Basic Books.

Richardson, G.H. (2002). *A border within: The Western Canada protocol for social studies education and the politics of national identity construction.* Retrieved from http://scholar.googleusercontent.com/scholar?q=cache:Q7sRfReQDrwJ:scholar.google.com/&hl=en&as_sdt=0,5

Roessingh, K., & Field, E. (2000). Time, timing, and timetabling: Critical elements of successful graduation of high school ESL learners. *TESL Canada Journal, 18,* 17–31.

Rossell, C.H., & Baker, K. (1996). The effectiveness of bilingual education. *Research in the Teaching of English, 30,* 7–74.

Rossiter, J.M., & Rossiter, R.K. (2009). Diamonds in the rough: Bridging gaps in supports for at-risk immigrant and refugee youth. *Journal of International*

*Migration and Integration, 10*(4), 409–429. http://dx.doi.org/10.1007/s12134-009-0110-3

Rutter, M. (1999). Resilience concepts and findings: Implications for family therapy. *Journal of Family Therapy, 21*(2), 119–144. http://dx.doi.org/10.1111/1467-6427.00108

Sapir, E. (1921). *Language: An introduction to the study of speech. I. Introductory: Language defined.* Retrieved from http://www.bartleby.com/186/1.html

Schieffelin, B. & Ochs, E. (Eds.). (1986). *Language socialization across cultures.* Cambridge, UK: Cambridge University Press.

Van Ngo, H. (2009). Patchwork, sidelining, and marginalization: Services for immigrant youth. *Journal of Immigrant & Refugee Studies, 7*(1), 82–100. http://dx.doi.org/10.1080/15562940802687280

Verad, M. (2010). *Growing up bilingual.* Retrieved from http://www.brainskills.co.uk/GrowingUpBilingual.html

Whorf, B.L. (1956). *Language, thought, and reality.* Cambridge, MA: MIT Press.

Zelasko, F.N. (2000). *Bilingual education: Need for bilingual education, benefits of bilingualism, and theoretical foundations of bilingual education.* Retrieved from http://education.stateuniversity.com/pages/1788/Bilingual-Education.html

# 12

## The Accelerated Basic Literacy Education (ABLE) program in the Waterloo Region District School Board

*Kimberly Hird-Bingeman, Michael McCabe, and Courtney Anne Brewer*

Immigration is on the rise in Canada. With this increase in people entering the country comes an increase in the number of students entering schools across Canada and, for the purposes of this chapter, Ontario. This chapter will define the various immigrant designations and examine the increase in the immigrant population across Waterloo Region in Ontario, Canada. It will also identify the adaptations that the Waterloo Region District School Board has made and will continue to need to make to accommodate the increased number of immigrant children entering our schools. We pay particular attention to the Accelerated Basic Literacy Education (ABLE) program within the Waterloo Region District School Board and the way this program relates to current policies mandated by Ontario's Ministry of Education. With many immigrants arriving in Ontario, English may not be an accessible language, and in many cases students may have limited exposure to this language of instruction. This recognition lends support to the need for programs such as ABLE to be implemented in school boards across Ontario.

In the Ontario Ministry of Education (2007) document *English Language Learners: ESL and ELD Programs and Services,* section 2.3.2 explains that expectations are placed on each school board in Ontario in relation to the teaching of children who are new to the school system: "If initial assessment indicates that the English language learner has had limited prior schooling, the board will provide additional support to the student" (p. 18). Policy section 2.5.1 states that "School boards will implement programs and services that will enable English language learners to continue their education while learning English" (p. 22). The document goes on to make the following recommendations:

> English Literacy Development (ELD) programs ... are for a student whose first language is other than English or is a variety of English significantly different from that used for instruction in Ontario schools. Students in these programs are most often from countries in which their access to education has been limited, and they have had limited opportunities to develop language and literacy skills in any language. Schooling in their countries of origin has been inconsistent, disrupted, or even completely unavailable throughout the years that these children would otherwise have been in school. As a result, they arrive in Ontario schools with significant gaps in their education. (p. 22)

## Immigration in Canada

When people arrive in Canada they are given one of two designations to identify their status in the country. These designations are *immigrant* and *refugee*. If entering in the latter category, individuals are given the subdesignation of *sponsored refugee* or *refugee claimant*.

### Immigrants

People who are designated *immigrants* are those who choose to come to Canada for a variety of reasons including employment or education. They apply through Canadian government programs designed to attract immigrants (Citizenship and Immigration Canada, 2010).

### Refugees

People who are designated *refugees* are those who are forced to leave their home country to seek safety in another country. Their home country is not able or not willing to protect their human rights, and therefore refugees must ask for help from another country. Refugees do not want to leave their home, but they must to protect their lives (Citizenship and Immigration Canada, 2010). There are two types of refugees: sponsored and claimants.

#### Sponsored refugees

Government-assisted refugees (GARs) are those refugees selected by the Canadian government to be resettled in Canada. These refugees will receive a year of support from the government upon arrival. This support includes housing, basic amenities, education, social development, health care needs, and support in family relations. The second category of sponsored refugees is privately sponsored refugees (PSRs). These refugees are sponsored by private groups, which include faith communities, ethnic associations, unions, and other groups that decide to help refugee families resettle in Canada (Citizenship and Immigration Canada, 2010).

**Refugee claimants**
This designation includes people who have left their own country, reached another country, and entered an application for asylum—in other words, those who have applied for refugee status (Citizenship and Immigration Canada, 2010).

## Immigration in the Waterloo Region
Waterloo Region has the fifth-highest proportion of foreign-born population in Canada behind Toronto, Vancouver, Hamilton, and Windsor (Region of Waterloo Public Health, 2009). Waterloo Region has a higher proportion of refugees than the Canadian average. In 2002, 11% of Canadian immigrants were accepted as refugees, whereas 18.3% of immigrants destined for Waterloo Region were refugees. In 2008, 2,700 immigrants settled in the Kitchener-Waterloo area (Region of Waterloo Public Health, 2009).

As of 2010, Waterloo Region had approximately 5,000 ESL/ELD students in elementary schools in the region (Newmaster, 2010). With the growing number of students with diverse needs, one of the local school boards developed an inclusive delivery model for second-language learners. This model includes English as a Second Language (ESL) teachers assigned to schools with high English-language learner (ELL) populations. An extension of this model includes specialized classes called Accelerated Basic Literacy Education (ABLE), which address the needs of a specific group of ELD students in our system.

## The Accelerated Basic Literacy Education (ABLE) program
ABLE was modelled after the Literacy Enrichment Academic Program (LEAP) in the Toronto District School Board (TDSB). As of 2010, TDSB has 40 half-day programs offered in elementary and middle-school settings for students between 11 and 16 years old and in 13 secondary schools for children up to 18 (Toronto District School Board, n.d.).

ABLE in the Waterloo Region District School Board began in 2004 with one class of 12 students housed in a portable at a local school. These students (10 males and 2 females) were mostly Sudanese refugees ranging from 11 to 13 years old (Newmaster, 2010). The local school has a population where 60% of the students are considered to be ELL. The need for additional classes across the region was great, and a Junior ABLE class was started at the local school in 2006, followed one year later by an additional Junior ABLE class at a different school and then a Senior ABLE class in yet another school. Currently, there are four full-day programs supporting the needs of 48 students in the Waterloo Region District School Board.

ABLE is a three-year program with a fourth-year option for integration in all subjects within the regular classroom. Each class is staffed with one full-time ESL teacher and one educational assistant for up to 12 students. In the Waterloo Region District School Board, ABLE is for students aged 9 to 13 who have recently arrived in Ontario schools with limited prior schooling. Students enter the program through a referral process at any point between grades 4 and 8. ABLE is intended to help identified ESL/ELD students who have been in Canada for one to three years to make significant gains in English-language development, literacy, numeracy, and academic skills and knowledge so they can successfully integrate into regular classroom programs (Waterloo Region District School Board, 2008–2009). Some of these students have not had prior opportunity to attend school before arriving in Canada; as a result, they are significantly behind their peers in literacy and numeracy. ABLE is accelerated so that students can potentially acquire knowledge and skills equivalent to two grade levels in one academic year.

Many of the students entering ABLE come from countries affected by war. Many have lived in refugee camps or have had limited opportunity to attend school in their country of origin, usually due to war, trauma, or poverty, but also for other reasons (The Community Social Planning Council of Toronto, 2005). Students who are appropriate for this program demonstrate a potential and motivation for learning. These students will have acquired basic oral English and a beginning reading level before entering the ABLE program. ABLE is not a remedial program for students who have experienced some learning difficulty in the past or in their first language. The students who apply should also not have any special-education needs identified in either this country or their home country (Waterloo Region District School Board, 2008–2009).

### ABLE program goals

Using the Ontario curriculum as a guide, ABLE students will, in one academic year, make significant gains in second-language development (all four strands for ELD Stage 1–2 in grades 4 to 8), literacy skills (alphabet, vocabulary, comprehension), numeracy skills (all five strands in mathematics), academic skills (research, writing process, computer skills, critical thinking), and knowledge (Canadian social studies/history and geography, science, language awareness, media works) (Waterloo Region District School Board, 2008–2009, p. 5). ABLE assists students to achieve these goals by providing intensive instruction in ESL and ELD, with an emphasis on the English-language skills needed for social and academic purposes; intensive support for accelerated literacy development and academic upgrading in core subjects to enable students to achieve their academic potential; support for students as they adjust socially and emotionally to their school environment; support during a one-year integration process into regular programs; and assistance with preparation for future goals such as secondary school placement and program/course selection (Waterloo Region District School Board, 2008–2009, p. 5).

## Roles and responsibilities

The success of the program depends on the coordinated efforts of staff within the home and ABLE schools as well as on people from outside of the schools. Students can be referred to the ABLE program at any time, but students usually start this congregated class placement at the beginning of the school year. A congregated class in Waterloo Region is a class located at a public school in a central location where students are transported from various home school locations.

The ABLE teacher must have ESL Part 1, although a Specialist in ESL is preferred. The ABLE teacher provides "intensive upgrading programs with an emphasis on literacy and numeracy" (Waterloo Region District School Board, 2008–2009, p 10). The teacher will provide individual and group instruction using appropriate instructional approaches and strategies for ELD students. The ABLE teacher will also collaborate with the regular classroom teachers, providing recommendations for the subject where integration into the regular classroom is possible.

Staffing for the ABLE class is reviewed every year, and programs may be closed and new ones opened in other locations of the region if demographic trends indicate a need for a location change. The program is supported centrally through an ESL/ELD consultant who provides staff development programs and works with other consultants in various subject areas to provide staff development and ongoing support.

Also connected to the ABLE program is a settlement worker assigned to the family of the enrolled student. Citizenship and Immigration Canada, settlement agencies, and school boards originally established a school-based outreach program called Settlement Workers in Schools (SWIS). There are SWIS programs in six communities in Ontario. The settlement worker is an additional support offered to the ABLE classes in Waterloo Region (Waterloo Region District School Board, 2008–2009, p 12).

The Settlement and Education Partnership in Waterloo Region (SEPWR) is also directly linked to the Newcomer Reception

Centre, the first place new immigrant families visit or are referred to when they arrive in the region. SWIS is a partnership of settlement agencies, the Waterloo Region District School Board, the YMCA, and Citizenship and Immigration Canada. SWIS connects with newly arrived families to align them with services and resources in the school and the community to promote settlement and foster student achievement. Learning about the education system is part of the settlement process, so the SWIS worker will explain essential school information such as school registration and refer the family to the appropriate school staff as necessary. The settlement worker assigned to the family by the Reception Centre aims to understand the needs of the family and stays connected with the family for up to five years. Workers can also take on new families who arrive at their school placement and who may not have gone through the Reception Centre process.

For those students who fit the criteria for the ABLE program, the settlement worker serves as a liaison between parent(s)/guardians, the ABLE teacher, and the ESL/ELD consultant once an application to ABLE is completed by the student's home school. The settlement worker can provide any necessary background or current information to support the needs of the student entering the program (SettlementAtWork.org, 2010).

## Curriculum focus

ABLE focuses on curriculum areas including language, mathematics, social studies, and sometimes science and technology. ABLE integrates language and literacy instruction with content from social studies (grades 1 to 8), history and geography (grades 7/8) and mathematics (grades 1 to 8) and may include science (grades 1 to 8). The language and literacy program for junior and intermediate students is based on modified curriculum expectations as outlined in *The Ontario Curriculum: Grades 1–8, English as a Second Language and English Literacy Development—A Resource Guide* (Ontario Ministry of Education, 2001). An essential component of the curriculum design is to begin at each student's starting point in language and literacy development, no matter how far behind the expected grade level this may be (Waterloo Region District School Board, 2008–2009).

The science and technology component of ABLE is based on the Orientation Strand for English Literacy Development in *The Ontario Curriculum, Grades 1–8: English as a Second Language and English Literacy Development—A Resource Guide*. Students start at their individual instructional level and work toward appropriate expectations from

*The Ontario Curriculum, Grades 1–8: Science and Technology* (Waterloo Region District School Board, 2008–2009).

For the remainder of the school day, students are integrated into programs where they can participate with some success and have some opportunities to interact with their peers. Subjects where this may occur include visual arts, music, health, and physical education. French may be included only if students have received French instruction or come from French-speaking countries (Waterloo Region District School Board, 2008–2009).

**Program evaluation**

Regular assessment procedures conducted by teachers in the ABLE program provide information on student progress. This information is important in evaluating the effectiveness of the program as well as individual student achievement. New placements are reviewed after six weeks to ensure that the placement is appropriate, and each student's placement is reviewed annually. ABLE teachers gather the following assessment information for each student during the academic year: the current ESL or ELD Tracking Report, clearly indicating the student's present level of development in oral language, reading, and writing; writing samples in three different genres (e.g., narrative, journal entry, lab report); math assessment information documenting growth in all strands (including work samples); reading comprehension scores on the Running Records or CASI (Comprehension Attitude Strategies Interests—a standardized reading assessment used by the local school board); a copy of the most recent report card; and other relevant information about achievement such as work habits, commitment to learning, and behaviour (Waterloo Region District School Board, 2008–2009, p. 16).

Students in the ABLE class are considered ready to return to the regular/mainstream classroom when they are performing at or near grade-appropriate levels in mathematics and literacy. They may continue to receive ESL/ELD support, if required, for up to one year before returning to their home school. Once they return to their home school or move to secondary school, students may continue to require program adaptation in some mainstream classrooms and subjects; this requirement is monitored annually for up to five years.

Before a student is returned to his/her home school or transitions to secondary school, an ABLE Program Exit Form is used to document a student's departure from the ABLE program. A copy of this form is sent to the ESL/ELD consultant, and a copy is placed in the Ontario Student Record (OSR) for future reference (Waterloo Region District School Board, 2008–2009).

One important aspect for success in the program is that the students remain connected to their own experiences to make the necessary connection with the world around them. This connection comes from Dewey's (1907) understanding that an experience has to be built on or connected to prior experience and becomes a pivotal aspect of future success in the integration of refugee students in the culture of mainstream schools in Ontario. Exposure to Canadian culture through experiential learning helps ABLE students not only identify the important aspects of the structure of the school environment but also, through the curriculum, develop a greater understanding of Canadian culture. Dewey (1907) also says, "All that society has accomplished for itself is put, through the agency of the school, at the disposal of its future members" (p. 19). If we believe that public schools can be mini-societies of a larger social structure, then the Ontario curriculum is the roadmap from which students can practise the skills necessary for the establishment of Dewey's democratic society. ABLE is one example of a program that attempts to assist students in gaining a better understanding of Canadian society while at the same time enhancing the chance for students' successes in school.

Looking forward, ABLE in the Waterloo Region District School Board is still developing and changing as its partners gain a better understanding of the unique needs of each child in the program. It must meet the academic, social, and emotional needs of this group and also address cultural issues that arise.

As ABLE develops, we gain a better understanding of not only the important aspects of the Ontario curriculum and how it can enrich the lives of these students, but also how these students can bring enriched experiences to the Ontario curriculum due to their diverse backgrounds. We must therefore provide opportunities for these students to receive programming based on their individual needs, "built on or connected to prior experience" (Noddings, 2007, p. 31), to gain a better understanding of the Ontario curriculum. These students must also be given opportunities to share their stories, not only with their small group of peers but with the larger student body in each school and with the school community. These students must become part of the fabric that makes up the schools they attend.

---

**REFERENCES**

Citizenship and Immigration Canada. (2010). *Immigrant designation.* Retrieved from http://www.cic.gc.ca/english/index.asp

The Community Social Planning Council of Toronto. (2005). *Renewing Toronto's ESL Programs: Charting a course toward more effective ESL program delivery.*

Dewey, J. (1907). *The school and society: Being three lectures by John Dewey supplemented by a statement of the University Elementary School.* Chicago: University of Chicago Press.

Newmaster S. (November 1, 2010). Personal email to Kim Hird-Bingeman.

Noddings, N. (2007). *Philosophy of education* (2nd ed.). Boulder, CO: Westview Press.

Ontario Ministry of Education. (2001). *English as a Second Language and English Literacy Development—A resource guide.* Retrieved from http://www.edu.gov.on.ca/eng/document/curricul/esl18.pdf

Ontario Ministry of Education. (2007). *English language learners: ESL and ELD programs and services.* Toronto: Queen's Printer for Ontario.

Region of Waterloo Public Health. (2009). *Immigrants in Waterloo Region* [fact sheet #1]. Retrieved from http://chd.region.waterloo.on.ca/en/researchResourcesPublications/resources/Immigrants_Status.pdf

SettlementAtWork.org. (2010). *Settlement workers in schools (SWIS).* Retrieved from http://wiki.settlementatwork.org/wiki/Settlement_Workers_in_Schools_(SWIS)

Toronto District School Board. (n.d.). *English as a Second Language/English Literacy Development.* Retrieved from http://www.tdsb.on.ca/HighSchool/YourSchoolDay/EnglishasaSecondLanguage.aspx

Waterloo Region District School Board. (2008–2009). *ABLE Program Guide* [Brochure]. Kitchener, ON: Waterloo Region District School Board.

# 13

# Building community capacity to support Karen refugee youth in schools

*Lisa Sadler and Nancy Clark*

> Nothing is holier, nothing is more exemplary than a beautiful, strong tree. When a tree is cut down and reveals its naked death-wound to the sun, one can read its whole history in the luminous, inscribed disk of its trunk: in the rings of its years, its scars, all the struggle, all the suffering, all the sickness, all the happiness and prosperity stand truly written, the narrow years and the luxurious years, the attacks withstood, the storms endured. And every young farmboy knows that the hardest and noblest wood has the narrowest rings, that high on the mountains and in continuing danger the most indestructible, the strongest, the ideal trees grow.
> — *Hermann Hesse, Bäume: Betrachtungen und Gedichte*

> A tree stands strong not by its fruits or branches, but by the depth of its roots.
> — *Anthony Liccione*

It has been suggested that a refugee is similar to a tree that has been cut off from its roots and transplanted into foreign soil (J. Bastin, personal communication, April 30, 2009). Without their roots, refugees do not have the capacity to be successful in their new lives. Rebuilding this root system takes time, patience, and a broad community support system.

Trees are made up of intricate, complex systems. Every leaf and every branch is connected to the tree trunk, but the health of the tree can be attributed to what is unseen: the large, complex root system below the ground that sustains the tree with water and nutrition. If the tree is cut off from its roots, it will quickly wither and die. Likewise, a tree that has been transplanted without special care does not thrive in its new environment. While the tree is not dead, it needs time, patience, and special care to graft a new root system to give life again and sustenance to allow the tree to thrive.

Generally, immigrants are able to tend to every root carefully, gently removing it from the soil, preparing for months, even years, to say goodbye to family, friends, and all of the pieces of their home that have been so firmly established. This period of mental and emotional adjustment and closure is critical, and while there are many challenges for immigrant families on arrival in Canada, the pre-migration experience plays a significant role in the adjustment of many newcomers.

On the other hand, the journeys of refugees usually begin with persecution causing them to flee their homes and homeland; unlike immigrants, they have been uprooted without a choice. As a result, refugees around the globe have endured some of the greatest resettlement challenges. Many refugees are persecuted due to their race/ethnicity, political affiliation, religion, or gender. In some cases forced migration has also been the result of war, genocide, and natural disaster (United Nations High Commissioner for Refugees [UNHCR], n.d.). Because of these experiences, many refugees have not had time to prepare for migration and to say goodbye to friends and family; they face ongoing uncertainty about their future. In the process of fleeing, many have been separated from loved ones or have witnessed and experienced horrible atrocities (Citizenship and Immigration Canada, 2008, 2012; Grove & Zwi, 2006). Their life stories often include trauma, torture, rape, lost loved ones, prolonged time spent in refugee camps, ongoing violence and insecurity, poverty, and malnutrition (Beiser, 2005, 2009; Keyes, 2000). This trauma can result in ongoing psychological challenges such as complex trauma and post-traumatic stress disorder (PTSD) when they arrive in Canada (Beiser, 2005, 2009; Keyes, 2000; Kinzie, 2006, 2008; Kirmayer, Lemelsen, & Barad, 2008). Furthermore, refugee trauma is related not only to pre-migration stress but also to ongoing experiences of discrimination, structural violence, lack of social support, and stress during the resettlement process (Agic, 2012; Beiser, 2005; Newbold, 2009; Porter & Haslam 2005).[1] This trauma is further compounded by challenges related to access to employment, language skills, education, and health (Dow, 2010; Morris, Popper, Rodwell, Brodine, & Brouwer, 2009; Porter & Haslam, 2005). These challenges make it difficult for refugees to rebuild healthy root systems in Canada.

In relation to the social and structural challenges of resettlement, refugee youth are considered to be one of the most vulnerable populations in Canada (Beiser, Hou, Hyman, & Tousignant, 2002; Doughty & Klingle, 2008; Kanu, 2008; Shakya et al., 2010). Globally, approximately, 44% of refugees and 31% of asylum seekers are children under the age of 18 (UNHCR, 2010). In Canada, refugee youth represent approximately 48% of all refugees accepted into Canada on humanitarian grounds (Citizenship and Immigration Canada, 2008). In addition to discrimination, social exclusion, poverty, intergenerational conflict, and resettlement stress, access to education is a challenge for refugee youth (Kanu, 2008; Kirk & Cassity, 2007; Shakya et al., 2010; Thomas & Collier, 1997). Education can play a pivotal role in the lives of refugee youth at a time when larger social structures such as racism and intergenerational conflict, as well as personal identity formation, affect youths' mental health and well-being (Hyman, Beiser, & Vu, 1996). Yet literature on refugee youths' access to education is limited. We argue, as do Shakya et al. (2010), that there is a pressing need for understanding and supporting refugee youth in accessing education that is culturally sensitive and trauma informed.[2] Culturally sensitive, trauma-informed practice will address the unique challenges and barriers that refugee youth face within the education system and will ultimately increase youth engagement and success. On the other hand, a lack of trauma-informed practice might lead to negative school experiences and ultimately affect youth mental health and well-being during resettlement. With this understanding in mind, our efforts to build community capacity to engage youth in the education system ought to address the complex root system that is required for enhancing the success and resilience of refugee youth.

Our community's unique circumstances necessitated the need for multiple partnerships to build community capacity to support refugee youth in schools. While Canada receives approximately 220,000 to 240,000 immigrants annually (Citizenship and Immigration Canada, 2008), the community of Langley, British Columbia, has remained fairly homogeneous: its citizens are predominantly white and middle class. However, during the period 2007 to 2009, more than 800 Karen refugees were resettled in British Columbia, landing mostly in Langley and neighbouring Surrey (ISS of BC, 2010). This large influx of refugees arrived from remote camps on the border between Burma (Myanmar) and Thailand with very high needs, including complex medical, educational, and social challenges. At the time of their arrival, refugee support services were non-existent in Langley, and the local school system was not prepared to receive such a large number of youth with various educational needs.

This lack of preparedness highlights the challenge to offer culturally relevant educational services for refugee youth faced in many smaller communities that do not normally receive high numbers of immigrants or refugees. Nevertheless, this challenge also presents a unique opportunity to develop collaborative partnerships that can strengthen the community and allow refugee youth to flourish. In this chapter we provide a narrative of experiences in Langley, located in the Metro-Vancouver region of British Columbia, Canada, where community capacity was built to support Karen refugee youth in schools.[3] This holistic community-development approach offers a helpful framework for educators and other social service providers to draw on as they support refugee youth in their education and resettlement as they rebuild their lives and root systems in communities across Canada.

## A community-development approach: Challenges and strategies for building capacity

Community development is a school of thought that seeks positive community engagement through empowerment, collaboration, and capacity-building and can be accomplished through tools and methods that build on the strengths or assets of a particular community or population (Brown & Hannis, 2008; Kretzmann & McKnight, 1993). While definitions of community development vary widely, for our purposes it is a process of building capacity within and between individuals and communities. In this context, a community-development approach is not a solution but rather a collaborative method that weaves a holistic support network around refugee children, youth, and families to develop new root systems and to mend broken ones. The process aims to strengthen and support existing assets and to empower individuals to effect change in their own lives and communities. Rather than a top-down approach, where goals and processes for change are imposed from above, there is growing support among scholars and activists for a bottom-up, grassroots approach to development, where the community determines its appropriate goals, objectives, and strategies (Brown & Hannis, 2008). Here we discuss our community's capacity-building process that has integrated service development and collaboration to address the unique challenges and experiences of Karen refugee youth in schools. While we highlight some unique challenges, we also wish to provide a framework for innovative strategies for success. In our community-development approach, we discuss how building both individual and community capacity through collaborative community relationships can holistically promote social inclusion, a sense of belonging within community, and access to education.

Social inclusion refers to a community's capacity to adapt to and accept newcomer groups in society. It is equally critical, however, for newcomers to feel a sense of belonging. More specifically, a sense of belonging includes a refugee youth's subjective experience of whether or not he or she felt included and the processes that facilitate a sense of belonging to a particular place. For example, Sampson and Gifford (2010) refer to sense of belonging to place as being shaped by environments that form therapeutic landscapes in refugee youths' everyday lives. Landscapes are social conditions of environments that are conducive to healing and promote well-being. In our context, building capacity for Karen refugee youth in schools includes facilitating environments that promote social inclusion, belonging, and learning. Thus, a community-development approach to education is holistic—it considers all aspects of a student's life, including psychological, physical, social, and spiritual domains that promote access to education. Teachers and those who work to help integrate belonging and social inclusion within schools must be aware of the pre- and post-migration conditions that challenge or support refugees in the context of their resettlement.

It is equally important to consider youth in the context of their family unit, as many refugee youth experience family resettlement stress (Hyman, Beiser, & Vu, 1996) and may require increased family support to be successfully engaged in education. Thus, rebuilding healthy root systems among refugee youth in schools requires ongoing collaboration and knowledge exchange among school staff and other community services, which may include health services, settlement workers, recreation services, volunteers, and other local non-profit organizations. Just as building a healthy root system requires various conditions, the building of relationships within community can support refugee families to ensure the retention of refugee youth in schools and maintain ongoing support in their adaptation to local communities in which refugee families are resettled.

Despite the resilience of refugee youth, they face many challenges to their success in the Canadian school system. Pre- and post-migration experiences and circumstances such as age on arrival, lack of previous education, culture shock, mental health problems related to trauma, the school environment, and the availability of social supports play a role in refugee youths' access to education and experience in schools. It is also important to note that these social categories are not exhaustive; further, they may be interrelated and may not be experienced by all refugee youth in the same way. However, acknowledgement and integration of the way these social categories play out in the context of resettlement for refugee youth in schools shaped the capacity-building strategy in our community.

## Educational challenges of refugee youth

On arrival, most refugee youth have very high needs. The difference between life in a refugee camp and life in Canada is enormous, and the learning curve is very steep. In many situations, students must learn English, adjust to a new culture, make friends, and learn basic life skills. In addition, refugee youth struggle with issues related to health, poverty, and identity (Anisef, 2005; Shakya et al., 2010; Wilkinson, 2002). Furthermore, immigrant youth who arrive in Canada as older students are more likely to drop out of secondary school than Canadian-born students and students who immigrate to Canada as younger children (Corak, 2011). Corak's (2011) study on the age of immigrant children and their education outcomes posits that children who arrive in Canada after the age of nine arrive during an important transitional stage in their lives, and "migration may have long-lasting impacts on their capacities to become successful and self-reliant adults, impacts that may be much more costly and difficult to remedy at a later stage" (Corak, 2011, p. 7). Refugee youth experience greater challenges compared to native-born youth. Additional stress for refugee youth may include lack of language ability and experiences of discrimination from their Canadian peers.

Moreover, the trend to drop out of secondary education may be more pronounced for refugee youth because of their lack of access to quality English-language education in their refugee camps. In addition, because of ongoing resettlement issues, refugee youth do not have the time to catch up to their peers academically. Simply put, refugee students do not have time to rebuild their roots in Canada because of the many social and cultural challenges they face, including trauma issues, culture shock, and the need to support their family. Citing figures from Citizenship and Immigration Canada, Shakya et al. (2010) note that "on average refugees 15 years and older are four times more likely than economic immigrants to have nine years or less of schooling" (p. 65). Refugees often have large gaps in their education; for many, schooling has been interrupted by war or unrest or is of poor quality due to protracted stays in refugee camps (Ministry of Education, 2009). Although access to education is a universal right, this right is not extended to many refugees who remain in camps for extended periods (Shakya et al., 2010). In particular, Karen refugees have experienced limitations on their access to education because of restrictions imposed by the Thai government (Shakya et al., 2010). In some cases, however, refugees living in Thai refugee camps have been able to access education beyond grade 10 through non-governmental organizations and international aid (Karen refugee, personal communication, January 2012). More specifically, the quality of education provided in many refugee camps is poor due to lacking teacher qualifications, inadequate school structures, and limited learning resources (Oh, 2010). This problem is not specific to Karen refugees but is reflected in many refugee camp populations (Shakya et al., 2010).

The lack of previous education creates immediate and long-term challenges for refugee students. On arrival in Canada, many Karen youth in our community were unable to read or perform at grade level in math and science. Several years later, we have found that some Karen youth have made great progress in their reading and writing while others continue to struggle with literacy and numeracy skills. This difference may be due to lack of access to education for youth who were living in refugee camps or to the fact that many of the youths' family members are illiterate in their own language and have not had access to education. Unfortunately, these young people also struggle to be successful in other academic classes, and the struggle affects their integration into the mainstream student body. Another finding from our work is that many of the Karen youth continue to struggle to catch up to their Canadian-born peers and grew too old to attend secondary school before they were able to obtain enough credits to graduate. This observation is reflected in research that shows that refugee students struggle to be successful in secondary school (Roderick et al., 2006; Wilkinson, 2002; Yau, 1996). Many refugees have "severe psychosocial and physical health concerns, limited or no labour market skills, little or no formal education, and, for children, greater developmental challenges" (Presse & Thomson, 2008, p. 95). Several pre- and post-migration experiences contribute to these challenges, and while not all of the problems have easy solutions, community strategies can support refugee youth to become successful in accessing education in their new country.

In our experience, the educational needs of Karen refugee youth became a pressing concern as many were not integrated well within the regular school system and required extra support to ensure their ongoing engagement and retention in school. We found that many Karen youth placed a great value on working hard to support their families. Many Karen refugee families experience great social and economic demands, and it is not uncommon for students to feel pressure to contribute to the family's income (Hyman, Beiser, & Vu, 1996). Finding a job was also related to the stress incurred by their need to pay off their transportation loans.[4] As a result, many Karen youth left school to take low-paying jobs to support their families. However, Karen youth also realize the importance of education and English-language skills to get a good job in Canada, and some go back to school as they continue to build their roots in the community. Our experiences are concurrent with the research of Shakya et al. (2010), which studied refugee youth in Toronto and suggests that refugee youth must often balance their family responsibilities against their own educational goals.

Meanwhile, while refugee youth face significant challenges on arrival, in our experience their needs evolve as they adjust to life in Canada. The resettlement and integration process can take many years; five years after their arrival in Canada, many Karen youth continue to face challenges related to literacy and language skills, posing ongoing challenges to their integration into mainstream academic classes. As a result, programs and support services must also continue to adapt to new needs that may emerge, such as connecting youth with job training or specialized education programs that can enhance language ability, individual skills, and connections with peers. Ongoing evaluation and collaboration with teachers and service providers can ensure that strategies for integration and engagement also evolve as the needs of refugee youth change or as new needs emerge.

## School environment

The school environment is critical for refugee students to feel safe, welcome, and supported; in fact, the school environment is a primary place for refugee youth to develop a sense of belonging (Kia-Keating & Ellis, 2007). Unfortunately, research shows that the opposite is often the case for immigrant students, who frequently feel isolated from the mainstream school population (Gunderson, 2000).

A safe social environment can have a significant impact on decreasing resettlement stress while fostering recovery from trauma and promoting well-being (Sampson & Gifford, 2010). In particular, Sampson and Gifford suggest that "during the early period of resettlement ... youth seek out and value places that promote healing and recovery" (p. 116). Creating an environment where youth feel valued may enhance engagement with education and promote retention in schools. Similarly, Kia-Keating and Ellis (2007) argue that the school has a particularly significant impact on the lives of refugee youth because it defines and affects one's sense of community. Importantly, the sense of belonging and connectedness that refugee youth experience also has positive effects on academic outcomes (Kia-Keating & Ellis, 2007).

We found that many Karen youth find it difficult to integrate and find spaces where they feel welcomed. Thus, creating safe spaces in schools for youth to tell their stories may increase awareness and understanding of youth experiences and build connections with existing community and peers. The place to start building a support network around a refugee student is within the school. In our case, this step included ongoing dialogue with classroom teachers, school administration, English-Language Learner (ELL) teachers, school counsellors, and settlement and multicultural workers who worked toward meeting both the collective and the individual needs of Karen youth. We were fortunate to have a Karen multicultural worker who was able to provide interpretation and translation services within schools and to offer valuable cultural insight in many situations. In addition, collaboration and networking within the school allowed ELL teachers to share their wealth of knowledge and experience in working with English-language learners and to provide useful information and resources that could assist refugee youth in the classroom setting. Many smaller school districts are not as fortunate to have built-in programs where multicultural workers and settlement workers are available for diverse refugees. Having the resources to integrate multicultural workers and translators can build a strong connection to schools and thereby create safe, supportive places.

Furthermore, many refugee students struggle with language differences, and this experience increases social isolation, stigma, and discrimination (Gunderson, 2000; Kia-Keating & Ellis, 2007; Sampson & Gifford, 2010). In schools it is therefore important to build bridges between Canadian students and refugee students that foster social inclusion. Gunderson (2000) found that because immigrant students are generally placed in English as a Second Language (ESL) classes, they have little opportunity to interact with Canadian-born students, although interaction may be the best way to learn Canadian culture, improve language skills, and ultimately adjust to Canadian society. Many refugee students find the stigma attached to taking specialized English classes makes them "second-class students" (Gunderson, 2000) and may further contribute to their sense of isolation and identity. From our experience, school staff worked to ensure that Karen youth felt safe and comfortable by introducing them to the school environment gradually, pairing them with a student who speaks the same language, and taking steps to understand their unique background, culture, and family situation when possible.

A supportive school environment may engage refugee students in leadership activities and extracurricular programs and may create opportunities for refugee students to give back and share their own unique strengths at school. Schools can create opportunities for student dialogue, sharing culture and empowerment, and ultimately offering a safe place where refugee youth can heal from their past and build a new life and identity. One promising activity we found was to identify potential student leaders, including Canadian students and previous refugees or immigrants, to work with Karen youth as peer mentors or cultural ambassadors. In elementary school, for example, these students might have the responsibility of showing a newcomer around the school, eating lunch with her/him, or playing on the playground with her/him. In secondary schools, a peer mentor may be trained and supported to provide homework support, in-class support, or friendship to a new student.

Schools are places of community, and supportive environments will help refugee students feel safe and engaged. However, to promote social inclusion and to ensure that refugee youths' holistic needs are met, a supportive and welcoming school environment must go beyond the academic system. Our community development approach is one example of how academic support can be enhanced through building social networks more broadly and may have positive implications for long-term educational engagement.

## Building collaboration and capacity within the local community

Local schools are the backbone of many communities and provide the perfect place to practise the community-development approach to refugee education and integration. Generally, there are several ways in which school staff can help refugee students to rebuild their root systems through community partnerships. While schools generally focus on a child's academic success in order for refugee youth to be successful and engaged with education, in our experience support services must be holistic. As such, we have built community partnerships to support the Karen youth outside of school. For example, we partnered with a community initiative designed to engage youth in sports and academics concurrently through recreation opportunities and an after-school homework club. Meanwhile, volunteer organizations, settlement workers, and other service providers have worked to provide family support and access to services. The recognition that Karen youth were part of family systems with complex, multi-faceted needs allowed school staff and community service providers to work together to support families in a way that would not have been possible if these resource staff had worked in isolation.

School engagement and success of refugee students is related not only to their migration experience but also to their personal resilience and social resources (Kanu, 2008). The social context, including the role of family and availability of resources, can promote or challenge refugee youths' engagement in schools. For example, parents may not be able to support a young person's learning as they are often struggling with accessing language services and in some cases may be illiterate in their own language. This reality presents challenges for youth who may benefit from extra parental support in relation to their educational needs such as reading and writing. However, strong partnerships among community agencies and schools can enhance resources for the unique learning needs of refugee youth. These kinds of partnerships may include collaboration between various organizations and services including sports and recreation, education, faith, culture, language, government, and business to enhance resources that can meet specific refugee youth needs.

The collaboration among various services and community volunteers led to the development of the Refugee Advisory Committee (RAC). RAC members included community volunteers, settlement workers, members of a local faith community, managers and frontline workers from immigration services, adult English-language service providers, and health service workers. The role of the RAC was to share experiences, collaborate on ongoing community needs related to Karen refugees, and partner with other organizations. Through this community-development approach, the RAC has remained open to various members of the community who serve refugees, and the membership has evolved as needs have changed or as new service providers have come forward. Meanwhile, the RAC has provided opportunities for knowledge exchange among service providers and teachers. Through this process the RAC has been able to identify areas of concern for Karen refugees in our community, which have included identifying youth at risk, mental health issues, problems with accessing health care, and language support. At the same time, advocacy and collaboration within the RAC have allowed members to develop strategic partnerships and innovative approaches to resettlement and integration such as recreation services, youth job-training programs, volunteer-run initiatives, and other programs to support refugee youth and their families. These increased supports would not be possible if the RAC had not been developed.

Refugee youth often face medical issues that can affect their schooling, or have family issues related to housing, employment, or settlement issues. The RAC was able to build strong connections with mainstream services such as local public health agencies to work collaboratively with schools and staff to identify needs and ensure that refugee youth and their families are able to access health care and other social services. Simich (2009) has discussed how creating opportunities for increasing health literacy for newcomer families requires going outside of medical settings to promote health and well-being for new immigrants. In addition there is a need to include broader social policy structures from all levels of government (local, provincial, national) and community to create conditions for health and human development. Working together, through taking a bottom-up and top-down approach, communities and governments (at all levels) can create conditions for the health and well-being of the whole community. For example, RAC members were able to provide educational, social, and health services on the frontline and are able to dialogue with managers and directors of community services who also sit on the RAC. Thus the RAC provides a space for ongoing dialogue for both service providers and policy planners on issues related to the community's needs, issues for newcomer youth, and the way policy influences access to education in schools. Through this forum we can work at initiatives that inform current policy on immigration and youth as well as collaborate on more local issues affecting refugee youth.

Thus, the RAC became an important forum for dialogue, networking, and advocacy to ensure that organizations like the school district, churches, community services, and public health agencies could work together to fill gaps and ensure that Karen refugees were able to access a broad spectrum of services so that that their needs were being adequately met. Many communities, particularly those in large urban centres, have a wealth of community services to offer refugee families, such as settlement workers, employment programs, or recreation programs. In our community, access to these specialized services and programs was difficult without the development of the RAC.

In addition to the development of the RAC, strategies for community development also included enhanced sports and recreational initiatives that could support Karen youths' engagement with education while building connections that could foster belonging and social inclusion. These recreation opportunities ultimately helped to create a stronger root system that enhanced a youth's individual capacity for learning and staying engaged with education. These activities are consistent with Citizenship and Immigration Canada's *Best Practice Guidelines* on promoting welcoming communities. Involving newcomer youth in sports can ultimately help to build knowledge, resources, and skills for newcomer youth and enhance belonging (Citizenship and Immigration Canada, 2012).

## Engaging youth through sports, recreation, and mentoring activities

Through ongoing collaboration and capacity-building with community organizations, school staff have been able to use recreation as a tool to enhance school engagement and help Karen refugee youth develop strong social networks. One of the most effective school–community partnerships for Karen youth has been an organization called PuCKS (Promoting Community Through Kids in Sport). Initially, this partnership created opportunities for many Karen youth to play hockey and receive academic support through an after-school homework club. This component of PuCKS is run by a collection of volunteers who help support youth in reading, writing, math, and science. While enhanced learning and literacy are an important component of the PuCKS program, the relational mentoring that has occurred with volunteer tutors has also shown itself to be significant for Karen youth. Anecdotal evidence and subjective reports from the youth themselves have shown that volunteers have been positive role models and have established important relationships with the youth at a critical time in their life. Furthermore, these relationships have increased the youths' sense of belonging and feelings of inclusion in the community. On the other hand, the Karen youth have also benefited from the tutoring support and having a space to complete homework that is outside of their school and within their community. Karen youth have self-reported that this has helped them to manage their homework and increase understanding of specific subjects such as math, science, and English. Many of the youth have brought their report cards to the after-school program associated with PuCKS and have shown improvement as a result of having extra support.

We have found that mentoring can foster relationships and provide positive role models at a critical time for refugee youth. Milliken (2007) has argued that mentoring should be the cornerstone of any program for at-risk youth or children, creating an environment where healthy relationships can flourish. He writes that "programs don't change kids—relationships do. Every child needs one adult who's irrationally committed to his or her future" (Milliken, 2007, p. 7). Many programs and community organizations like Big Brothers and Big Sisters offer in-school mentoring programs that encourage youth to stay in school, avoid risky behaviour, and have healthy attitudes and relationships with their families and peers (Big Brothers

Big Sisters, 2011). Furthermore, many immigrant-serving organizations offer programs that connect youth or adults with community volunteers to assist in settlement and integration (ISS of BC, n.d.). School–community connections through initiatives such as PuCKS can help build self-esteem, increase the sense of belonging, and promote engagement with other youth in Canada. While adult mentors can provide positive role models and much-needed guidance for refugee youth, mentoring can also take place within the school environment, where specially trained peer mentors can help youth build relationships and connections across cultural boundaries.

In addition, we found that sports are an equally important component of refugee youth engagement. Playing sports fosters individual skills sets and contributes to being a member of the team. For many students, sports can be a carrot that keeps them from dropping out of school while it increases their sense of belonging. One Karen youth explained that he likes to play football because he likes to help his school team—they rely on him. Karen women and girls have also benefited from involvement in sports. Women and girls represent approximately 47% of refugees of concern (UNHCR, 2010) and many have experienced gender-based violence, a lack of access to education, and significant pre-migration trauma (Norsworthy & Khuankaew, 2004). As we have noted, many refugee girls struggle to fit in and experience racialization, making them increasingly vulnerable to social isolation and consequently to negative mental health outcomes (Berman & Jiwani, 2008). Less is known about gendered experiences of youth migration and resettlement and the ways in which social environments and community supports include or exclude refugee youths' engagement with education. In our community capacity-building approach with the PuCKS program, many Karen girls have been able to access sports such as local soccer and hockey teams. Thus, programs such as PuCKS may promote equal opportunities for sport. Our experience in creating opportunities and access to sports has also provided opportunities for Karen boys and girls to build connections with their Canadian peers and increase their sense of confidence, while at the same time fostering engagement with mainstream educational systems. In addition, through sports and recreation, Karen youth have had opportunities to engage in mainstream school activities as well as to show off some of their traditional skills such as playing caneball with their Canadian-born peers.[5] These opportunities promote cultural exchange and enhanced learning for mainstream youth. It has been our experience in working with refugee youth that every child has a unique passion or an ability he or she excels at. Finding that passion or ability can help students gain confidence and resilience in the midst of a tumultuous time in their life.

Refugee youth face complex challenges that will require many community supports to rebuild their lives and identity. While positive, caring relationships will help youth to rebuild their roots through confidence and trust, such relationships are simply the foundation for addressing many of the complex challenges that refugee youth face during resettlement. Overall, the collaborative relationship between PuCKS, local schools, and other community organizations has built capacity and resilience in refugee youth by promoting a sense of belonging through sports in addition to caring relationships with volunteers, coaches, and other adults. These community strategies and capacity-building approaches may facilitate other communities to help support refugee youth to achieve their educational goals and dreams.

## Conclusion

Clearly, refugee youth and their families face many challenges associated with resettlement. Arriving in Canada without a healthy, supported root system places these youth at risk for mental health issues, despite the fact that they also arrive with many unique gifts, abilities, and strengths. We argue that increasing community capacity to support refugee youth in schools must go beyond the educational system itself and provide opportunities for stakeholders and service providers to engage in dialogue and initiatives that address the various challenges for refugee youth. As the backbone of many communities, local schools can employ many strategies to build a supportive environment to engage refugee youth in systems of education. This process requires great collaboration among various levels of service providers and communities of practice and can increase educators' understanding of the challenges that refugee youth and their families face in relation to their pre-migration and resettlement contexts. Creating safe spaces for dialogue and community engagement as we have experienced with the RAC has broadened our knowledge of refugee experiences. Community initiatives such as PuCKS can also promote engagement in educational systems that seek to foster belonging and connection among diverse refugee youth. Through this community capacity-building process we have not only increased services and supports for Karen youth but have been changed by gaining increased cultural understanding of the significance of engagement in education for Karen youth and the strategies needed to build a strong root system that will allow refugee youth to flourish.

## NOTES

The authors would like to acknowledge our community partners who have contributed to the ongoing settlement of Karen refugee youth, including Zipporah Devadas, Karen Multicultural Worker; Margaret Kunst, PuCKS Program Operations Director; Sharon Kavanagh, CARL Project Coordinator and Volunteer; Karen Initiative volunteers, staff, and teachers at Langley School District; and many others who have acted as supporters, advocates, and mentors.

1 Structural violence is a complex term that refers to violence exerted systematically and indirectly by a particular society (Farmer, 2004). Structural violence is experienced in various forms such as racism, gender inequality, and violation of human rights, as well as widely through genocide and epidemic disease. In this chapter, we refer to social structures that violate refugee youths' inability to access systems such as education due to inadequate and inflexible systems that create barriers in education.

2 The term *trauma-informed care* has evolved out of capacity-building in immigrant and refugee health and mental health services (Poole & Greaves, 2012). In the context of education, trauma-informed care would require teachers and staff to develop an increased understanding about the factors that shape the resettlement process for refugee youth. Many refugees have experienced trauma during their migration; however, the stress of resettlement may compound youths' previous traumatic experiences. Thus it is important that people working with refugee youth tailor education not only to be mindful about the refugee experience but also to recognize the way mainstream education might add to youths' stress. Compounded mental health issues may be seen when educational practices fail to integrate refugee youth into mainstream systems of education.

3 Karen people represent one of many ethnic minority groups in the former British colony known as Burma, now referred to by the current government as Myanmar. In 2006, Canada resettled approximately 8,000 Karen people as Government-Assisted Refugees into communities across Canada.

4 Government-Assisted Refugees in Canada are required to pay back the transportation costs incurred during their resettlement process. These costs include medical expenses, transportation expenses, and a service fee. Canada is one of a few countries that require refugees to pay for their transportation and medical costs. If the loan is not repaid within three years, the government charges interest on the principle amount owing (ISS of BC, 2010).

5 Caneball, also known as *sepak takraw*, is a traditional game in many Southeast Asian countries, including Thailand, Burma (Myanmar), and Malaysia. It is similar to kick volleyball, where players use their feet, knee, head, or chest to touch a ball made of rattan (Sepak Takraw Association of Canada, n.d.).

## REFERENCES

Agic, B. (2012). Trauma-informed care for refugees. In N. Poole & L. Greaves (Eds.), *Becoming trauma informed* (pp. 121–123). Toronto: Centre for Addiction and Mental Health.

Anisef, P. (2005). *Issues confronting newcomer youth in Canada: Alternative models for a national youth host program.* Toronto: Joint Centre of Excellence for Research on Immigration and Settlement.

Beiser, M. (2005, Mar–Apr). The health of immigrants and refugees in Canada. *Canadian Journal of Public Health, 96*(Suppl 2), S30–S44. Medline:16078554

Beiser, M. (2009, Dec). Resettling refugees and safeguarding their mental health: Lessons learned from the Canadian Refugee Resettlement Project. *Transcultural Psychiatry, 46*(4), 539–583. http://dx.doi.org/10.1177/1363461509351373 Medline:20028677

Beiser, M., Hou, F., Hyman, I., & Tousignant, M. (2002, Feb). Poverty, family process, and the mental health of immigrant children in Canada. *American Journal of Public Health, 92*(2), 220–227. http://dx.doi.org/10.2105/AJPH.92.2.220 Medline:11818295

Berman, H., & Jiwani, Y. (2008). Newcomer girls in Canada—Implications for interventions by mental health professionals. In S. Guruge & E. Collins (Eds.), *Working with immigrant women—Issues and strategies for mental health professionals* (pp. 137–155). Toronto: CAMH.

Big Brothers Big Sisters (2011). *In-school mentoring*. Retrieved December 18, 2012, from Big Brothers Big Sisters: http://www.bigbrothersbigsisters.ca/en/home/mentoringprograms/inschoolmentoring.aspx

Brown, J.D., & Hannis, D. (2008). *Community development in Canada*. Toronto: Pearson Education Canada.

Citizenship and Immigration Canada. (2008). *Facts and Figures: Immigration overview Permanent and Temporary Residents. Research and Evaluation Branch, Citizenship and Immigration Canada*. Ottawa: Author.

Citizenship and Immigration Canada. (2012). Best practices in settlement services. Retrieved from: http://www.cic.gc.ca/english/department/partner/bpss/index.asp

Corak, M. (2011). *Age at immigration and the educational outcomes of children*. Ottawa: Minister of Industry, Statistics Canada. http://dx.doi.org/10.2139/ssrn.1971980

Doughty, W., & Klingle, Y. (2008). Immigrant and refugee child and youth needs research study. Final Report.

Dow, D.H. (2010). An overview of stressors faced by immigrants and refugees: A guide for mental health practitioners. *Home Health Care Management Practice, 23*(3), 210–217. http://dx.doi.org/10.1177/1084822310390878.

Farmer, P. (2004). An anthropology of structural violence. *Current Anthropology, 45*(3), 305–325. http://dx.doi.org/10.1086/382250

Grove, N.J., & Zwi, A.B. (2006, Apr). Our health and theirs: Forced migration, othering, and public health. *Social Science & Medicine, 62*(8), 1931–1942. http://dx.doi.org/10.1016/j.socscimed.2005.08.061 Medline:16242227

Gunderson, L. (2000). Voices of the teenage diasporas. *Journal of Adolescent & Adult Literacy, 43*(8) 692–706.

Hyman, I., Beiser, M., & Vu, N. (1996). The mental health of refugee children in Canada. *Refuge, 15*(5), 4–8.

ISS of BC. (2010). *Changing faces, changing neighbourhoods*. Vancouver: Immigrant Services Society of British Columbia.

ISS of BC. (n.d.). *Settlement mentors*. Retrieved January 12, 2013, from http://www.issbc.org/settlementmentors

Kanu, Y. (2008). Educational needs and barriers for African refugee students in Manitoba. *Canadian Journal of Education, 31*(4), 915–940.

Keyes, E.F. (2000, Jun). Mental health status in refugees: An integrative review of current research. *Issues in Mental Health Nursing, 21*(4), 397–410. http://dx.doi.org/10.1080/016128400248013 Medline:11249358

Kia-Keating, M., & Ellis, B.H. (2007, Jan). Belonging and connection to school in resettlement: Young refugees, school belonging, and psychosocial adjustment. *Clinical Child Psychology and Psychiatry, 12*(1), 29–43. http://dx.doi.org/10.1177/1359104507071052 Medline:17375808

Kinzie, J.D. (2006, Dec). Immigrants and refugees: The psychiatric perspective. *Transcultural Psychiatry, 43*(4), 577–591. http://dx.doi.org/10.1177/1363461506070782 Medline:17166947

Kinzie, J.D. (2008). PTSD among traumatized refugees. In L.J. Kirmayer, R. Lemelsen, & M. Barad (Eds.), *Understanding trauma: Integrated biological, clinical, and cultural perspectives* (pp. 259–274). Cambridge: University Press.

Kirk, J., & Cassity, E. (2007). Minimum standards for quality education for refugee youth. *Youth Studies Australia, 26*(1), 50–56.

Kirmayer, L.J., Lemelsen, R., & Barad, M. (Eds.). (2008). *Understanding trauma: Integrated biological, clinical, and cultural perspectives*. Cambridge: University Press.

Kretzmann, J.P., & McKnight, J.L. (1993). Introduction. In J.P. Kretzmann & J.L. McKnight (Eds.), *Building communities from the inside out: A path toward finding and mobilizing a community's assets* (pp. 1–11). Evanston: Institute for Policy Research.

Milliken, B. (2007). *The last dropout*. New York: Hay House.

Ministry of Education. (2009). *Students from refugee backgrounds: A guide for teachers and schools*. Victoria: British Columbia Ministry of Education.

Morris, M.D., Popper, S.T., Rodwell, T.C., Brodine, S.K., & Brouwer, K.C. (2009, Dec). Healthcare barriers of refugees post-resettlement. *Journal of Community Health, 34*(6), 529–538. http://dx.doi.org/10.1007/s10900-009-9175-3 Medline:19705264

Newbold, B. (2009, Jun). The short-term health of Canada's new immigrant arrivals: Evidence from LSIC. *Ethnicity & Health, 14*(3), 315–336. http://dx.doi.org/10.1080/13557850802609956 Medline:19263262

Norsworthy, L.K., & Khuankaew, O. (2004). Women of Burma speak out: Workshops to deconstruct gender-based violence and build systems of peace and justice. *Journal for Specialists in Group Work, 29*(3), 259–283. http://dx.doi.org/10.1080/01933920490477011

Oh, S.-A. (2010). *Education in refugee camps in Thailand: Policy, practice and paucity*. Paper commissioned for the EFA Global Monitoring Report 2011, The hidden crisis: Armed conflict and education.

Poole, N., & Greaves, L. (2012). *Becoming trauma informed. CAMH.* Toronto: Centre for Addiction and Mental Health.

Porter, M., & Haslam, N. (2005, Aug 3). Predisplacement and postdisplacement factors associated with mental health of refugees and internally displaced persons: A meta-analysis. *Journal of the American Medical Association, 294*(5), 602–612. http://dx.doi.org/10.1001/jama.294.5.602 Medline:16077055

Presse, D., & Thomson, J. (2008). The resettlement challenge: Integration of refugees from protracted refugee situations. *Refuge: Canada's Periodical on Refugees, 25*(1) 94–99.

Roderick, K., Janzen, R., Ochocka, J., Westhues, A., Jenkins, J., & Sandbeck, B. (2006). *Pathways to success: Immigrant youth at high school*. Kitchener, ON: Centre for Research and Education in Human Services.

Sampson, R., & Gifford, S.M. (2010, Jan). Place-making, settlement and well-being: The therapeutic landscapes of recently arrived youth with refugee backgrounds. *Health & Place, 16*(1), 116–131. http://dx.doi.org/10.1016/j.healthplace.2009.09.004 Medline:19837625

Sepak Takraw Association of Canada (n.d.). Retrieved January 12, 2013, from Sepak Takraw Association of Canada: http://www.takrawcanada.com/

Shakya, Y.B., Guruge, S., Hynie, M., et al. (2010). Aspirations for higher education among newcomer refugee youth in Toronto: Expectations, challenges, and strategies. *Refuge: Canada's Periodical on Refugees, 27*(2), 65–78.

Simich, L. (2009). Health literacy and immigrant populations. Policy report submitted to Public Health Agency of Canada and Metropolis Canada.

Thomas, W., & Collier, V. (1997). *School effectiveness for language minority students*. Retrieved August 18, 2008, from http://www.thomasandcollier.com/1997_Thomas-Collier97-1.pdf

United Nations High Commissioner for Refugees [UNHCR]. (2010). Global trends. Retrieved from www.unhcr.org

United Nations High Commissioner for Refugees [UNHCR]. (n.d.). *Who we help*. Retrieved January 12, 2013, from United Nations High Commissioner for Refugees: http://www.unhcr.org/pages/49c3646c11c.html

Wilkinson, L. (2002). Factors influencing the academic success of refugee youth in Canada. *Journal of Youth Studies, 5*(2), 173–193. http://dx.doi.org/10.1080/13676260220134430

Yau, M. (1996). Refugee students in Toronto schools. *Refuge: Canada's Periodical on Refugees, 15*(5), 9–16.

# 14

# Fostering solidarity in the classroom

## Creative expression workshops for immigrant and refugee students

Caroline Beauregard, Marie-France Gauthier, and Cécile Rousseau

For the past 15 years, the Transcultural Research and Intervention Team (TRIT) has been offering creative expression workshops to children and youth in multi-ethnic schools. Three programs are offered, targeting the developmental needs of different age groups. One of the common features of these programs is that they offer a space where fostering solidarity becomes possible through play and creative expression. Although this type of intervention provides benefits for both students and teachers, addressing personal and social relations within a classroom also raises important challenges. We will first explain the rationale and theoretical framework structuring the workshops and then describe the three programs using vignettes to illustrate the complexity of the relational dimension of these interventions.

## Effects of migration on social and family networks

The process of migration engenders a disruption in the life of migrants, and they have to reconstruct their social networks following resettlement. After arriving in the host country, immigrants and refugees have to face not only a new culture but also the multiple losses of their homeland, culture, family members, work, and social status, among other things. Refugees' predicament is unique and distinct from other immigrants' experiences in that they are more often exposed to organized violence in their homeland and they often remain in uncertainty for prolonged periods after arriving in the host country, making them vulnerable to various mental health issues (Silove, Steel, McGorry, & Mohan, 1998). Some refugees may have been exposed directly or indirectly to war, but in this context, organized violence is also understood as a type of structural violence that emanates from official institutions. For instance, governmental agents can exert intimidation and oppression on citizens, imposing constraints that can be psychologically destructive. In that sense, all refugees have experienced organized violence. At the community level, organized violence shatters various social links, producing mistrust and suspicion among its members (Rousseau, 2000; Rousseau, Drapeau, & Corin, 1997). This disruption in social and family networks can exacerbate mental health problems. Indeed, when the social fabric disintegrates, people are more likely to be subjected to isolation, which renders them more vulnerable to develop mental health issues.

TRIT has examined the effects of organized violence on refugees' social and family networks. The team's previous work with asylum seekers confirmed that refugees who have been exposed to insecurity, persecution, and organized violence in their homeland face difficulties in rebuilding their social network after migration (Morantz, Rousseau, & Heymann, 2012). This context has an impact not only on family life before migration, but also on the family resettlement process and on the children's adjustment to the host country. The extent to which refugee families have difficulty in rebuilding their social network is different for parents and children. Indeed, the network restoration process is easier for younger children than it is for their older siblings. This difference is even greater between young children and their parents. This divergence in experience has an impact on family life. For instance, parents might have experienced multiple losses, traumas, and separations, leaving them emotionally distant and unavailable to respond to their children's needs (Howard & Hodes, 2000). The effects of parental distress also have an implication for mental health services offered to refugee children.

Despite exposure to adversity, refugees are underrepresented as mental health service users. This fact could be explained by structural deficiencies regarding help offered to immigrant and refugee families, while families may have to overcome differences in cultural practices, a fear of stigma, language difficulties, barriers in accessing information, and insufficient financial resources (Saechao et al., 2012). Negative past experience with health authorities in their country of origin can pose another barrier to mental health service access for refugees. For instance, some refugee families have experienced betrayal by official institutions that were unable, perhaps, to protect them from violence and who, in some cases, may even have been perpetrators of that violence. This experience and various cultural differences partially explain refugees' lack of trust in government agencies and in particular their reluctance to seek help from health services. There is a consensus in the literature that schools are the best environment to reach refugee children and offer them intervention (Jaycox et al., 2010; Salloum & Overstreet, 2008; Stein et al., 2003) and prevention programs (Hodes, 2000; McArdle et al., 2002). When access to mental health services is difficult and/or embarrassing, schools can be a more accessible service site as well as a non-stigmatizing gateway to such support (Pumariega, Rogers, & Rothe, 2005).

Some school-based programs use creative expression as a way to promote refugee and immigrant students' well-being. For instance, various creative activities were used to support increased connections among middle-school–aged girls in a US inner-city school (Sassen, Spencer, & Curtin, 2005). In Germany, music was used to promote respect, diversity, and social integration in high school with the effect of improving the regulation of affect and aggression (Nöcker-Ribaupierre & Wölfl, 2010). Positive social bonding to peers and adults resulted in decreased isolation and improved self-image and confidence for youth participating in a group storytelling program (Nelson, McClintock, Perez-Ferguson, Shawver, & Thompson, 2008). These programs share the reinforcement of a sense of solidarity in the classroom. In this context, *solidarity* is defined by a feeling of sharing a common experience with others that can lead to collective action. The creative expression programs we offer to children and youth in multi-ethnic schools share this belief by presuming that improving solidarity in a classroom setting has a positive effect on students.

## Rationale for creative expression programs

Relying on scientific literature and on its clinical experience with refugee families, in the late 1990s TRIT started to develop and implement preventive school-based intervention programs for children based on creative expression. Families in crisis came to our attention in our clinical work. Children often exhibited severe symptoms of anxiety, suicidal ideation, and selective mutism, accompanied by learning and behavioural difficulties that were usually linked to trauma (experienced or transmitted through parents and/or extended family), migration process, and resettlement in the host country. TRIT realized that to help these families, we could be more constructive if we offered school-based preventive programs where children could express their difficulties before they built up to a state of crisis. Therefore, to foster solidarity in the classroom, the team focused on three key elements of intervention: prevention, expression, and inclusion. First, we work upstream with whole classrooms to promote children's self-esteem and awareness of the other simultaneously, to develop links between individual and collective expressions. Providing a safe space of expression is the second important aspect. Immigrant and refugee children have often lived through difficult situations and at times have had very traumatic experiences. It could be too threatening to talk about these events directly, but by using play and various mediums (sand and figurines, stories and drawing, fabrics, musical instruments, and theatrical exercises) and by being supported through the process, children can safely express how they feel and build renewed self-confidence as well as a sense of identity. In this safe space, children and youth express what is important to them; active and respectful listening is encouraged. Third, all students are included in the workshops. This inclusion is done in opposition to targeting only a few "at-risk" students with the potential risk of stigmatizing them in the process. In many schools, intervention regarding students exhibiting difficulties consists of taking the child away from his/her classroom to receive the service needed (school psychologist, psycho-educator, social worker, etc.) (Brindis et al., 2003). This situation creates an opportunity for easy labelling from school workers and also from peers, which could affect the student's self-confidence and social ability. Instead, some researchers believe that providing interventions in the classroom is a better way to attenuate students' learning and behavioural difficulties (Hong, Yufeng, Agho, & Jacobs, 2011). These same researchers also imply that teachers are in a good position to implement the interventions. We offer students the opportunity to work together through various situations; we encourage and value multiplicity when differences have been a source of exclusion and persecution for students or their families. TRIT believes these are the fundamental bases of its work.

Through the years, we developed three programs targeting specific age groups: Sand Play (3 to 7 years old), Art and Storytelling (8 to 11 years old), and Drama Plurality (12 to 16 years old) (see Rousseau & Heusch, 2000; Rousseau, Lacroix, Bagilishya, & Heusch, 2003; Rousseau, Singh, Lacroix, Bagilishya, & Measham, 2004; Rousseau, Drapeau, Lacroix, Bagilishya, & Heusch, 2005; Rousseau, Gauthier, Lacroix, et al., 2005; Rousseau, Lacroix, Singh, Gauthier, & Benoit, 2005; Lacroix et al., 2007; Rousseau et al., 2007; Rousseau, Benoit, Lacroix, & Gauthier, 2009). These creative expression programs combine verbal and non-verbal modes of expression to offer students multiple alternatives to express themselves, both individually or collectively, and are meant to foster empathy and solidarity in the classroom (Rousseau, Lacroix, Singh, Gauthier, & Benoit, 2005).

## Creative expression workshops with refugee students

In this section, we examine how fostering solidarity in the classroom through creative expression workshops could affect the class dynamics and social networks. We briefly introduce each of the programs to provide a general outline of the workshops and the materials used for the intervention. Then we present vignettes to illustrate how students build a sense of solidarity and acceptance while strengthening their sense of self. These workshops allow for the individual and collective explorations needed to influence class dynamics and the restoration of students' social networks.

### Sand Play

The Sand Play program is generally offered to preschoolers, but children up to grade 2 may also benefit from the workshops. This expressive modality is especially appropriate for young children who have not yet developed the fine motor skills to represent their experiences graphically. Using figurines and ready-made objects, young participants can easily create a concrete representation of their experience (Lacroix et al., 2007). Young children also have difficulty expressing in words what is going on inside them, and such expression is all the more difficult when the experience deals with loss or trauma. Interventions based on symbolic play can give refugee children tools to express themselves in a non-verbal way (Adler-Nevo & Manassis, 2005). Based on these principles, the Sand Play workshops allow for symbolic expression and exploration through play and are used to facilitate the social adjustment of immigrant and refugee children who are at their first steps in the Canadian school system. These workshops foster solidarity by offering the opportunity to share with peers in a tolerant, respectful, and open manner.

When participating in the Sand Play program, the class is divided into groups of four children who share a set of figurines and two blue sandboxes (50 cm × 70 cm × 12 cm each) that are divided by a removable piece. The children can create three-dimensional images in the sand with figurines representing different worlds and countries: people, deities, animals, as well as objects related to transportation, housing, food, and nature. Introducing a choice of figurines representing a variety of religious and cultural elements is important when working with children from diverse ethno-cultural backgrounds as it offers culturally relevant ways to express their experience (Lacroix et al., 2007). The Sand Play follows a structure that is repeated week after week to secure a routine with children so they can anticipate what will happen. As a means to create continuity, the class sings the same action song at the beginning of each workshop. The opening ritual facilitates the transition from normal school activity to Sand Play. Next, children are invited to share with others through answering a question that deals with themes common to all but that allows personal expression as well (e.g., What is your favourite game? Who is taking you to school?). Non-directed play time, which constitutes the main portion of the workshop, follows. During this period, children have the opportunity, if desired, to tell the story of their three-dimensional image to their teacher or their peers while playing. The workshops end with the same action song, which acts as a closing ritual.

The Sand Play workshops foster solidarity through different channels. Because children share a sandbox, every image they create is influenced by their subgroup and by the social activity in the class, so their creations are often individual *and* collective expressions.

### VIGNETTE 1

Two six-year-old girls took advantage of the possibility to remove the wood separation of the sandbox to play together. They started by playing with

**Figure 14.1** A non-threatening island. This image illustrates the final state of the sandbox created by the two girls. Fishes and sharks had disappeared at that point.

human figurines, mostly girls, and decided to invent an island in the sandbox. They wanted the island to be a volcano and shaped the sand to make a mountain, decorating it with feathers, miniature trees, and foliage.

Because the sandbox is painted blue, during their play the girls used the empty coloured space at the bottom to place various fishes and corals. They also added beaches and umbrellas to the scene, as well as people eating on the sand. This world was non-threatening for both of them, regardless of the sharks and the volcano. Since kids play in groups of four in the workshops, the girls' image influenced the scene that the two other children were making. They started to create an island as well, using different materials and placing them according to their own story. In this sandbox, sharks were eating people and people had to retreat under a canopy of very dense foliage because of a devastating storm.

This vignette illustrates how the concrete space of the sandbox allowed an experience lived by one of the girls' families to be replayed; she shared some of her anxiety with the others while they were helping her to be protected during that storm. The four children finally created a world where both safe and threatening islands can cohabit, thereby developing empathy and a sense of belonging together. At the end of the workshop, children from other subgroups

**Figure 14.2** A devastating storm. Again, in the process of transforming their image, the children took out some foliage. But the devastating effects of the storm are clearly visible.

were able to feel that something important had happened in these scenes. Although they were not verbally expressing their emotions, their body language showed how well they were listening and being attentive to their peers' story. No sound could be heard in the classroom, but the quality of their silence reflected the solidarity that unified the group that day, in that moment.

Another example where family dynamics and those from society at large (e.g., war, natural disasters) were represented through play was the way in which the 2005 tsunami was replayed within the workshops, two weeks after it occurred in the Indian Ocean. At that time, TRIT coincidentally offered the Sand Play program to preschoolers coming predominantly from South Asia. Many stories were directly or indirectly related to that natural disaster (Lacroix et al., 2007). When such dynamics are re-enacted and transformed through play into something else, the outcome can influence the child and the class's solidarity in return.

Another important actor in these workshops is the teacher. By allowing children to play without interfering, the teacher agrees to modify his or her usual role of leader to one of active observer. When reflecting on her experience with the Sand Play workshops, one teacher declared that she liked the way non-verbal relationships were encouraged, the way a child looked to her for encouragement, and the way she would encourage the child without directly intervening. Bonds of solidarity between the teacher and her students were created in these gazes, and both children and teacher came to perceive one another differently. By being attentive to the children's play, the teacher shows genuine interest toward her students, which they perceive. This interest may allow the children to feel comfortable enough to share their emotions with their teacher, who may perceive her students differently now that she knows more about them. It is in these transformative processes that the objectives of the intervention can be met.

## Art and Storytelling

The Art and Storytelling program was created for elementary-school–aged children, especially grades 3 to 6. It is particularly appropriate for students between 7 and 11 years. At this age, drawings progressively get more complex as children achieve more control of the drawing tools, materials, and techniques (Joyal, 2003). Later, children are usually increasingly concerned with reproducing reality in their image, a concern that may inhibit them from drawing when they are in high school (Duncum, 1999). The workshops are also appropriate for elementary-school–aged children in relation to children's narrative developmental stages. During the latency age, children develop the complexity of their narrative abilities (Bento & Befi-Lopes, 2010). When they reach the age of 10 or 12, they normally demonstrate growing control over expressive elaboration, which becomes more than solely information transmission (Ukrainetz et al., 2005). The use of creative activities and stories is also well adapted for immigrant and refugee children. When arriving in a new country, these children may experience gaps among the different cultural worlds in which they exist (home, school, home and host society, etc.). In this context, drawing and storytelling give immigrant and refugee children tools to represent those gaps symbolically and create bridges between them (Rousseau et al., 2003). The evolution toward mastery of both drawing and storytelling might enable children to express themselves in a way that communicates both information and emotions. This communication can enhance the feeling of empathy among children and lead to a growing sense of solidarity in the classroom.

The workshops centre on drawing and storytelling. They usually start with a facilitator asking students to form a circle and take part in a mirror game, in which each child is invited to do a movement and a sound that represent how he or she feels. This opening ritual is usually transformed with time as children bring in their own ideas. The movements frequently refer to small games students play during recess time, like hand-clapping games. Most children already know these games, but playing them as a group in the classroom is different from playing them during recess, and children usually feel an increased sense of connection to one another.

The workshops then continue with a storytelling period. Throughout the program, the story can be told in three different manners. At the beginning of the program, the workshop facilitators decide on various stories that reflect themes such as exclusion, migration, acceptance of the other, social justice and sharing, and rituals. To encourage children's participation, the story is told without a book and is adapted to allow children to get involved by making sounds and gestures or by bringing new elements to the story. By mid-program, children have the opportunity to tell stories related to a trip or a journey that they undertook, or the facilitators may guide them through a visualization activity. In the last Art and Storytelling workshops, children are invited to tell the class stories they were told by a family member. The stories can come from their country of origin and may be inspired by real life, or they can be fairy tales and folk tales. The storytelling period provides an interesting opportunity to value multiplicity, especially when children tell the stories themselves. For instance, a child will often tell a fairy tale known by his peers to be similar to "Little Red Riding Hood." When this happens, children usually raise their hands and say, "I know this, but in my story the wolf is a bear!" or "For us, the girl goes in the woods with a friend to visit an old lady who is sick." However, there often are small differences in the story that can reflect cultural variations on the same fairy tale or reflect how a child appropriates the story for him/herself (Rousseau, Bagilishya, Heusch, & Lacroix, 1999; Rousseau et al., 2003). It is therefore interesting to have a small discussion on what is similar or different in the stories while insisting that there is no superior version. By emphasizing acceptance and respect of the other, the Art and Storytelling workshops foster a sense of solidarity that grows as the children go along in the workshops.

The last part of the workshops consists of a free drawing period. At that time, the children are usually invited to form groups of four sitting together at their desks. Each child makes an individual drawing with oil pastels; the drawing may be related to the story told but not necessarily. Even though each child has his or her own sheet of paper, the images produced are often the reflection of a collective creation.

### VIGNETTE 2

In one class, boys were sitting together during the drawing period and each created a unique yet similar image. The theme of the castle and the flaming dragon was adopted by two of them, and it was impossible to disentangle who created what first.

Both children more than probably influenced each other without noticing it, creating a sense of oneness and solidarity in the drawing.

At times, children consciously decide to draw the same subject as their friends; they find pleasure in this similarity. This is what happened when two girls drew a sunset and one of them turned her drawing upside down to complete the sun as a circle. From the looks on their faces, they evidently found pleasure in completing the image together. That moment was a reflection of their solidarity.

By way of combining drawing with myth and storytelling, the intervention aims to foster solidarity by offering a safe and respectful space where students can share their experience. The following vignette illustrates how this process can strengthen relations within the group.

### VIGNETTE 3

During a series of workshops, we were at the stage of progression where children were telling stories about their family or stories

**Figure 14.3** Castles and flaming dragons. Credit: Erit.

that were told to their parents when they were young. We were in a welcoming class during midterm when three children from China joined the class. They did not speak a word of French or English and were obviously feeling very shy and out of place. This group worked well together and manifested their solidarity toward these newcomers when two boys from Bulgaria offered to mime the story told by one of their peers. The story was one of pride because the youngster's grandfather saved people in his village during the Second World War

**Figure 14.4** Rainbow drawings. Credit: Erit.

and received a medal for his bravery. The story was told with details and the two "actors" were taking their role very seriously, wanting to be as close as possible to the original story. Little by little, the story unfolded, and the three Chinese children were touched by the story itself and by the group's joint effort to make them understand the story and therefore be part of the class.

This experience may be about building bridges between past and present, home and school environment, and the here and there

**Figure 14.5** Complementary suns. Credit: Erit.

of students' experience of family history. But it is also about fostering solidarity in the classroom since all the students present worked toward an understanding of the story and created an atmosphere of joy in being together.

In Art and Storytelling, students may express themselves by drawing and telling stories individually, and they can also create together, choosing to modify their creations to share their perception of their real and imaginary worlds. Non-verbal interactions between peers and with the teacher also take part in this process. Both aspects have an impact on how students see themselves and one another, creating solidarity in the classroom.

### Drama Plurality

Our third program consists of theatrical expression interventions that are offered to high school students. Drama activities are appropriate for children because they encompass play, storytelling, and role-playing, activities usually associated with childhood (Moneta & Rousseau, 2008). Theatrical interventions also offer a suitable outlet to adolescents, who are experiencing a transition phase to adulthood that can be emotionally confusing and disturbing. In this sense, drama can offer them a space where they can express their difficulties but also their strengths (Emunah, 1985, 1990). Further, it is possible for adolescents to express their conflicting experiences and try out alternate solutions with peers (MacCormack, 1997). Same-age peers who share similar interests and experiences are in a good position to support one another in their struggles. Indeed, the Drama Plurality program assumes that one way to prevent the exacerbation of behavioural and emotional difficulties that can stem from adolescence, as well as from migratory experiences, is to foster solidarity among high school students.

The Drama Plurality workshops are based on improvisation and, as with our other programs, no performance on the part of the students is sought. This series of workshops unfolds the same way every week for at least 12 weeks; each session lasts 75 minutes. To begin, we share an opening ritual that supports the adolescents in their transition from school to the theatrical space. The opening ritual takes into consideration the level of energy of each participant and allows for the raising or calming of the group's energy to pursue the main objective: create a safe space where adolescents may feel they can express themselves while being supported by the others. The second part of the workshop brings everyone together in a playful game. It allows for the creation of a bond within the group while connecting individuals to their childhoods and ideally to a pleasant experience when they played similar games. A sense of "I know this and I had fun with my friends" is present in the group. Often we will hear "Oh, we have another name for that game!" and "Ha! We used to do three turns instead of one before sitting!" The third part of the workshop gives participants an opportunity to learn theatrical tools while they access emotions and prepare to share them with the group. These theatrical exercises vary from week to week. Some encourage observation and listening while others focus on building a scene together, using fabrics and musical instruments to give a sense of atmosphere, time, and place. The fourth step of the workshop is about telling stories and being able to find alternative scenarios. To do this, participants tell narratives to each other in small groups. The narratives are usually inspired by their personal lives. In their small groups, participants choose one of the narratives to be "played" in front of the large group. The choice of a story often reflects the energy and the capacity of the subgroup to contain and honour the story that emerged at that time. Another time and group would mean the choice of another story. These stories are personal and often find an echo in other participants.

### VIGNETTE 4

A Romanian boy was telling a story about walking with his friends in the forest. In the story, as the day progressed, they enjoyed themselves, eating and swimming in a pond. Soon after, they decided to go back and realized they were lost. They eventually found their way back and arrived at sunrise. This story evoked memories in other adolescents in the class, who narrated also being lost in the forest with friends, family, or alone. These forests, for other members of the larger group, were Amazonian, Asian, and Russian. At last, a new version of the story was made to accommodate all these forests and situations. Thus, the adolescents came to realize that their differences in culture and experience can also be an opportunity to grow emotionally close to one another and that one's story can trigger memories in others.

The closing ritual allows participants to make the transition back to being in school and ready for what follows that day. It is the occasion for them to reflect on the workshop and how they are feeling, what they would like to keep in memory, and what they would like to leave in the theatrical space.

Drama is used as a means to work together as a group. We offer a safe, caring, and playful environment where adolescents can share their thoughts, feelings, and experiences. Students often feel honoured when they hear what their classmates and teachers have to share with them, and they usually receive the stories with respect. Adolescents are encouraged to support one another, and this support can lead to a new solidarity and the collective creation of something meaningful by easing the exploration of various scenarios.

## Conclusion

Fostering solidarity among refugee students is a good way to compensate for the loss of social and family networks they may have experienced when migrating. School-based preventive intervention programs offer a constructive alternative to traditional health services underused by refugee children and youths. The creative expression workshops described in this chapter are especially beneficial for refugee students who might still be experiencing adversity in their daily lives. The novelty of these preventive programs resides in their use of creative arts to promote the creation of a playful atmosphere that allows students to come together and have fun while expressing themselves. These programs also encourage respectful negotiations among peers and allow for increased connections among themselves and with the teacher. The sharing of experiences in a non-threatening way usually generates empathy and understanding and creates solid bonds among youths. These newly created bonds provide the basic support that refugee students need to overcome some of their difficulties.

This chapter has explained how creative expression interventions benefit refugee students by fostering solidarity in the classroom.

While these programs are beneficial to these students in particular, they are likely to have positive effects on non-immigrant students as well. We believe that by offering various ways of communicating and by fostering solidarity, tolerance, and resilience in Canadian classrooms, we are participating in the growth of this generation.

## REFERENCES

Adler-Nevo, G., & Manassis, K. (2005). Psychosocial treatment of pediatric posttraumatic stress disorder: The neglected field of single-incident trauma. *Depression and Anxiety*, 22(4), 177–189. http://dx.doi.org/10.1002/da.20123 Medline:16180209

Bento, A.C., & Befi-Lopes, D.M. (2010, Oct–Dec). Story organization and narrative by school-age children with typical language development. *Pro-Fono*, 22(4), 503–508. http://dx.doi.org/10.1590/S0104-56872010000400024 Medline:21271107

Brindis, C.D., Klein, J., Schlitt, J., Santelli, J., Juszczak, L., & Nystrom, R.J. (2003, Jun). School-based health centers: Accessibility and accountability. *Journal of Adolescent Health*, 32(6 Suppl), 98–107. http://dx.doi.org/10.1016/S1054-139X(03)00069-7 Medline:12782448

Duncum, P. (1999). A multiple pathways/multiple endpoints model of graphic development. *Visual Arts Research*, 25(2), 38–47.

Emunah, R. (1985). Drama therapy and adolescent resistance. *Arts in Psychotherapy*, 12(2), 71–79. http://dx.doi.org/10.1016/0197-4556(85)90025-5

Emunah, R. (1990). Expression and expansion in adolescence: The significance of creative arts therapy. *Arts in Psychotherapy*, 17(2), 101–107. http://dx.doi.org/10.1016/0197-4556(90)90019-M

Hodes, M. (2000). Psychological distressed refugee children in the United Kingdom. *Child Psychology and Psychiatry Review*, 5(2), 57–68. http://dx.doi.org/10.1017/S136064170000215X

Hong, L., Yufeng, W., Agho, K., & Jacobs, J. (2011, May). Preventing behavior problems among elementary schoolchildren: Impact of a universal school-based program in China. *Journal of School Health*, 81(5), 273–280. http://dx.doi.org/10.1111/j.1746-1561.2011.00592.x Medline:21517867

Howard, M., & Hodes, M. (2000, Mar). Psychopathology, adversity, and service utilization of young refugees. *Journal of the American Academy of Child and Adolescent Psychiatry*, 39(3), 368–377. http://dx.doi.org/10.1097/00004583-200003000-00020 Medline:10714058

Jaycox, L.H., Cohen, J.A., Mannarino, A.P., et al. (2010, Apr). Children's mental health care following Hurricane Katrina: A field trial of trauma-focused psychotherapies. *Journal of Traumatic Stress*, 23(2), 223–231. http://dx.doi.org/10.1002/jts.20518 Medline:20419730

Joyal, B. (2003). *L'évolution graphique: du premier trait gribouillé à l'œuvre plus complexe.* Sainte-Foy: Presses de l'Université du Québec.

Lacroix, L., Rousseau, C., Gauthier, M.-F., Singh, A., Giguère, N., & Lemzoudi, Y. (2007). Immigrant and refugee preschoolers' sandplay representations of the tsunami. *Arts in Psychotherapy*, 34(2), 99–113. http://dx.doi.org/10.1016/j.aip.2006.09.006

MacCormack, T. (1997, Jun). Believing in make-believe: Looking at theater as a metaphor for psychotherapy. *Family Process*, 36(2), 151–169. http://dx.doi.org/10.1111/j.1545-5300.1997.00151.x Medline:9248825

McArdle, P., Moseley, D., Quibell, T., et al. (2002, Sep). School-based indicated prevention: A randomised trial of group therapy. *Journal of Child Psychology and Psychiatry, and Allied Disciplines*, 43(6), 705–712. http://dx.doi.org/10.1111/1469-7610.00091 Medline:12236606

Moneta, I., & Rousseau, C. (2008). Emotional expression and regulation in a school-based drama workshop for immigrant adolescents with behavioral and learning difficulties. *Arts in Psychotherapy, 35*(5), 329–340. http://dx.doi.org/10.1016/j.aip.2008.07.001

Morantz, G., Rousseau, C., & Heymann, J. (2012). The divergent experiences of children and adults in the relocation process: Perspectives of child and parent refugee claimants in Montreal. *Journal of Refugee Studies, 25*(1), 71–92. http://dx.doi.org/10.1093/jrs/fer025

Nelson, A., McClintock, C., Perez-Ferguson, A., Shawver, M.N., & Thompson, G. (2008). Storytelling narratives: Social bonding as key for youth at risk. *Child and Youth Care Forum, 37*(3), 127–137. http://dx.doi.org/10.1007/s10566-008-9055-5

Nöcker-Ribaupierre, M., & Wölfl, A. (2010). Music to counter violence: A preventative approach for working with adolescents in schools. *Nordic Journal of Music Therapy, 19*(2), 151–161. http://dx.doi.org/10.1080/08098131.2010.489997

Pumariega, A.J., Rogers, K., & Rothe, E. (2005, Oct). Culturally competent systems of care for children's mental health: Advances and challenges. *Community Mental Health Journal, 41*(5), 539–555. http://dx.doi.org/10.1007/s10597-005-6360-4 Medline:16142537

Rousseau, C. (2000). Les réfugiés à notre porte: Violence organisée et souffrance sociale. *Criminologie, 33*(1), 185–201. http://dx.doi.org/10.7202/004743ar

Rousseau, C., Bagilishya, D., Heusch, N., & Lacroix, L. (1999). Jouer en classe autour d'une histoire. Ateliers d'expression créatrice pour les enfants immigrants exposés à la violence sociale. *Prisme, 28,* 88–103.

Rousseau, C., Benoit, M., Gauthier, M.-F., et al. (2007, Jul). Classroom drama therapy program for immigrant and refugee adolescents: A pilot study. *Clinical Child Psychology and Psychiatry, 12*(3), 451–465. http://dx.doi.org/10.1177/1359104507078477 Medline:17953131

Rousseau, C., Benoit, M., Lacroix, L., & Gauthier, M.-F. (2009, Jun). Evaluation of a sandplay program for preschoolers in a multiethnic neighborhood. *Journal of Child Psychology and Psychiatry, and Allied Disciplines, 50*(6), 743–750. http://dx.doi.org/10.1111/j.1469-7610.2008.02003.x Medline:19207622

Rousseau, C., Drapeau, A., & Corin, E. (1997, Apr). The influence of culture and context on the pre- and post-migration experience of school-aged refugees from Central America and Southeast Asia in Canada. *Social Science & Medicine, 44*(8), 1115–1127. http://dx.doi.org/10.1016/S0277-9536(96)00243-2 Medline:9131736

Rousseau, C., Drapeau, A., Lacroix, L., Bagilishya, D., & Heusch, N. (2005, Feb). Evaluation of a classroom program of creative expression workshops for refugee and immigrant children. *Journal of Child Psychology and Psychiatry, and Allied Disciplines, 46*(2), 180–185. http://dx.doi.org/10.1111/j.1469-7610.2004.00344.x Medline:15679526

Rousseau, C., Gauthier, M.-F., Lacroix, L., et al. (2005). Playing with identities and transforming shared realities: Drama therapy workshops for adolescent immigrants and refugees. *Arts in Psychotherapy, 32*(1), 13–27. http://dx.doi.org/10.1016/j.aip.2004.12.002

Rousseau, C., & Heusch, N. (2000). The trip: A creative expression project for refugee and immigrant children. *Art Therapy, 17*(1), 31–40. http://dx.doi.org/10.1080/07421656.2000.10129434

Rousseau, C., Lacroix, L., Bagilishya, D., & Heusch, N. (2003). Working with myths: Creative expression workshops for immigrant and refugee children in a school setting. *Art Therapy, 20*(1), 3–10. http://dx.doi.org/10.1080/07421656.2003.10129630

Rousseau, C., Lacroix, L., Singh, A., Gauthier, M.-F., & Benoit, M. (2005, Aug). Creative expression workshops in school: Prevention programs for immigrant and refugee children. *Canadian Child and Adolescent Psychiatry Review, 14*(3), 77–80. Medline:19030511

Rousseau, C., Singh, A., Lacroix, L., Bagilishya, D., & Measham, T. (2004, Feb). Creative expression workshops for immigrant and refugee children. *Journal of the American Academy of Child and Adolescent Psychiatry, 43*(2), 235–238. http://dx.doi.org/10.1097/00004583-200402000-00021 Medline:14726732

Saechao, F., Sharrock, S., Reicherter, D., et al. (2012, Feb). Stressors and barriers to using mental health services among diverse groups of first-generation immigrants to the United States. *Community Mental Health Journal, 48*(1), 98–106. http://dx.doi.org/10.1007/s10597-011-9419-4 Medline:21655942

Salloum, A., & Overstreet, S. (2008, Jul). Evaluation of individual and group grief and trauma interventions for children post disaster. *Journal of Clinical Child and Adolescent Psychology, 37*(3), 495–507. http://dx.doi.org/10.1080/15374410802148194 Medline:18645741

Sassen, G., Spencer, R., & Curtin, P.C. (2005). Art from the Heart: A relational-cultural approach to using art therapy in a group for urban middle school girls. *Journal of Creativity in Mental Health, 1*(2), 67–79. http://dx.doi.org/10.1300/J456v01n02_07

Silove, D., Steel, Z., McGorry, P., & Mohan, P. (1998, Mar). Trauma exposure, postmigration stressors, and symptoms of anxiety, depression and post-traumatic stress in Tamil asylum-seekers: Comparison with refugees and immigrants. *Acta Psychiatrica Scandinavica, 97*(3), 175–181. http://dx.doi.org/10.1111/j.1600-0447.1998.tb09984.x Medline:9543304

Stein, B.D., Jaycox, L.H., Kataoka, S.H., et al. (2003, Aug 6). A mental health intervention for schoolchildren exposed to violence: A randomized controlled trial. *Journal of the American Medical Association, 290*(5), 603–611. http://dx.doi.org/10.1001/jama.290.5.603 Medline:12902363

Ukrainetz, T.A., Justice, L.M., Kaderavek, J.N., Eisenberg, S.L., Gillam, R.B., & Harm, H.M. (2005, Dec). The development of expressive elaboration in fictional narratives. *Journal of Speech, Language, and Hearing Research: JSLHR, 48*(6), 1363–1377. http://dx.doi.org/10.1044/1092-4388(2005/095) Medline:16478377

# 15

## "More than winning the lottery"

### The academic experiences of refugee youth in Canadian universities

Martha K. Ferede

> I can't tell you how it feels like. It's like even more than winning a lottery ... you had no hope that you are going to university, even though it's the thing you most wanted to do. And then the second thing is not only are you going to university but also you are going to Canada ... so it's ... I can't explain it to you. It's the best thing that has ever happened to me.

Viola values the opportunity she gained through the World University Service of Canada (WUSC) Student Refugee Program "more than winning a lottery." She is not alone in her exulting assessment. Other refugee youth express gratitude, in large part for WUSC's provision of "access to university" that has given them a "second chance in life" without which they say they may have been "on the streets," "doing nothing in the camps," or simply "somehow surviving." However, as much as resettlement into Canada and entry into university are substantial improvements from a harsh refugee existence, this new life, whereby students are thrust into demanding academic programs within weeks of arrival, is not without its challenges. The academic experiences of WUSC refugee students are varied and complicated, a patchwork of struggles and triumphs.

In this chapter, the multifaceted narratives of students' post-secondary education are organized in three parts. First, I examine refugee youths' academic challenges, grouping them under those arising from misaligned expectations and those they experience without preconceptions.[1] Next, I explore the supports and resources that refugee students say facilitate their academic adjustment. Then I provide detailed profiles of three students; two embody recurrent trajectory patterns, while one, who counters the trends, stands distinct from the others. The purpose of these profiles is to discern the arc of the academic trajectory of WUSC students. By their very definition, trajectories require a sweeping gaze across time; it is only through understanding students' narratives in their complicated wholeness and integrity that the neatly contained snapshots of evidence come together to create an authentic image of students' lived experiences.[2]

## Research impetus

There are many reasons to care about the university education and experiences of refugees. We know that a university education—and completion of a bachelor's degree in particular—offers important individual and social benefits including a gateway to upward social and economic mobility (Baum & Ma, 2007; Bowen, Kurzweil, Tobin, & Pichler, 2005). Yet very little is known about refugees' experiences and trajectories in Canadian universities. While there is a growing body of research on the higher education experience of refugees in other top resettlement countries such as the United States, Australia, and the United Kingdom, there is little scholarship specific to the Canadian context.[3] Due to the Canadian government's privacy laws and a lack of systematic collection of refugee status by Canada's educational systems, refugees are often combined with other immigrants in educational research (Kaprielian-Churchill & Churchill, 1994). However, since refugees' pre-arrival experiences often differ in important ways from those of voluntary immigrants, research that discerns their distinct experiences is warranted (Herman, 1992). Since only refugees are sponsored into the Student Refugee Program, researchers are able to target this population to understand their unique experiences.

The study also contributes to the methodology that informs the nature of what we understand about refugees' experiences. Existing research on refugees in Canada is largely quantitative and focuses predominately on economic outcomes and mental health issues. These are important topics that require attention; however, they do not tell the whole story. Through research that uncovers perceptions, narratives, and lived experiences founded on rich contextual information, this study fulfills the urgent need for qualitative work.

## Organizational context

The World University Service of Canada (WUSC) is the organizational site of the study. While there are other Canadian sponsoring agencies, churches, and organizations that resettle refugees—sponsorship-agreement holders (SAHs)—WUSC's Student Refugee Program (SRP) is the only one with an explicit post-secondary education agenda.[4] The SRP is also unique in that it is primarily a student-driven endeavour mobilized by groups of students, faculty, and staff on university campuses across Canada. These local committees, present at 80 universities and colleges, espouse WUSC's goal to "promote global understanding and cooperation and increase understanding of international development issues on campus and in the community" and agree to have at least one WUSC-related activity per year (WUSC, 2012). Not all WUSC local committees decide to be involved in the Student Refugee Program; as of 2011, out of 80 universities and colleges with local committees, 61 local committees sponsored refugee youth on their campus. From 1978 to 2011, local committee members sponsored 1,216 refugee youth into Canada.

## Refugee youth and education

Little has been written about the higher education access and experiences of refugee youth in the Canadian context. However, the existing Canadian literature and scholarship in other Western resettlement countries such as the US, Australia, and the UK provide insights as to pertinent considerations.

A Toronto-based study using focus groups and personal interviews with Afghan, Karen, and Sudanese refugees determined that refugee youth develop high aspirations for higher education as a positive response to their limited educational opportunities before arrival (Shakya et al., 2010). Youth also aspire to higher education because they view these credentials as providing them with an easier entryway into the Canadian labour market. However, despite high aspirations, refugees face considerable challenges in accessing and completing their post-secondary studies. Shakya et al. (2010) indicate that while other migrant youth also face post-migration familial responsibilities such as needing to translate documents for their parents, for refugee youth, familial responsibilities are more difficult and "acutely" experienced. This difference is due in part to many refugee youths' becoming the family's breadwinner, a role reversal that often complicates their educational goals.

Pre-arrival factors appear to contribute to higher education access. One study (Hannah, 1999) used interviews and document review to examine the higher education access and support of refugees in Sydney, Australia. Pre-arrival factors such as interrupted education, trauma, having little financial capital, and non-recognition of credentials were related to limited access to post-secondary education. Trusting relationships with advisors working at migrant resource centres were positive for access, allowing refugees to connect with valuable information, guidance, and support in familiarizing refugees with the Australian higher education system. The study concludes with recommendations that include having institutions become aware of and responsive to refugee students' needs, maintaining strong data on how students from refugee backgrounds fare within institutions, and educating refugees at the outset about the academic and social support services available to them.

Another Australian-based study that examined the university experiences of students with refugee backgrounds recommends that higher-education institutions offer specific programs for refugee youth to induct them into the university environment and culture (Joyce, Earnest, De Mori, & Silvagni, 2010). Using semi-structured interviews with 11 participants from Eritrea, Liberia, Sierra Leone, Somalia, Sudan, and Uganda, the researchers determined that university students with refugee backgrounds face several challenges that are not recognized by higher education institutions. These challenges include language barriers, financial stress, and differences in educational style from their country of origin. They also include refugees' feelings of anxiety and stress at not being able to understand the university system. Joyce et al. (2010) report that "for many students the university is a culturally alienating place [and that] programs may need to be developed that enable students to become active members of a learning community and have a sense of belonging to this culture" (p. 94).

Education seems to contribute to refugee youths' enhanced coping and positive identity formation (Rutter & Jones, 1998). Mosselson's (2006) study on US refugee youth in secondary institutions offers an intriguing assessment of the empowering function of education. First, the process of gaining an education provides refugee adolescents with a sense of control in a life that has been mainly defined by chaos. While material objects may be lost or taken, education is perceived as being inalienable. Refugee youth are comforted by the security that their education cannot be taken from them. Second, being a *student* allows refugee youth to transition more smoothly from the immediate designation as *foreigners*. Moreover, since the label of student is imbued with notions of success, it bolsters a positive frame of reference. Mosselson (2006) asserts that education allows refugee youth to "create both a sense of a more secure future and a more secure present" (p. 27). Although this study is based on refugee students at the secondary level, the positive identification associated with being a student may well hold true for university students as well. In fact, we may expect it to be enhanced since university degrees are highly sought after and widely perceived as an essential pathway to social and economic mobility and security.

## Methodology

### Participant selection

The study is limited to refugee youth sponsored into universities. Universities and colleges are distinct institutions in Canada. Universities generally offer three- or four-year bachelor's and graduate degree programs. Colleges typically offer two- to three-year applied arts and science diploma or bachelor's degree programs.[5]

Participants were selected using purposeful sampling (Maxwell, 2005) derived from the population of refugee youth who were sponsored into Canadian post-secondary institutions through the SRP from 2007 to 2011 ($N = 321$). Limiting the study to refugee youth who arrived from 2007 to 2011 allowed for timely and up-to-date inquiry. Moreover, encompassing a range of refugees' arrival years enables understanding of how refugees' academic experiences shift over time—from recent arrivals who were in the country just three months to those who have lived in Canada for half a decade.

### Data collection and analysis

Interview transcripts from over 100 hours of audio recordings, detailed observation notes, and participant profiles provided the main source of data used in analysis. I used in-depth interviews to attend to students' experiences in the context of their life stories. Specifically, I employed a modified version of the three-meeting series interview protocol as outlined by Irving Seidman (2006). In this model, three 90-minute sessions are designed to allow participants to share their life history, provide details of their experiences under study, and offer reflections on these experiences. Altogether, I interviewed a total of 25 refugee youth over 60 days spread across five months; these interviews were conducted in November and December 2011 and April, May, and June 2012. Due to issues of identity protection, one participant's responses had to be removed from the study, leaving a total of 24 participants.[6]

Rich descriptive data from informal observations of campuses, visit sites, and interview sessions provided an important contextual layer for analyzing students' spoken statements. Review of documents included program records and training manuals, correspondence sent by WUSC executives, WUSC publications for public consumption, and news articles in campus, city, province, and national media outlets.

In addition to organizational documents, I also reviewed and analyzed the 13 academic transcripts that were submitted. I read each transcript, taking note of participants' course selections and progress (such as dropping, retaking courses, or advancing), scrutinizing how particular grades related to course averages, and, for participants who arrived before 2011, examining the development of their GPA across academic years. Since institutions had different evaluation systems, with some offering letter grades and others percentages, I could not conduct a numeric evaluation of the transcripts across participants (for instance, identifying and comparing the average grade percentage at year of entry, second year, etc.). Rather, I took detailed notes on course selections and organized transcripts according to patterns in the way participants tended to progress through their university tenure. By checking participants' academic transcripts against their interview responses, searching for points of corroboration and discrepancy, I was able to triangulate the data and strengthen the integrity of my findings.

The study has several limitations. First, those who volunteered for my study may differ from those who chose not to participate—it is plausible that those who have not adjusted academically or socially were less responsive. Certainly, during interviews I learned that there were students who had discontinued their studies or taken time off to work. However, despite my best efforts to reach out to this group, no student who had left university decided to participate. Furthermore, my study participants are young adults who enter Canada through a unique program. Consequently, I will not be able to generalize the findings to all refugees resettled in Canada. However, while distinct, study participants share crucial pre-arrival experiences with refugees as a whole and in particular with those who have matriculated into universities. Therefore, through careful analysis, I have been able to draw important insights that may be helpful to understanding the higher education experiences of younger generations of refugees resettled in Canada.

## Characteristics of study participants

There were 24 participants in this study (see Table 1). Fifteen participants were male (62.5%) and nine participants were female (37.5%).[7] WUSC-sponsored refugees arriving in 2011 participated at a higher rate than those arriving in 2007, 2008, 2009, or 2010. All study participants originated from African countries and had asylum in the African countries of Kenya and Malawi (see Table 2). Ten of the 24 participants were Rwandese, 6 South Sudanese, and 5 Somali. One participant each originated from Ethiopia, Congo, and Kenya. Seventeen participants (71%) had been sponsored from the asylum country of Kenya, while 7 (29%) of the participants were Rwandese and had been sponsored from Malawi.

**Table 1.** Gender of study participants, by year of entry, 2007–2011

| Characteristic | N | | | % | | |
|---|---|---|---|---|---|---|
| Year of Entry | Total (24) | Female (9) | Male (15) | Total (100%) | Female (37.5%) | Male (62.5%) |
| 2007 | 2 | 0 | 2 | 8.3% | 0.0% | 100.0% |
| 2008 | 5 | 3 | 2 | 20.8% | 60.0% | 40.0% |
| 2009 | 4 | 1 | 3 | 16.7% | 25.0% | 75.0% |
| 2010 | 4 | 2 | 2 | 16.7% | 50.0% | 50.0% |
| 2011 | 9 | 3 | 6 | 37.5% | 33.3% | 66.7% |

Note. $N = 24$

**Table 2.** Study participants' country of asylum, by country of origin, 2007–2011

| Country of Asylum | Country of Origin | 2007 | 2008 | 2009 | 2010 | 2011 | Total | Percent of N |
|---|---|---|---|---|---|---|---|---|
| Kenya | Sudan | 2 | 1 | — | — | 3 | 6 | 25.0% |
| | Somalia | — | 2 | — | 2 | 1 | 5 | 20.8% |
| | Rwanda | — | 1 | 2 | — | — | 3 | 12.5% |
| | Ethiopia | — | 1 | — | — | — | 1 | 4.2% |
| | Democratic Republic of Congo | — | — | 1 | — | — | 1 | 4.2% |
| | Kenya (born into refuge) | — | — | — | — | 1 | 1 | 4.2% |
| Kenya Total | | 2 | 5 | 3 | 2 | 5 | 17 | 70.8% |
| Malawi | Rwanda | — | — | 1 | 2 | 4 | 7 | 29.2% |
| | | | | | | | Total | Percent of N |
| Total Across All Countries | | 2 | 5 | 4 | 4 | 9 | 24 | 100% |

Note. $N = 24$

## Findings

### Academic expectations and challenges

The thrill students experience when they are first accepted into the WUSC program gives way to apprehension during the first few weeks in Canadian universities. The adjustment students need to make is profound; they undergo what I call "academic culture shock."[8] Sometimes the reality of university work and life runs counter to students' stated expectation; at other times, students encounter significant difficulties that they had not anticipated (see Table 3).

**Table 3.** Expectations versus reality of Canadian institutions

| Expectation | Reality |
|---|---|
| Easy, not hard work | Very hard work |
| Professors follow up on you for work | You must be responsible for own work |
| Can start right away in career track major (such as medicine and law) | Some career tracks require undergraduate work first |
| Majority male classrooms | Gender-balanced or heavily female classrooms |

Nearly half of the refugees imagined that the work in Canadian universities would be easy, requiring little effort on their part. This seems counterintuitive; after all, students are entering a higher level of schooling. When I asked Munira why she expected not to have to work hard in university, for instance, she told me that the stubborn "myth that Western education is easy" is based on a pre-arrival belief that "everything is done by computers ... you have a lot of resources [so] you don't have to do a lot of work." This is precisely what Christopher thought; he "had this feeling things were going to be simple." After a few weeks in the academic environment, a sobering reality set in. Munira admitted that although "you have a lot more resources, you still have to put in the work," while Christopher "wishe[d] someone had told me the reality, that it is not really simple and I'm going to actually study hard, harder than I ever had." Somebody most likely did tell him "the reality," even though he never registered hearing about it. As part of their pre-arrival training, WUSC students are provided with orientation on the nature and difficulty of Canadian universities. Yet some students' lingering belief of the ease of post-secondary academic work suggests other dynamics are at play. Since there is considerable difference between hearing something and experiencing it in person, the WUSC briefing on academic work may not be resonating on a meaningful level for many refugee youth. It is also possible that the cognitive dissonance is too great: the myth that students have internalized and what they are told could be too divergent to reconcile. Finally, with all the apprehension about leaving their family and transitioning into a new life and culture, perhaps minimizing the academic element is a coping mechanism that helps students to lessen their anxiety.

While only some students are surprised about work difficulty, nearly every refugee student was surprised to find that Canadian university professors have a less hands-on teaching style than educators in

African high schools. They anticipate teachers who conduct "roll call," follow up with them to see whether assignments are complete, and administer punishment if they are not. Nadifa describes the "great difference" between her high school teachers and university faculty:

> When I was in high school it was like it is spoon feeding because teachers used to write everything, they used to say everything. So here it was all different—the professor will just stand there and just says. In high school, the teacher may ask you directly a question, "How are you finding this? Have you done the homework?" But here the professor will just say an assignment is due on that day. ... There is no punishment. In high school if you don't do your exercise, teachers used to punish students but here, there is no punishment.

Like Nadifa, Victor from South Sudan also finds it strange that "everything is voluntary." Without prompting, he failed to attend lectures or complete problem sets. He reflects,

> Actually like the first semester, I did poorly, because I sat there waiting everything that used to be done to me in Africa. I thought the professor would tell me, "Why are you not bringing it to me? Can you bring me your assignment for marking?"

According to Victor, the difference boils down to the "teacher-centred" classrooms he was used to and the "pupil-centred" Canadian teaching style.[9] He shared that back in the "teacher-centred" classroom, "you followed what they [the teachers] do. If the teacher doesn't say that *do this*, you cannot do that. But here you have to discover it." It was not until nearly the end of his first semester that he recognized "nobody cared about what you are doing." At that moment, Victor experienced an important perspective shift. When he thought attending lectures and completing assignments were mandatory, he waited for someone to push him to do the work. Yet when he realized the responsibility fell to him, Victor says that he began to view doing academic work as a "right" and an opportunity to "be disciplined."[10]

In addition to discovering student-centred education, many refugee students arrive expecting to enroll immediately in study areas that are graduate-level programs in Canada—particularly in law and medicine. Victor reveals that he "would have preferred to be a lawyer, but when I came here I found out the road to law school is blocked." He elaborates on what he means:

> In Africa, if you want to be a lawyer you just go to a law school, right from first year—you are a lawyer ... When you finish your high school, if you go decide to be a doctor, you go to med school, if you have decided you want to be a teacher, you go to teacher school. But when I came to Canada, it's different. There's an undergrad degree and there's a grad degree.

Of course, the pathways to law and medicine are not literally blocked. However, since they cannot be studied at the undergraduate level, for refugee students like Victor, the road is much longer and more onerous than they expected.

Finally, students arrive expecting the heavily male composition they are used to in Kenyan and Malawian high schools. To their astonishment, in Canada they discover university classrooms with more gender parity and even some classes where women constitute the majority of students.[11] Ayan describes her surprise when she entered her first class:

> My first class, Chemistry, was quite shocking ... there were like 90 students and I would say maybe 15 or even less than that were guys in the class. And to me that was so shocking because ... I'd never been to a classroom where there were like 80 girls and there are like 10 boys, you know? So it was the reverse of where I went to school. I was like *Wow, this is really crazy. What are all these girls doing here?*

Similar to understanding the professor's role or what constitutes undergraduate versus graduate degrees, becoming accustomed to the new class composition requires a calibration of expectations grounded in experience. These mental adjustments are neither severe nor prolonged. In this manner, they differ from the other challenges that students say feel "overwhelming."

The majority of refugee students express experiencing tremendous academic difficulties in their first academic year. These numerous challenges span instructional and curricular concerns.[12] They also include difficulties with language and navigating relationships with faculty.

### Accents and silence

To be eligible for the WUSC program, refugee students are required to have a working knowledge of English or French—the two official Canadian languages.[13] Since English is the teaching language of Kenyan and Malawian high schools, students arrive with years of exposure and training. However, due to English often being their third or fourth language, many are functionally but not fully fluent, especially in terms of grammar.[14] As just one example, Steven, a 23-year-old South Sudanese who was a refugee in Kenya, spoke Lokuto, Lopit, Toposa, Arabic, and Kiswahili before he learned English (he told me Lokuto is his "real mother tongue").

Through their WUSC pre-arrival training, students attend language lessons to help them with the Test of English as a Foreign Language (TOEFL), which is part of most universities' admissions criteria. However, students are trained by non-native speakers and thus become familiar with hearing English imbued with Kenyan or Malawian accents. They are not consciously aware that this difference is an issue until they arrive at the first day of their university lectures and are shocked and horrified to find that they have little idea of what their professor is saying:

> Molende (2009): So like you know in the Kenyan English we have like in *Give me wata*, ER is like A like open mouth but here ER is like ERR [like] *watur* ... and other small differences like African accents inside the English. So the first day of lecture ... I was like *Wow, what is she talking about?*

> Munira (2008): If you sit in an hour-long lecture and you don't understand a single thing that anyone says, you feel very dumb and you ... feel very frightened, that you are going to fail and stuff.

> Christine (2011): Like my first days I was finding it hard; especially Biology because the professor would pronounce words very fast. He had that speed, he had very, very quick speed and I couldn't get him that much.

In initial lectures, refugee students grasp little of the material covered because of professors' rapid speech combined with their "Canadian" English accents. With time and repeated exposure, however, students increasingly understand more and more. As Victor states, his ears began to adjust to the Canadian way of speaking in a matter of a few weeks:

> When I came I couldn't hear.... I didn't understand my professor. I tried to move to a closer seat on the front bench. I still didn't get it. So I went to my local committee member and said, "I should drop this course." He said, "No, just wait. You'll get it." So after two weeks, I said, "Oh! This professor, I think his English has improved."

Comprehending professors' accents is one challenge that all refugee students in the study seem to overcome within the first semester. However, many students find that understanding cultural references, examples, and jokes takes much longer. This is true not just of professors' words but of classmates' comments and questions. For example, Munira's sense of isolation was so deep that she shrouded herself in silence for years. She describes feeling unlike the gregarious student she had been in Kenya:

> I didn't even talk in the class for the first two years here.... I couldn't do the conversation; I cannot get the jokes.... Unless I see someone from back home, that I met somewhere, I wouldn't even giggle. [In Kenya] I was laughing all the time, getting thrown out of class for laughing and sent home. And then I come here, I cannot keep up with the jokes. Like if the professor makes a reference and you have no idea where that comes from. But [back at] your place, you spend all this time being a social person, feeling good about yourself, having

a good self-esteem, being confident to speak up in a group. And then you come here and it was just ... I was just telling one of my [WUSC] friends, at registration [who] was scared. I said, "I didn't speak in class for the first two years. If I knew everything that I feel I know now, I would talk. I wouldn't care about accents, I wouldn't care about people not getting me; I would still say something. But I didn't. For the first two years, I just went to class, I sat there, I did my exams. I didn't talk."

Munira's revelation that in hindsight she "wouldn't care about people not getting me" points to another important concern for refugee students when it comes to feeling and being understood—their *own* accents. Not only do refugee students think their accent is incomprehensible to others; they also fear that it will alert others to their foreignness and, perhaps by proxy, signify a lack of intelligence. Patrice says he felt his accent would bring unwanted attention, something that he found particularly embarrassing in large lecture auditoriums. Like many other students, he preferred to remain silent by avoiding questions or clarifications (leaving holes in his own understanding of course material) rather than be exposed:

If you ask a question, and you're in a class of let's say of a hundred students, and you raise your hand and you ask a professor a question, because of your accent he makes you repeat it like maybe two times. And by that time the whole class is looking at you, so they get to say, "Who is this person?" And they realize that you look different. They realize that you have this strange accent ... There were some questions that I was like *Maybe this is stupid to ask because maybe everybody else knows it except me?*

Even in instances when students know the answers to questions posed in class, they limit their participation for fear of not being understood. Ayan describes what stops her from responding:

[The professor] was asking a question, and I'm thinking, if I raise my hand—I know the question—maybe he wouldn't understand my accent. I had that fear, you know? Like maybe what if what he says *Oh, I don't get you?*

On the other hand, refugee students feel somewhat less shy and self-conscious about approaching professors during office hours, outside the critical gaze of hundreds of other students. Ayan told me that "after a month" she "still didn't ask questions in the class" but instead summoned up her courage and met with her biology professor during office hours. She remembers feeling nervous, thinking,

So, the first time I was like *OK, I really don't know how this will go, but I just have to go,* you know? And I asked him, I went and he was like *OK, sit down* and he was really, really kind to me. And when he didn't understand what I was saying, he was like *Can you say it again?* ... He was really patient with me. I was like *OK, now I can talk to my professor, I can talk to anyone!*

Although there is variation among individuals, as a group, female students in this study took longer to approach and build connections with faculty. Jeanne, who is on the extreme end, told me it took her two years to approach her professors. When she finally did, she found her professors "really helpful." When I asked her why she waited so long to speak with them, she admitted that she didn't realize how to take the initiative to establish a connection. She "regrets" recognizing so late that faculty "won't just come up to you and like help you. You, actually, have to be the one approaching them and ask for help." Even when Jeanne finally spoke up, she didn't know how to ask to be placed on projects, a fact she now feels put her at a disadvantage for medical school applications. Again she did not know she could "ask them if they would be willing to direct me to something or even someone or if they knew of any [research] opportunity." Ayan explained that refugee students have difficulty interacting with faculty members because of a disconcerting informality they notice with other students. She elaborates:

> There is a high amount of respect between the student and a teacher [in Kenya] and that's the kind of life I grew up. And I came here and I'm like whoa ... The relationship between professors and students is like two friends, kind of people who are peers, that is the way it is ...
> I guess maybe because it is a university and the professors themselves are thinking the students are more mature.

The casual student–faculty relationship confounded Ayan. She was also shocked when students were openly dismissive, "saying some negative things about the professors or like reading in the class." Like Ayan, Christine was also surprised with the familiarity between student and teacher. Unlike her peers, she refuses to address her professors by their first name:

> If he's like, Mr. Chris and the surname, they just call him by the first name.... I can't do that to my teacher because I respect him a lot. I call him Sir. I can't call him by his first name because I respect him. He is older than me but students here they just call, if it's Jane, *Hey, Jane* or Katherine, *Hey, Katherine*. But I can't do that, I'm not used to that.

For newcomers, trying to understand the rules of a new environment is par for the course. However, for refugee students, it is difficult to understand how to communicate with professors who differ from one another in either encouraging or discouraging a formal association with their students. In this case, the data shows that regardless of their peers' behaviour or professors' suggestion, refugee students seem comfortable maintaining a much more formal and "respectful" distance with their teachers.

## Making progress

The layered and intersecting issues of missing knowledge content, gaps between high school and university, and the unrelenting volume and pace of Canadian university curricula pose significant challenges for refugee students. Yet despite these considerable setbacks, every participant in the study reported making academic strides and improvement. How were they able to do so? In this section, I explore this question, paying particular attention to the resources and relationships students identify as catalyzing their academic progress.

### Academic resources

For WUSC students, the difference between the access to resources in Kenya and Malawi and that in Canadian universities is not a contrast between less and more. It might better be described as the difference between scarcity and abundance. Overnight, students shift from having a handful of books that are often shared, little to no technology, and limited skills support to having practically every academic resource at their fingertips.

In addition to resources such as computing centres and libraries, WUSC students make extensive use of university offices dedicated to academic support. This is particularly true of writing centres. Most refugee students, but particularly those in writing-intensive programs (such as political science), have much to learn about formulating well-researched, correctly cited, and effectively written essays and reports. Charlotte, a global studies major, shared that her local committee directed her to the writing centre, where "they taught me how to write from the ground, how to first put my thoughts together and explain my paragraph and do the conclusion, and all that." She acknowledges struggling initially, but by "the second term I had already gotten all the concepts that I needed to write an essay." Many students also use math centres that offer directed help. In addition, a few students like Victor are able to apply for bursaries through their math departments for private tutoring.

### Academic support from teaching faculty, study groups, and advisors

Although libraries, computers, writing centres, and math centres provide important supports, refugee students claim that it is the advice and guidance from faculty and peer study groups that provide the essential supports of their academic development.

Once students learn to connect and establish relationships with faculty, professors become important sources of support. Eric said that his math professor gave him books to help him become familiar with the content covered in Canadian high schools. Telling Eric he "has to catch up," the professor also provided additional time to "offer clarifications" as needed. In addition, if refugee students explained their challenges, some faculty members were willing to provide a certain leeway, such as extensions on assignments or not counting initial weak exam scores.

Jacob told me that after his first year he learned that building relationships with faculty was important to "pass[ing] my courses." He discloses:

> I started being close to the profs; that's one of the key things in Canada. That's what I've realized ... if you know the profs it would be easy to access [them], to ask them questions even if you're at home and you're doing assignment then you e-mail them ... Then they reply to you. You can do your assignment and you pass it. So I started being close to the profs.... that's how everybody else is doing, those who pass.

Teaching assistants also serve as important supports. Jeanne shared that she really began to make academic strides in the summer following her first year. When I asked her what happened, she said she began "attending tutorials that are offered by other people, student groups, people that were just there volunteering, or even talking to my TA." In these conversations, she learned about past exams that were sold by her school's math association—exams that proved to be tremendously helpful in understanding the types of questions to expect.

Students also say classmates are important for helping their academic progress. Asad told me he sets out "to build relationships" with classmates. He does so by finding "someone who is answering a question" in his various courses and then approaching them afterward to "make contact." Clearly, Asad is strategic in targeting and acquainting himself with those he perceives are informed classmates. While to a lesser degree of intentionality, Mor-Anyar believes that rather than "locking yourself in" and studying alone, it is more "productive" to collaborate with classmates who may help you grasp concepts that would "take a week to figure out yourself." Jeanne also shares his views, touting the value of study groups sharing:

> I really found them really helpful because there's always this one thing you just wouldn't get and there's someone in the group who actually has got it. So it's people coming together with maybe different ideas. Everyone has something that they really understood that you didn't get or didn't even think it was necessary. And when they explain it to you, it's really nice. And when you're even explaining to the people in your group, it actually enhances your understanding more and you're even able to remember so much better, I find.

On the other hand, although he agrees that study groups are "very good," Jacob is wary about students who "do not care what grade they get in a specific course; [and they] will free-ride and then that's not a good thing." Still, he finds that most students are "serious with their work."

The majority of students also mention that university academic advisors are important sources of support in navigating the academic pathway. This guidance is especially important in the first few years, as students are familiarizing themselves with the course catalogue and program options. Not all students find advisors helpful, however. A few students, including Asad, trust students much more than they do their academic advisors. Asad believes when he asks students "which course is harder," they will not "lie" to him. On the other hand, he says advisors "don't know anything because they didn't do the course." In fact, he believes that advisors direct him to a *more* difficult path:

> It is good to talk to students if they did the course instead of talking to academic advisors. Talk to the students and tell them, "You know what, Eco 209 and Eco 200, if there are these two substitutes, which one do you think I should take and which professor is better?" And they said, "You know what, do not even attempt to go to this." Students are way better than to go to the academic advisors. They [advisors] recommend the hardest course and the hardest professor [because] they want to make money. Students drop the course, take it again, and the university makes money.

In his comments, Asad appears suspicious of advisors, believing them to be in cahoots with a greedy university that is failing students to earn additional tuition revenue. This seems to be a rather cynical perception. Perhaps Asad's distrust is an extension of the palpable fear of failure that seems to be rampant among WUSC students. This fear seems to take root when WUSC students, who were often top elementary and high school students, arrive and face numerous challenges and barriers in Canadian universities. If they receive low grades on their first few exams or assignments, panic sets in.[15] Even if they make a strong performance, no longer being the top student seems to shake these refugee youth to the core. This change may skew their perception of just how well they are doing. For instance, Asad told me several times that he wished his grades were higher. When I reviewed his transcripts, I was surprised to find his grades in difficult courses were much higher than the class averages.

## Three academic trajectory trends

Here I use student profiles to illustrate the three trajectory patterns that have emerged among study participants: *Steady Risers*, *Dippers*, and *Instant Achievers*. Mor-Anyar exemplifies the most common trajectory arc of WUSC students, the Steady Riser. As a Dipper, Munira is emblematic of the second-most typical trajectory pattern, and as an

Instant Achiever, Molende stands out for his immediate and consistent high grades.

## Mor-Anyar: A steady riser

In 1995, with his "teachers on the battlefields" during the war between the Sudanese government and the "rebels," young Mor-Anyar had no opportunity for schooling. Comforted by the blessing of his widowed mother who saw no other way, he separated from her to flee to Kenya with an uncle and cousin. Mor-Anyar entered school in the second grade and completed his elementary education in Kakuma refugee camp. "There was some insecurity," he recalls; "the locals were not happy about the refugees who they thought were living better lives."[16] At the time, Jesuit Refugee Service (JRS) provided scholarships for the top 15 refugee students to attend Kenyan high schools. Mor-Anyar worked diligently, did well on his exams, and successfully secured a scholarship.[17] Situated far from the camp in the Kenyan countryside, the boarding school environment was difficult, with "water shortage," "high temperatures," and "food that wasn't that great." However, Mor-Anyar benefited from a high-quality education.

His plane ride to Toronto as a WUSC-sponsored student was punctuated by musings: *What will Canada be like? And how do I settle? What if somebody doesn't show up? What's my future?* To his relief, Mor-Anyar was warmly received at the airport. He was immediately placed in his campus dorm, which, two weeks before the start of the term, felt "a little bit empty." Mor-Anyar had been "away from school for like two years" and felt "excited" about university, spending his initial weeks reflecting on how useful his degree in electrical engineering would be to the development of South Sudan, where he hoped to return. Mor-Anyar's first two classes of physics and chemistry went well; these were subjects he had studied in high school. Yet Mor-Anyar soon found "things very strange" as he entered into courses where "it was the first time seeing them." He "struggled" with the course Engineering Graphics and Calculus. He describes feeling bewildered and confounded by his requirements, thinking,

> Okay, electrical engineering, so [I thought] I will be dealing with circuits, I would be dealing with transistors, I would be dealing with, what do you call it? Electronics? But here I was, dealing with computers; [I wondered] why would I be doing a programming course when I'm an Electrical Engineer? Why would I being doing Geography?

Bewildered, Mor-Anyar spoke with his professors, who referred him to teaching assistants, who in turn helped him "go through Excel and things to do with Microsoft" so that he could do his reports and "compile all my data." Still, he found it "really tough." In hindsight, he believes part of the problem was that he "locked himself in his room" trying to "figure out problems by myself." Over a period of two years, however, Mor-Anyar opened up, making friends and studying with other students. He recalls the benefits of creating an academic community:

> If you lock yourself, you'll be struggling and yes doing the work but not being that productive. But then if you connect with other people and you chat, even over random stuff, just a friendly chat, talking, you will have a different mood after that, and you will be a little bit happy. And when you come back it will be good break from your studies and when you begin you are fresh, and you'll do really good work. And for most of the case you will be talking with your classmates about things that you studied in class. So you will get different views, maybe someone will be telling you something that is different from the way you know it.

Mor-Anyar's academic transcript is a testament to an unrelenting spirit. From 2007 to 2011, Mor-Anyar retook several courses multiple times until he earned passing grades and credit. For instance, he took Calculus 1 in his first term (Fall 2007) and second term (Winter 2008) and finally passed it in his third term (Fall 2008). There are other examples of course repetitions, providing evidence of a persistent approach; he retook the courses Intro to Computers in Engineering, Practical Engineering Modules (both A & B) and Micro-Processing Systems each at least twice. With the exception of Computing Science for Engineers in Fall 2010, in which he received a grade of 28%, every year, as he became more familiar with the curriculum and began to work more with classmates, Mor-Anyar's grades gradually rose. In his final academic term (Winter 2011), he earned 90% in his capstone Electrical Engineering Project class.

Mor-Anyar exemplifies the most common trajectory arc of WUSC students: Steady Risers. These students' progression pattern is defined by considerable struggle at entry and the experience of steep learning curves. They tend to fail, drop, or do poorly in their first-year classes. However, within the first two years, Steady Risers make incremental improvements; they settle on a major, they drop fewer courses, and their GPAs increase. There are still setbacks, such as struggling to establish a work–study balance, but these issues are not as daunting as the flood of work and new skills development during the initial term and year. Steady Risers like Mor-Anyar are the refugee students who, despite initial difficulties, persevere as they inch toward their academic goal of a Canadian university degree.

### Munira: A dipper

Her smile is radiant. Holding 12 pink long-stem roses bundled in a cellophane wrapper that sparkles under the flash of the camera,

Munira stands tall and proud. In her other hand, decorated in an elegant henna design, she clutches a large, crisp crimson envelope containing the bachelor's degree awarded to her that very morning, June 5, 2012. To understand the significance of this accomplishment fully, we need to travel back to when Munira's walk across the graduation stage really began: more than 20 years ago in Mogadishu, Somalia.

In 1991, unaware of the mounting chaos of Somali's civil war, two-year-old Munira clung to her mother as the family fled a home where they no longer felt safe. With three young daughters, her parents took incremental steps toward Kenya, stopping for periods here and there, not completing the 200-mile walk to Dadaab refugee camp for close to a year. Munira remembers it mostly as a place where "there's never enough of anything ... never enough food, never enough books, never enough teachers, classrooms." Yet despite an existence defined by scarcity, Munira considered herself one of the "lucky" ones who still had her family.

The 6:30 a.m. rousing for primary school changed to a 5 a.m. start for high school. Both started with early-morning prayers and a 25-minute walk to school. With the strong Kenyan sun beating on tin roofs and "about 200 students" in each class, elementary school felt "crowded" and "really hot." The crowding was less of an issue in high school, but there were other concerns. Munira recalls teacher shortages: "Ten teachers were needed but they would hire five teachers. So every class has to go without one subject and you still have to do the test, like the exam in the end of the semester." Afternoon classes ended at 4:30 p.m.; however, Munira often stayed behind to study since "you have to work two or three times as much as you would in a normal school life kind of situation, because you have to share books." Munira would sometimes stay in school as late as six or even eight at night, crediting her ability to study after hours to her parents, who were "serious about school" and defied cultural norms. She explains:

> Most female students will have to go home and cook and help with the housework but I didn't have to. I wasn't expected or forced or asked to do anything at home. My mom would just say, "Stay in school instead as much as you can, just come home before dark." That was the only condition.

With older sisters who were able to assist at home, Munira had more freedom to study than is generally available to other female students.[18] Munira thrived and academically "was usually the first female student" and fourth overall with "three or four boys ahead of me." Male students threatened her, insisting, "I'm supposed to be more successful than you." The self-described "stubborn" Munira approached being academically successful as a "competition ... like a war." She believes that the boys' jealousies were further intensified by the additional attention and encouragement she received with the "girl child education campaign" that had taken root in the camp. She explains that the boys "hated" that the "teachers were always giving me the books and asking me to be responsible for the stuff we have to share." As she progressed through secondary school, Munira noticed there were "a lot less girls," perhaps "seven female students" out of a class of "forty students."

> Everyone was dropping out, but the girls would drop out double as the guys. The girls, they get married, they have to work at home, they have to help with whatever the family is doing for economic purposes [such as] selling things in the market.

Munira has fond memories of "good teachers" who taught her well and under whose guidance she earned "really great grades." She recalls a Kenyan school system where "education is very strict, you just have to study and study and study, and of course, there is the cane and the punishment—if you don't behave." In grade 11, Munira heard about the WUSC program from other students who had graduated and applied through Windle Trust, the local NGO that administers the program. Motivated to "get an education and go to university," Munira submitted an application following her high school graduation, feeling both thrilled and terrified to reach the semi-final interview:

> [It's] the most like scary thing that you can imagine feeling. At that point you feel like your whole life depends on this interview. So just sitting there and being very scared. You know nothing about a career because there's not career counseling or academic advising, or looking up [on] the Internet. It was just difficult.

Successful in her interview and following a year of English classes, computer training, and security clearance by Citizenship and Immigration Canada, Munira arrived in Canada on August 23, 2008. From professors' accents to the selection of courses, Munira was just as startled as other refugee students when her classes started and she understood little of what was happening. Adding to her confusion, she could not decide on a major, taking "everything":

> I did some Biology classes, I did a couple of English Literature classes; I really didn't know but I was leaning more into Sociology, but then like thinking of International Relations and [so] I took a Global Development class—[but] it was nothing like I was thinking. [I decided] *This is not what I wanted to do.*

To pass her classes, Munira relied on a strategy that had served her well in high school. She says she studied hard and managed by "memorizing every single thing in the textbook because if you, if you get almost every question that comes from the textbook, so even if you don't get [the lecture] you end up with, you know, a middle, a mid-70." Munira's transcripts reflect a strong first year, with all grades above class averages. For instance, her grade in Politics in the Global World is a B while the class average is B−, and her grade in Literature for Our Time is a B+ while the class average is a C+. Munira discloses that her academic struggles did not start until the summer following her first year. In Summer 2009, the grades she received for science courses fluctuated; for example, she earned a B (above the class average of C) in Introduction of Evolution and Evolutionary Genetics, but a D+ in her Diversity of Organisms course (below the class average of C−). Munira identifies two potential reasons for the dip in her grades. First, after the success of her first year, she felt she could relax a little and not be so serious about school, describing that she felt "kind of confident. I was like I don't really need to study because now I know I can catch up with stuff." Second, at the end of her 12 months of funding, she moved off campus with a Kenyan friend who did not charge her rent, explaining "once you get into second year, you don't live in residence; you don't have the meal plan." Even though it meant she could no longer stay and study late at the library as she used to, Munira was not initially concerned about the long commute. However, reality soon set in and along with it panic. Munira describes her dramatic reaction to the low marks she started to receive:

> The grades, I wanted to cry. I would come home and I will have two Cs. All I can do is just like, I would just cry at home because I was like, *Oh my God! If I keep getting this and I don't finish school and I don't have good grades, I will have nothing to do in life. I am going to be homeless.*

Munira got through her difficult second year and, after spending hours consulting with her advisor, decided to focus on social work, transferring to a university in another city that offered the program. The new university, fortunately, accepted her transfer credits, and she took out student loans for tuition and living expenses (in addition to part-time work she found that allowed her to send money to her family). Finally feeling more settled in her third year, Munira rediscovered the confidence she had temporarily lost. She credits her "above average" grades in her third and fourth years (all As and Bs) to a combination of "really good professors" and helpful resources.

As a Dipper, Munira reflects the second-most typical trajectory of WUSC students. In this pattern, refugee students do well in their first year and then slide in subsequent terms (mainly within their second and third years). This slide is followed by improvement in the fourth or fifth year. Many factors appear to contribute to the post-first-year decline. With academic success in their first year, some become overconfident and take a more lax approach in their second year. Most often, the decline seems to correspond with personal issues, such as the death of a family member or the end of a romantic relationship. Grade declines also occur at the end of students' financial support from the SRP; at this time, many students describe feeling additional burden and stress in having to support themselves, afford tuition, and still find some way to send money back home. Once some of these issues are resolved, students regain their footing and seem to be able to refocus on their academic work. At this point Dippers, their confidence renewed, begin to earn passing grades that will ultimately allow them to make their way across their own graduation stage.

**Molende: An instant achiever**

Molende, a 2009 arrival, is unique. From the first semester of his first year, he shone academically. A review of his transcript reveals that he earned all As in his freshman term (one of them an A+), and three As and a B in his second term. A pattern of high grades continued throughout his second and third years. This trend of immediate and consistent high marks is highly unusual. Why was he alone able to be instantly successful at managing and navigating university in Canada?

Closer examination reveals that Molende diverges from other refugee students in this study in many important respects. Having lived four and half years in Kakuma refugee camp, he spent the least time in refuge. He is also the only student who completed all his primary and secondary education in his home country of Congo before entering the refugee camp. In addition, Molende's parents are the most highly educated of the whole group: his mother earned a nursing degree and his father has a PhD in geology. With both his parents and all his siblings alive, he has not had to face the loss of immediate family members. Moreover, he has two older resettled siblings who work and send money home, eliminating any pressure on Molende to provide remittances. Finally, at 28 years of age, he is one of the oldest study participants. The image of Molende that emerges is in stark contrast to other refugee students: he arrived with more experiential stability, two highly educated parents, fewer financial responsibilities, and perhaps more developmental maturity.

A rigorous educational background appears to play a role in Molende's current academic achievement. He told me that he arrived feeling well prepared to enter Canadian university. When asked why, he says that although "my country [Congo] may have lots of issues, we do also have a strong education system. I attended a good school back home, so I was very confident about myself."

Molende was also self-assured enough to speak up immediately in class or consult his professor when he did not understand a concept or a lesson. "I never felt shy to ask something," he says, "because I'm new here, I have to get as much information as possible." He credits his "open" personality for his tendency to ask for help, saying, "It's just the way I am ... if I feel like asking you something, I will just ask you. So I'm that type of person." He told me he was initially so shaken by not understanding his professors' accents that he immediately worked hard to overcome it. When I asked him how he adjusted in just "three weeks" he told me,

> I started watching movies in English only day and night, day and night, and then I got the accent straight and I thought *Okay, good, now I can get it.* So after around two, three weeks I was into it.

Although other refugee students also approach faculty, many wait at least a week or two, losing precious time by remaining "lost" in lectures. Since he immediately asked for help, Molende positioned himself for academic success. Molende also approached a wide variety of people in addition to faculty members to receive the guidance he needed. He actively sought out teaching assistants, local committee members, "academic and program" advisors, classmates, and study groups. He believes "it is a combination of all that that helped me to kind of get good grades."

Molende is evidently a planner. Since he is not responsible for sending money to his family, he is not obligated to work. Nevertheless, to avoid student loans, he decided to find a job in his second term with the thinking that "after two years, I have no scholarship but if I work now, I can save money." He is currently paying for his third-year tuition and living expenses from past and current earnings. Similar to other students, Molende also worries about balancing workload and schoolwork. The difference is he treats his limited schedule as an advantage by creating and sticking to a strict schedule. He explains:

> It wasn't easy because at some point you're like, *Oh my God, I have to go to work. There is this assignment, what am I going to do?* But that's actually helped me have discipline. I have a schedule: I will write Monday to Sunday, 8:00 to 12:00 school, 1:00 to 3:00 library, this is friend time, this is work time. So when you call me when you're not supposed to, I can't do anything. Like when you're calling me when I have to study, I really know if I don't study during that time, it's not going to work and I'm not going to have other opportunity to catch up. So that helped me to kind of ... to be more disciplined. I had my friends, some other students who were sponsored as well but who never worked, but I happen to have higher grades than them [even though] they had more time than me. So the point is when you get too much free time, you forget that focus.

As an Instant Achiever, Molende stands out for his consistently high grades. His strong educational and stable background likely played a role. Part of his success also appears to be related to a confident and assertive personality, however. For instance, he asked for the help he needed sooner rather than later. In addition, Molende is highly disciplined and has developed and stayed committed to a schedule that helps him to balance the rigours of studying and work. Thus, Molende's accomplishment as an Instant Achiever seems to reflect a unique interplay of his personality traits, a stable and academically strong background, and disciplined time-management skills.

## Discussion

I have considered the academic challenges faced by refugee youth and how they overcame them. There are several important points to pull from these pages of investigation and analysis. Refugee students face a tremendous range of issues: not understanding professors' and classmates' accents, being silenced by their own, having to learn how to draft university-quality papers, getting lost in the rapid pace of lectures and assignments, taking courses when they do not have the necessary grounding, and needing to balance their studies with employment.

Despite the myriad of challenges, all study participants persevered and progressed.[19] Their improvement seems to develop from supportive relationships as much as it does from newfound access to the riches of resources on university campuses. Often it is by connecting with professors, teaching assistants, classmates, local committee members, and academic advisors that students are able to navigate their way through Canadian universities. The "university village" assists refugee youth to understand academic norms, receive the guidance they need, and learn about and access resources.

To provide a more holistic and authentic portrayal of students' current experiences, student profiles were infused with rich, pre-arrival contextual details. Taken together, the three trajectory patterns of WUSC-sponsored refugee students indicate that refugees take divergent pathways through Canadian universities, informed in part by their pre-arrival conditions and personality traits. As signifiers of the trajectory patterns of study participants, these profiles teach us that refugee youth navigate university in distinctive ways. Steady Risers start struggling and make academic progress at a slow and steady pace. Dippers start strong but struggle with courses before getting back on track. Instant Achievers are highly successful from the start.

As narratives of three lives (apart from the trajectory patterns they signify), these profiles illustrate that pre-arrival factors matter for how students manage and navigate their academic pathways in Canada. Refugee youth are not entering on a level playing field; they differ in ways that are more nuanced than simply by country of origin or asylum. For instance, although it may be unusual to discuss privilege when it comes to refugee students (since it is not a label often associated with the population), we see that privilege is relevant for Molende. He is a well-educated child of well-educated, living Congolese parents, was fortunate to spend just a few years in the refugee camp, and left Kenya without feeling any financial obligations to his family. With all these relative advantages, it is not surprising that Molende excelled academically from the start of his university tenure. On the other hand, we see both Mor-Anyar and Munira had to negotiate a more difficult existence before they even set foot on campus. Although it is difficult to infer the extent to which these pre-arrival factors have affected the students' academic achievement and experiences, I believe they have. Mor-Anyar wishes to return to South Sudan, to develop the country with his engineering degree; however, he likely also wishes to return to his only living parent, from whom he needed to separate as a child to attend school. Munira, who stated that she had to counter cultural gender norms simply to be educated, demonstrated a similar post-arrival resiliency by picking herself up after her academic struggles in her second year of university. These trends provide us with a broad overview of the ways in which refugee youth navigate Canadian universities.

## Recommendations

### WUSC local committees

In view of students' initial challenges with the English accent of professors and students, WUSC local committees could send mobile-phone–enabled MP3 podcasts of Canadian voices to refugees at the pre-arrival stage. Mobile phones could also be used to connect current WUSC students with future arrivals for discussion on the Canadian university system and courses—a mentorship model.

In addition, local committees should conduct specialized orientation with faculty and student-support officers to inform or remind them of the needs and challenges of this population. If they are not already doing so, local committee members would do well to introduce newly arrived student youth to research librarians, contacts at support offices, and the writing centre personally. The gaps in refugee youths' curricular knowledge and years away from academic routines may require specialized attention and explicit instruction. Current and former WUSC-sponsored youth, who best understand these challenges and pathways, are essential to any orientation planning and delivery of this nature.

### Institutional

Recognizing schedules and costs, universities could sponsor week-long remedial training for newcomer refugee youth before the start of the academic year. This approach would familiarize refugees with Canadian university expectations and course load, and teach or highlight skills—such as time management—that are critical for academic success. Many universities have already committed to the SRP; they would simply need to bolster their support and use current students to lead workshops and seminars, enabling Canadian students to develop and practise leadership and teaching skills.

In addition, many refugee youth are sponsored for only one year of study. If university housing could be subsidized for students' second year, they could better focus on their studies, rather than work many hours to send financial remittances to their family in refuge *and* support themselves in Canada.

### Faculty

According to refugee youth, professors are essential to their academic success and emerge as important figures in the lives of these young people. Faculty could insist on mandatory attendance at office hours during the first week of classes. This way, the onus for reaching out is removed from refugee youth, who may be bewildered, shy, or unaware, and these important relationships can be developed sooner. Such a strategy may prove particularly useful for female students. Faculty also set the culture of classrooms. Creating a welcoming culture and providing opportunities for refugee students to participate, while taking care not to be demeaning, are essential to helping refugee youth find their voices.

## Conclusion

Refugee students often perceive and frame their education as a collective opportunity. This view is palpable in their intense fear of failure, for if they were to fail, it would not be an individual failure but rather a group failure, which could seem much worse. In this way, the social and academic worlds of refugee youth collide. This understanding provides another perspective by which to understand students' deep gratitude for the access to higher education gained through WUSC's Student Refugee Program. At one level, it is a notable accomplishment and improves life conditions of individual refugees who are resettled in a safe country with abundant resources. At the same time, it is about more than personal achievement and security; it is about what this degree grants students: the opportunity to improve the lives of loved ones in developing homelands or in refuge. It means being a bridge, a conduit, and a catalyst of support. Ultimately, it means hope.

## NOTES

1 Here, I distinguish between challenges where students clearly indicate expecting something different from what they face in Canadian universities and challenges they encounter without vocalizing that they anticipated it to be otherwise. It is a subtle but important distinction. In the first instance, they calibrate their previous expectations, whereas in the second instance, they develop new understanding.

2 I include pre-arrival conditions and experiences. We have to understand where students are coming from to understand the nature of their progression in Canadian universities.

3 *Resettlement* refers to placing refugees in safe third countries where they "gain legal protection—residency and often eventually citizenship—from governments who agree, on a case-by-case basis, to open up their communities to new members" (United Nations Association of Georgia, 2005).

4 Under Canada's Private Sponsorship Program, sponsorship-agreement holders—made up of humanitarian, religious, ethnic, community, or service organizations—have a special affiliation and contract with Citizenship and Immigration Canada that allows them more flexibility than other types of private sponsors.

5 For further clarification, visit the Association of Universities and Colleges of Canada (AUCC) at http://www.aucc.ca/.

6 After data collection was completed, one participant requested that critical aspects of his identity be hidden (including religious affiliation, country of origin, and asylum). To protect his identity, I would have had to hide or change it to such a degree that it would not have been possible to include his highly divergent story and still present an authentic exploration of the experiences of refugee youth. His data was not analyzed and is not part of this study. Henceforth, I refer to only 24 study participants.

7 There is a higher proportion of females who participated in the study (37.5%) than the proportion of females who arrived in 2007–2011 (22.4%).

8 By academic culture shock, I mean students' reactions (from surprise, to fear, to alarm) to the academic work and environment they encounter.

9 The definitions of "teacher centred" and "pupil centred" here are Victor's. They should not be confused with how these terms are traditionally conceived in educational literature.

10 This leap in assuming responsibility may be similar for Canadian students who are finding they have to take more ownership of their own time and work. So, it may not simply be differences in Kenyan versus Canadian styles but rather the difference between high school and university expectations.

11 Surprisingly, none of the male students made any comments on the gender composition of Canadian universities. I say surprisingly because it would also be a change for them.

12 Students also faced tremendous technological challenges that are too extensive to discuss in this text and will be a topic for future publications.

13 All the students I interviewed were in English-speaking universities and required to study in English. Therefore adjusting to French accents is not addressed.
14 All participants speak multiple languages, which often include the language of their homeland or asylum country and, in many instances, dialects of each.
15 Students seem to feel ashamed when they do not do as well as they expect to do. Many of the students who decided not to share their transcripts with me said they did not want to show some of their low grades.
16 Students discuss local Kenyans being upset by the UNHCR food rations and other support provided to refugees. With remittances sent from abroad, some refugees are also able to start little shops, further exacerbating tensions.
17 Nearly every single student in the study received a scholarship, supported mostly by JRS, to attend a Kenyan or Malawian high school (outside of the camp compound). High schools in the refugee camp are often taught by other refugees who, although they have high school diplomas, are not trained teachers.
18 Munira indicates that her sisters took on additional housework so that she could study. There seems to have been a family effort on to ensure that she continued her education.
19 Of course, there are many WUSC students who are not part of the study, who may have dropped out, and who could not take the mounting pressure and challenges. I am not disregarding them by airbrushing them out of the emerging picture. I am simply saying that the refugee youth of this particular study manage to find their way successfully.

## REFERENCES

Baum, S., & Ma, J. (2007). *Education pays 2007.* New York, NY: College Board Publications.

Bowen, W., Kurzweil, M.A., Tobin, E.M., & Pichler, S.C. (2005). *Equity and excellence in American higher education.* Charlottesville: University of Virginia Press.

Hannah, J. (1999). Refugee students at college and university: Improving access and support. *International Review of Education, 45*(2), 153–166. http://dx.doi.org/10.1023/A:1003640924265

Herman, J.L. (1992). *Trauma and recovery: The aftermath of violence—From domestic abuse to political terror.* New York: Basic Books.

Joyce, A., Earnest, J., De Mori, G., & Silvagni, G. (2010). The experiences of students from refugee backgrounds at universities in Australia: Reflections on the social, emotional and practical challenges. *Journal of Refugee Studies, 23*(1), 82–97. http://dx.doi.org/10.1093/jrs/feq001

Kaprielian-Churchill, I., & Churchill, S. (1994). *The pulse of the world: Refugees in our schools.* Toronto, ON: OISE Press.

Maxwell, J.A. (2005). *Qualitative research design: An interactive approach.* London, UK: Sage.

Mosselson, J. (2006). Roots & routes: A re-imagining of refugee identity constructions and the implications for schooling. *Current Issues in Comparative Education, 9*(1), 20–29.

Rutter, J., & Jones, C. (1998). *Refugee education: Mapping the field.* London, UK: Trentham Books.

Seidman, I. (2006). *Interviewing as qualitative research.* New York: Teachers College Press.

Shakya, Y.B., Guruge, S., Hynie, M., et al. (2010). Aspirations for higher education among newcomer refugee youth in Toronto: Expectations, challenges, and strategies. *Refuge: Canada's Periodical on Refugees, 27*(2), 65–78.

United Nations Association of Georgia. (2005). What type of durable solutions exist for refugees? Retrieved from http://una.ge/pdfs/publications/rcg/resettlement%20-ENG.pdf

World University Service of Canada. (2012). Local Committees. Retrieved from http://wusc.ca/en/local-committees

# 16

# Managing expectations through building cultural capital

## The student refugee program experience

*Ashley Korn, Michelle Manks, and Jacqueline Strecker*

When the government of Canada implemented the Immigration Act that resulted in the Private Sponsorship of Refugees program in 1978, World University Service of Canada (WUSC) was among the first organizations to agree to provide care, lodging, settlement assistance, and financial support to Canada's first privately sponsored refugees (Citizenship and Immigration Canada, 2005b). In addition to the traditional assistance offered by private sponsors, the organization recognized the role that education plays in human development and became the first—and still the only—organization in the world to combine refugee resettlement with tertiary education through an initiative known as the Student Refugee Program (SRP). This unique youth-led program not only provides resettlement and a minimum of one year of post-secondary education to young refugees, but also offers hands-on experience in refugee protection to youth across the country and endeavours to raise awareness among Canadians about forced migration, newcomer integration, and diversity.

At present, the program has resettled and provided post-secondary education to more than 1,250 refugees, collaborating with nearly 65 Canadian post-secondary institutions to sponsor approximately 80 students annually. Because of its unique peer-to-peer sponsorship model and the extensive pre-departure preparations sponsored students receive, the SRP continues to be recognized by partners in resettlement and refugee protection for its best practices in integration and public education.

This chapter explores the experiences of the SRP's sponsored students to expound the importance of providing pre-departure orientations and to identify ways in which cultural capital, or a lack thereof, can affect a student's experience in the classroom. Cultural capital encompasses the cultural competencies needed to navigate within a social or cultural group successfully (Bourdieu, 1973, 1986). Traditionally, cultural capital theory suggests that upward mobility can be restricted if an individual lacks the cultural knowledge and symbols that characterize the unfamiliar social group (Bourdieu, 1973; Torres, 2009). Bourdieu (1973) uses the terms *codes* and *tools* to refer to the linguistic and cultural competencies included within a society's cultural capital. These competencies allow an individual to function in a particular social class or society. Lacking the required cultural codes and tools could exclude one or limit one's participation in a new social class, culture, or society (Bourdieu, 1973). Cultural capital is naturally acquired through familial or cultural socialization. Those who do not have avenues of inculcation must deliberately seek opportunities to acquire cultural capital (Bourdieu, 1973, 1986).

When we apply cultural capital to the analysis of the role of pre-departure orientations in resettlement of refugees, the orientation sessions take the place of socialization. By receiving relevant and accurate information through cultural training, refugee students can more thoroughly grasp the cultural codes and tools needed and use them to navigate the new cultural and academic milieu. Orientations allow for youth to become familiar with cultural norms and ways of doing and thinking relevant to Canadian society and culture (Korn, 2009). In turn, cultural capital encourages individual autonomy and a more complete contribution to the receiving society (Bourdieu, 1973, 1986).

Facilitating cultural training through pre-departure orientations enables organizations to manage the expectations of participants by imparting knowledge about the receiving country. The International Organization for Migration (IOM) has documented that many of the refugees who are accepted for resettlement arrive straight from refugee camps, with little or no knowledge of the social and economic practices of capitalist countries (IOM, 2004). The information that refugees do acquire is amassed through an eclectic network of government bodies, partner organizations, media, and transnational contacts, which at times can blur reality with fiction, building false expectations and negatively affecting the resettlement process (Horst, 2006). Misinformation or a lack of information can produce unrealistic expectations. Failure to meet these pre-migration expectations can lead to distress for resettled refugees and can ultimately result in poor mental health (Simich, Hamilton, & Baya, 2006). Pre-departure orientations are therefore pivotal not only in building cultural capital but also in confronting preformed expectations of resettlement because they foster greater understanding about the process, culture, and challenges that will likely be encountered.

The importance of providing pre-departure training has also been supported by the United Nations High Commissioner for Refugees (UNHCR), who affirms that "refugees should have as much information as possible of what awaits them upon arrival in the resettlement country ... concerning the language, culture, climate and population of the country as a minimum" (UNHCR, 2004). This is why UNHCR has worked with the IOM and receiving countries to provide basic pre-departure orientations for all refugees selected for resettlement.

## Pre-departure orientations for refugees destined for Canada

In the days and weeks leading up to migrating to Canada, refugees and other migrant groups are invited to receive a Canadian Orientation Abroad (COA) session delivered by the IOM. The COA curriculum was developed by IOM in collaboration with Citizenship and Immigration Canada (CIC). These orientation sessions can be delivered over one day or several days, depending on the time before departure and the urban or rural environment refugees originate from.[1]

Although on paper the COA curriculum includes information and knowledge required for migrants/refugees to succeed when migrating to Canada, CIC identified several constraints to the COA. CIC believes there is a "lack of systematic knowledge of the orientation needs of immigrants and convention refugees from different countries and cultural groups" (Citizenship and Immigration Canada, 2005a, p. 3). They contend that the COA participants' manual is under-translated and therefore less accessible to the diverse populations it has been developed for; further, some materials are out of date and at times only partially distributed to pre-migration migrants (Citizenship and Immigration Canada, 2005a). CIC also reports that although facilitators are well trained in the facilitation approach employed by CIC and the IOM, those who implement the COA have been found to lack direct knowledge of Canada; in addition, the time allotted to complete the COA is insufficient (Citizenship and Immigration Canada, 2005a). Importantly, the COA does not provide significant exposure to the knowledge and tools required to navigate

Canadian education systems successfully. The COA is a valuable part of the migration process; however, there is need for program reform.

Although all SRP students participate in the COA, WUSC recognized the need for much more thorough training to ease the transition and manage the expectations of refugee youth once in Canada. While the COA provides a general overview of life in Canada, WUSC pre-departure orientations include an overview of their welcoming groups and what can be expected of them, how they fit into Canada's larger immigration system, in-depth sessions on Canadian culture and the Canadian education system, and tips on managing one's expectations. In addition to building cultural capital, the WUSC orientations provide a safe space for students to express their concerns and receive knowledgeable answers to their questions without any anxiety that it will "jeopardize their status." This anxiety is a current limitation of the COA initiative (Citizenship and Immigration Canada, 2005a).

## The SRP model and experience

For nearly two decades, WUSC has been working with partners in countries of asylum to provide sponsored students with the training and skills needed to succeed in Canada. This information has included English-language proficiency courses and tests, computer training, and research and writing courses. In recent years, WUSC has also delivered more substantial orientations for students destined for Canada, to supplement COA sessions. These orientations began informally with volunteer students in 2008, but were shown to be extremely beneficial to the students' integration on arrival. When evaluations were conducted six months after the students' resettlement, individuals who had received the training in their country of asylum indicated that the training received before departure was an important factor in building cultural capital and assisted in understanding Canada and its post-secondary education system (WUSC, 2011). WUSC has therefore found that orientations beyond the COA are beneficial, if not necessary, to the successful placement of students on campuses and their integration into their new communities. The examples highlighted in the following sections demonstrate how cultural capital, or a lack thereof, has affected SRP-sponsored students' educational experiences.[2]

### Language acquisition and proficiency

Many universities and colleges require proof of language proficiency to admit students with international transcripts. For this reason, WUSC has worked with partners to provide several months of

English and French language training followed by an official language assessment test, a critical aspect of the admissions process. Although sponsored students must have a functional knowledge of one of Canada's two main languages to be admitted to a post-secondary program, they also require language confidence. Acquiring confidence in their language abilities requires familiarity with academic terms and acknowledgement that different accents can present challenges for all students, even those who score well on assessment tests. Sponsored students reflecting on their experiences noted the following:

> I felt like no one understood me, and I was struggling to make people understand me. I use to compare myself to others, and it took me a while to get confidence to talk. I use to have to tell people two to three times what I was saying. It was really frustrating, especially in class. (Interviewee A, Student Refugee Program Interviews, 2012)

> I can say there is two kinds of English, there is conversational and academic. I can speak here, but in class the prof is talking and I don't get it. It is English but it sounds like German. There are terms for specific courses that I don't understand, and you just can't get around it. (Interviewee B, Student Refugee Program Interviews, 2012)

Attaining proficiency in the official languages of the receiving country can facilitate independence and lead to the development of social resources and coping strategies for refugees (Beiser & Hou, 2001). Korn (2009) affirms that "language acquisition is notably the most important element of resettlement in Canada, as it is imperative to finding meaningful employment and integrating into the wider community" (p. 10). The diversity of dialects, academic jargon, and slang terms may be exceedingly difficult for many sponsored students, who often expect to communicate seamlessly on arrival at their universities (Student Refugee Program Interviews, 2012). The pre-departure orientations attempt to manage some of these expectations by informing students of the difficulty of past peers, providing tips for interacting in different settings, and familiarizing students with different approaches for seeking academic support.[3] Although sponsored students continue to struggle with language acquisition and proficiency, acknowledging the issues before the sponsored students' departure assists in preparing them for the challenges ahead and gives them strategies for coping. One SRP alumna articulated her experience:

> Even though you might be comfortable in speaking in English, there is an accent attached to it. So I had problems, because I would speak but they wouldn't understand me, and at times I couldn't understand them. This is because of our accents. My strategy was to adopt their accents and embrace how they talked. (Interviewee C, Student Refugee Program Interviews, 2012)

Language continues to be one of the greatest challenges for all resettled refugees (Citizenship and Immigration Canada, 2005b). Building cultural capital through the provision of language courses in advance of resettlement and creating awareness around continuing language challenges can provide a significant advantage for sponsored students.

## Canadian culture

Creating cultural capital through language training is also linked to the larger issues of cultural differences. Building understanding and awareness around different values and norms, as well as creating awareness about culture shock, is another important aspect to pre-departure orientations. Sponsored students experience varying degrees of cultural adjustment when they relocate to Canadian universities. In many ways, their resettlement is similar to the adjustment experienced by international students, which is found to depend on social factors before departure (Ward, Bochner, & Furnham 2003). Jackson (2004) notes that cultural differences such as a new diet, differing health beliefs, and general displays of affection can be triggers that exacerbate feelings of cultural shock or homesickness. Two sponsored students describe the impact of these types of triggers:

> It was really hard to adjust to food when I came. The first food I ate was in the morning after flying. I ordered eggs that were sunny side up, and the eggs came raw. I was like, "I am supposed to eat this?" When adjusting to food, I thought I was to look for the food I was used to. But I couldn't find it ... I know there were some guys who don't eat at all, this really impacted their ability to study. (Interviewee C, Student Refugee Program Interviews, 2012)

> It's generally cultural that in Africa we aren't so much strangers, everyone you meet there and talk to become [part of] your family. Especially when they are in your class. If you are different people will approach you. It's not like that in Canada. [In Canada] people have their high school friends, so it's not the same. It's not that easy to expend the time and effort into forming friendships. In Africa you don't have to put effort into talking to people. (Interviewee A, Student Refugee Program Interviews, 2012)

Preparing sponsored students for cultural shock and providing tips for countering and addressing cultural differences are two of the main objectives of WUSC pre-departure orientations. Korn (2009) notes that "if students are not appropriately prepared for their intercultural interactions, it can lead to awkward moments and unsettling encounters, which may increase the likelihood of being withdrawn in their new environment" (p.15). In contrast, Martin (1989) acknowledges that students who have strong self-confidence, cross-cultural communication skills, and the ability to tolerate uncertainty tend to adapt and integrate effectively in a new school. To build students' capacity with these abilities, pre-departure orientations teach sponsored students about cultural values, the stages of culture shock, tips for engaging in different cultures, and approaches for addressing culture shock. Sessions also include several activities that role-play common situations faced by SRP alumni. Participants are asked to identify the different values motivating actions and to strategize ways of addressing these cultural conundrums. Feedback from these sessions has been extremely positive, with students continually referring to the cultural-capital benefits they gained:

> All workshops and sessions helped a lot. Every time we got into a restaurant we had a certain play we did ... The orientations were useful for everyday life. (Interviewee E, Student Refugee Program Interviews, 2012)

> The pre-departure orientation provided me with a foundation to Canadian college life. The education system I had known was very different from the Canadian one and having someone explain to me how things work prior to my departure was very beneficial. I remember attending my very first university lecture in a big lecture hall filled with up to 1,500 students. I felt so insignificant and wondered whether the professor would ever know that I existed or even address my questions. Then, I recalled being taught to never feel intimidated and always feel free to talk to the professors, as they are approachable. If it weren't for the pre-departure orientation I would have never known. (Interviewee F, Student Refugee Program Interviews, 2012)

> Before we came, we were told a lot of things about culture. We knew how to interact, it helped us not get shocked. It was helpful ... We came here with a different culture, but you have to keep your own culture. People do their own stuff; you just respect other people's culture. Of course there are things that I can embrace, but I keep my own culture. (Interviewee D, Student Refugee Program Interviews, 2012)

Korn (2009) found that sponsored students "felt that understanding the culture shock curve [gained from pre-departure orientations] was quite useful during their resettlement and adjustment period. They were able to identify what stages of culture shock they were experiencing, which gave them a reference point to connect their feelings with their experiences" (p. 39). Building cultural capital through instilling confidence in intercultural exchanges is also imperative for helping students navigate through the Canadian education system.

## Understanding post-secondary education systems

The post-secondary education system in Canada provides another significant challenge for resettled refugee students. Secondary education systems in the countries of origin, or in countries of asylum prior to resettling in Canada, are different from the Canadian system.

These systems generally place more emphasis on testing as a method to evaluate knowledge acquisition. Secondary schools are often overpopulated, with high student-to-teacher ratios. Students do not have access to computers, online learning forums, or large libraries. Refugee students may not be familiar with participatory teaching styles found in Canadian institutions. After arriving in Canada and starting their studies, sponsored students experience great challenges navigating the Canadian post-secondary system. Challenges may include interacting with professors and other academic supports, in-class etiquette, confidence in presenting and sharing knowledge, a lack of computer skills (specifically typing speed and online research processes), and feeling a lack of required academic knowledge specific to their post-secondary studies. When facing these challenges, sponsored students feel that they are not able to learn at the same level as their peers who were prepared in the Canadian secondary education system. Sponsored students believe they are behind in lectures and course work, as they have to deal with all of the challenges in navigating the system.

Kilbride, Anisef, Baichman-Anisef, and Khattar (2001) recognize that newcomer youth may face several barriers to succeeding in the educational system based on myriad factors, which are echoed by the sponsored student experiences. Canadian culture, expectations of the education system, roles of educators, acceptable behaviour, and mainstream values are areas of cultural knowledge refugee youth identified as important to their success in the post-secondary education system (Korn, 2009). Sponsored students agree:

> The system was the hardest thing. When you come from Africa the systems are different and the resources are limited. (Interviewee C, Student Refugee Program Interviews, 2012)

> In Kenya, we learn to study for exams. People are developed to become educated but in Kenya we learn to pass exams. In Canada you learn researching, larger perspective issues. In Kenya we learn to solve chemistry questions, so when I came to Canada I saw that people are becoming learned. (Interviewee A, Student Refugee Program Interviews, 2012)

> Getting to university and some of the things like computer knowledge. We learnt computers in the camp, but it is different some how. You go to class and professor says to go here and get this file, and I can't follow. (Interviewee D, Student Refugee Program Interviews, 2012)

When refugee youth receive information regarding anticipated academic experiences and knowledge through pre-departure orientations, they are better prepared to deal with challenges they face. Through orientation, refugee youth are exposed to the cultural competencies needed to navigate the broad Canadian socio-cultural system and specifically to promote success in the Canadian post-secondary education system. Sponsored students who received extensive pre-departure orientations stated:

> No matter how much fear I had at the university I remembered that we should make profs my friends, that I should take time to meet them. If I didn't know that I wouldn't make it.... All workshops and sessions helped a lot. (Interviewee E, Student Refugee Program Interviews, 2012)

> I had two Canadians come to the camp to talk. [They] told us about talking to professors and walking in and telling them exactly what you don't know. I would have been so much stressed in my first year if I didn't know that. I was use to achieving success, and in my first class I wasn't happy with my achievements so I met with my professor and they were so happy. The professors were also so happy and always smiling ... I just survived my first year based on my orientation. (Interviewee A, Student Refugee Program Interviews, 2012)

It is important that the cultural training enables transmission of Canadian cultural competencies to refugees so they have the tools to understand and participate in Canadian society during resettlement (Korn, 2009). Through acquisition of the necessary cultural competencies within cultural capital, refugees destined for Canada are better prepared to succeed within the post-secondary education system and their initial settlement and integration.

The testimony from sponsored students speaks to the value of pre-departure orientations. Other studies have documented the effects of pre-departure orientations for international students and arrive at similar conclusions. Preparing students intellectually, behaviourally, and emotionally helps them to cope with culture shock and increases their ability to study effectively in a new, different environment (Martin, 1989). Students who are adequately equipped with knowledge about their new study environment and the skills required for intercultural interaction and communication are also more likely to succeed in forming intercultural relationships (Ying, 2002).

Providing pre-departure orientations to sponsored refugee youth is therefore imperative for easing refugee resettlement and integration, especially with international scholarship programs. These orientations not only provide knowledge about the countries of resettlement but equip refugee youth with tools for navigating and interacting in these new environments. In addition, pre-departure orientations assist in managing the expectations of the students by fostering understanding and filtering the information gathered from transnational networks. These orientations are an important way of building cultural capital, ensuring that sponsored students are informed and prepared to address the uncertainty and cultural differences that accompany resettlement and life in post-secondary education.

## Conclusion

Since introducing pre-departure orientations in 2008, WUSC has worked with a team of WUSC staff, committee members, and alumni to standardize pre-departure modules that can be delivered by volunteers in the field. These modules cover priority topics identified through SRP evaluations and staff observations, some of which have been discussed in this chapter. Although orientations can never cover all subjects and situations, giving students the tools for managing cultural differences and conflict has empowered sponsored students to make confident, informed decisions. Unfortunately, due to resource limitations, the provision of pre-departure orientations has not always been feasible within all countries of asylum. WUSC has accounted for this gap by providing post-arrival orientations for all available sponsored students in the late fall each year. While both orientations are beneficial, students who have received pre-departure orientations have a distinct advantage as these earlier orientations have played a pivotal role in managing expectations, curbing initial culture shock, and the early adaptation of sponsored students. As a result, WUSC continues to strive to provide all sponsored students with updated orientations, observing the strong correlation between pre-departure sessions and students' cultural understanding.

The SRP orientation model, which includes both pre-departure and post-arrival orientations, prioritizes the need for students to acquire and build cultural capital within their countries of resettlement. While this chapter has established the importance of pre-departure orientations within the SRP, further advocacy is needed to ensure that orientation systems are in place in other resettlement programs. Orientations must be based on appropriate and relevant information and delivery methods to ensure refugee youth are acquiring the information and applying it to their experiences after they arrive in Canada. Tapping into the alumni groups or youth who have already come through the SRP is an important element of informing the ongoing development of orientations, as these youth are the experts with lived experiences and strategies. Although orientations require an investment of time and resources, the facilitation of pre-departure orientations enables refugees to have the time and confidence to build cultural capital. Through this cultural capital, refugees are able to develop an understanding of how to navigate within

Canada's social, cultural, and academic milieu, providing them with the tools and knowledge they need to adapt successfully to Canadian post-secondary classrooms.

## NOTES

1 Topics covered may include facts about Canada (geography, political system/government structure, languages), transit, culture shock, families in Canada (relationships, nutrition, hygiene, diet), the concept of social welfare, communication, climate, finding a place to live, adjusting to Canada, settlement services, education (levels and teaching styles), employment, cost of living, living in a multicultural society (respect, diversity, equity), and rights and responsibilities. The IOM has developed a youth-specific curriculum, focusing on the above information through a youth lens. The youth sessions include other relevant topics for youth, such as dating, in-class culture, youth employment, and bullying.
2 The topics selected are based on areas of frequent concern for sponsored students but are not an exhaustive list of challenges experienced by refugees and students in the SRP.
3 Some approaches include seeking out one-on-one support from professors, teaching assistants, or peer tutors; joining study groups that provide smaller group discussions and learning; and acknowledging problems early with educational staff, to make them aware of difficulties.

## REFERENCES

Beiser, M., & Hou, F. (2001). Language acquisition, unemployment and depressive disorder among Southeast Asian refugees: A 10-year study. *Social Science and Medicine, 53*(10), 1321–1334. http://dx.doi.org/10.1016/S0277-9536(00)00412-3

Bourdieu, P. (1973). Cultural reproduction and social reproduction. In R. Brown (Ed.), *Knowledge, education and cultural change: Papers in the sociology of education* (pp. 71–112). New York: Harper and Row.

Bourdieu, P. (1986). The forms of capital. In J.G. Richardson (Ed.), *Handbook of theory and research of the sociology of education* (pp. 241–260). New York: Greenwood Press.

Citizenship and Immigration Canada. (2005a). *Report on the evaluation of the delivery of the Canadian Orientation Abroad initiative.* Retrieved on February 19, 2009, from http://www.cic.gc.ca/english/resources/evaluation/orientation.asp

Citizenship and Immigration Canada. (2005b). *Summative evaluation of the Private Sponsorship of Refugees Program.* Retrieved on November 20, 2012, from http://www.cic.gc.ca/english/resources/evaluation/psrp/psrp-summary.asp

Horst, C. (2006). Buufis amongst Somalis in Dadaab: The transnational and historical logics behind resettlement dreams. *Journal of Refugee Studies, 19*(2), 143–157. http://dx.doi.org/10.1093/jrs/fej017

International Organization for Migration. (2004). *Pre-departure orientation/cultural orientation.* Retrieved from http://www.iom.int/jahia/webdav/site/myjahiasite/shared/shared/mainsite/published_docs/brochures_and_info_sheets/pre_departure.pdf

Jackson, J. (2004). Language and cultural immersion: An ethnographic case study. *Regional Language Centre Journal, 35*(3), 261–278.

Kilbride, K.M., Anisef, P., Baichman-Anisef, E., & Khattar, R. (2001). Between two worlds: The experiences and concerns of immigrant youth in Ontario. Toronto: Joint Centre of Excellence for Research on Immigration and Settlement (CERIS).

Korn, A. (2009). *What to expect? Examining the role of pre-departure cultural orientations* [MA thesis]. Ryerson University.

Martin, J.N. (1989). Pre-departure orientation: Preparing college sojourners for intercultural interaction. *Communication Education, 38*(3), 249–258. http://dx.doi.org/10.1080/03634528909378761

Simich, L., Hamilton, H., & Baya, B.K. (2006, Sep). Mental distress, economic hardship and expectations of life in Canada among Sudanese newcomers. *Transcultural Psychiatry, 43*(3), 418–444. http://dx.doi.org/10.1177/1363461506066985 Medline:17090626

Student Refugee Program Interviews, A, B, C, D, E, F. (2012, Nov). Student Refugee Program participants. Ottawa, Canada.

Torres, K. (2009). "Culture shock": Black students account for their distinctiveness at an elite college. *Ethnic and Racial Studies, 32*(5), 883–905. http://dx.doi.org/10.1080/01419870701710914

United Nations High Commission for Refugees (2004). *Supporting next steps in integration initiatives: An inventory of opportunities and needs in the integration of resettled refugees.* Retrieved on February 19, 2009, from http://www.unhcr.org/protect/PROTECTION/4173839e4.pdf

Ward, C., Bochner, S., & Furnham, A. (2003). *The psychology of culture shock* (2nd ed.). New York: Routledge.

World University Service of Canada. (2011). *Mid-term evaluation for sponsored students.* Ottawa: Author.

Ying, Y.-W. (2002). Formation of cross-cultural relationships of Taiwanese international students in the United States. *Journal of Community Psychology, 30*(1), 45–55. http://dx.doi.org/10.1002/jcop.1049

# 17

# How do I get in?

## *Exploring the underemployment of immigrant teachers in Canada*

Christine L. Cho

As a researcher in teacher education, specifically focused on immigrant teacher candidates (ITCs), I was recently invited to give a two-hour workshop at the local immigration counselling service in the city in which I live. Fifteen participants attended, eager to hear what they might do to become teachers in Ontario. I spent the first hour listening to the attendees tell their individual stories and describe their qualifications. This was a group of 14 women and 1 man who individually and collectively speak multiple languages and have multiple degrees, including bachelor of education degrees, some of which were obtained at Ontario universities. The attendees also shared their experiences from many years of teaching in their home countries. One attendee explained that teaching was in her heart and she has been working as a custodian and occasional education assistant in Canada for the past 10 years. There was palpable desperation in the room. The attendees' overarching question was "How do I do it? How do I 'get in' here? How do I become a teacher in Canada?" My ongoing query has been, "What is keeping immigrants out of the teaching profession?"

Why are so many citizens who immigrated to Canada underemployed (or mal-employed) in the education sector? In 2010 the Ontario College of Teachers found 68% of certified teachers who are immigrants to Canada are not employed in any form of teaching job in their first year post graduation; 84% of those actively seeking teaching jobs are underemployed or mal-employed. By comparison, 36% of

Anglo-Canadian certified graduates are without jobs in their first year (McIntyre, 2011). The underemployment trend among immigrant teachers reveals an under-utilization of human resources. Teachers who have immigrated bring to Canada, and to the dominant-group learners in their classrooms, important cultural resources: competencies, skills, attitudes, divergent knowledge, and alternative ways of thinking and knowing. However, most teachers who have immigrated to Canada are not seen as a resource, particularly in a tight employment market.

## The project

To contextualize my recent experience with the attendees at the immigration counselling workshop I facilitated, I am going to draw from a critical ethnographic project I undertook with several teacher candidates enrolled in a bachelor of education (BEd) program in Ontario, Canada, who self-identified as immigrants. The project invited immigrant teacher candidates (ITCs) to share their experiences on placement and in coursework through a series of focus groups and individual interviews. Participants also shared narrative works written for a mandatory foundations course. The data was analyzed inductively, using the techniques described by Bogdan and Biklen (1998). Analysis included process coding and an initial "analysis in the field" phase using both socio-culturally grounded speculation and the generation of ideas about the themes that were identified and categorized from the interview and focus-group transcripts, as well as triangulation of the participants' written reflections and course assignments.

### Participants

The participants were representative of the BEd program in which this project was conducted. The program offers two divisions for credentialing: primary–junior and intermediate–senior, with part-time and full-time enrollment options. In all, seven ITCs participated: one male and six female participants. Five of the participants were qualifying in the primary–junior stream.[1] Two of the participants were enrolled full-time in the intermediate–senior division. English was the first language for the male participant, who immigrated first from Guyana to England and then to Canada in 1973.[2] English was an additional language for the rest of the participants, who came from Egypt, India, Iran, Pakistan, and Sri Lanka and who immigrated to Canada between 1992 and 2006. Six of the seven participants were visible minorities. There was one Caucasian participant from Germany, who immigrated to Canada in 1997.

## The challenges

In Ontario, when students successfully complete the requirements of the BEd degree, they are recommended for certification with the Ontario College of Teachers (OCT). Individuals who immigrate to Ontario with a BEd from another country must have their credentials assessed to be granted certification to teach in the province of Ontario. ITCs face numerous challenges in obtaining documentation that is acceptable to the various accrediting bodies. The Ontario College of Teachers website recently posted a document entitled "Requirements for Becoming a General Education Teacher in Ontario" (OCT, 2011). This document, which did not exist in its current form when my participants were either applying for or enrolled in the BEd program, strives to make the application process for certification more transparent and outlines specific requirements for certification by OCT. The document states, "It is our responsibility to ensure that everyone who is licensed to teach in this province is qualified" (OCT, 2011, p. ii). However, when I was asked to speak at my local immigration counselling service, expressly invited to discuss the accreditation process in Ontario, the attendees immediately remarked they knew the "technicalities" of the process. They wanted to know why they still could not get hired. The attendees' frustration mirrors the frustration ITCs in my project have experienced searching for the elusive explanation of how to get hired as a teacher in Ontario, as well as ascertaining the criteria needed to obtain an Ontario teaching certificate (see Cho, 2013a, 2013b).

I begin with a discussion of language proficiency because it is generally the most-raised concern with the respect to teachers who are immigrants.

### Language proficiency

University entrance and OCT regulations require potential teachers to demonstrate language proficiency if their degree was granted in a language other than English or French. Elke, a teacher from Germany, was unable to obtain OCT certification when she first immigrated to Canada. Private schools were her only option for employment, so she decided to enroll in a BEd program in Ontario; she experienced challenges with her language-proficiency test scores. She explains:

> I applied to [another university], too. In the TOEFL [Test of English as a Foreign Language] test I got a 28 out of 30 and [the university] wanted 29 so they did not accept me there. I wanted to apply to [a third university] but they would not accept anything that I have and [a fourth university] it was not the right translations from the [German] university. They wanted to have it directly from the [German]

university, which was hard enough to get already for the College of Teachers, right, so [the university at the centre of this project] at least accepted all my notarized copies and translations and so that's how I got in to [the university]. (Interview, July 30, 2009)

There is little consistency in terms of an acceptable TOEFL score for university entrance; acceptable scores vary from institution to institution. The institutional requirement for applicants to secure acceptable translations, where the definition of "acceptable" again varies from institution to institution, can delay opportunities to apply for admission or certification. It is not clear from Elke's account on which component she scored 28, but her story does reveal that some universities may have score requirements even higher than the OCT's. As Pollock (2006) reports,

> Tests such as the TOFEL test for language proficiency do not test for occupation-specific language and the subtle nuances of word meanings, leaving many IETs [Internationally Educated Teachers] unaware of the present "politically correct" discourse. This can lead to several negative outcomes such as being perceived as not suitable to teach and not called back for supply work or hired for any type of permanent teaching position. In addition, the dialects some IETs have can also carry a negative value. (p. 3)

When some people hear their first language spoken with an L2 dialect, what Lippi-Green (1997) describes as "breakthrough of native language phonology into the target language" (p. 43), they presume that the speaker might not be proficient in the language.

Khayrah speaks with frustration about obtaining acceptable documentation. Because of bureaucratic red tape, she is forced to give up opportunities to apply for teaching jobs. After graduating with her BEd from an Ontario university with recommendation for an Ontario teaching certificate, she has had to produce additional documentation to OCT (transcripts from her undergraduate degree). She states,

> I just thought that since I've done this paperwork for [World Education Services] and I've done it for [the university], it should be okay for OCT. I should have started [the paperwork] the moment I got here. I did it in April and it's now July and I've heard from [the university] there are still things that need to come from [Pakistan] and I'm sitting here and I'll miss even the next batch of postings that would come up because I don't have [the OCT certification]. (Khayrah, Focus Group 2, July 29, 2009)

Most universities' student handbooks instruct teacher candidates on what to do near the end of their BEd year to obtain OCT certification and how to apply for membership with their respective teachers' association that oversees contractual issues as well as stipulating salary grid placement (such as QECO, OECTA, or OSSTF).

The handbooks do not direct ITCs to begin the process early if they require transcripts from another country. There is also no forum for ITCs to share their experiences with each other to facilitate the navigation of various institutions that they will encounter.

Sometimes graduates hide their foreign credentials by completing a domestic degree so they do not have to produce transcripts from another country. ITCs are implicitly required to present domestic degrees so they can begin to fit into the Ontario or Canadian system. A domestic degree may give the impression that ITCs will be able to deliver the curricular content in Ontario schools because they have successfully demonstrated their learning in a Canadian environment (and have demonstrated success in school in either French or English). However, obtaining a BEd in Ontario when an ITC already has a teaching degree from outside of Canada serves to mask the teacher's experience and credentials, as Elke explains: "But people don't know that you still have experience. They don't know the background. And then on top of that, it's probably when they see a foreign name that's a second reason they wouldn't request you" (Interview, July 30, 2009). Elke's four-year teacher-education degree from Germany was not useful for gaining employment in Canada and does not appear on her transcript or OCT certificate of qualifications as a teaching degree, but rather appears as a non-specific undergraduate degree. On paper, she appears as every other student newly graduating from a BEd program. As she observes, only her foreign name will create an additional barrier to being called for an occasional teaching job. As a result of the stripping away of previous credentials and experiences (on paper), ITCs may interpret their previous work and education as not valued or not good enough for Canadian standards. In this way, ITCs are being stripped of their difference and then moulded and manufactured into the Canadian cultural norm of a teacher with Canadian credentials and Canadian experience. They are also sent a message that what they have achieved is of no value, or of minimal value, to Canadian society. They are placed in a position where they are perpetually proving themselves and working to fit in.

Sadly, one of the attendees at the local immigration counselling service workshop was a former student of mine and a previous participant in a pilot project that preceded this larger project (Cho, 2010). Prior to her arrival in Canada, she had been a teacher in her home country. In 2004 she had her credentials approved by OCT and obtained an Ontario teaching certificate. However, with no job prospects, she determined it might be useful for her to obtain a domestic BEd, and she did so in 2006. It has been seven years since she graduated, and while she is on the occasional teacher list in a school district two hours away, she has been unable to get on the occasional teacher list for the local school board and was at the meeting to discover what else she could do to make herself more marketable.

Within our society there exists a hierarchy of difference. As research has shown, difference is something to be *tolerated* with respect to the students in the classroom (Causey, Thomas, & Armento, 2000; Cockrell et al., 1999; Echols & Stader, 2002; Olmedo, 1997), but it is taken for granted in the literature that the teachers themselves will be prototypical.[3] The over-representation of underemployed immigrant teachers suggests the teaching workforce is not ready for or prepared to contend with a diverse representation among teachers. Insofar as there is a concept of the prototypical teacher in Canadian schools, there also exists a prototype for the ideal immigrant, or what Suzuki (2002) has termed the "model minority," to which my participants also seem to be trying to conform. There is a tension at the intersection of existing norms and perceived difference. Identity-conformity expectations seem particularly rigid in the domain of teaching. My research reveals how certain aspects of difference are tolerated: those that can be understood or that fit existing schemas. However, some aspects of difference that cannot be easily understood are questioned or even shunned. Differences seen as less invasive or not a threat to the fabric of Canadian life are ignored so that they do not interfere with the process of assimilation (James & Schecter, 2000). The continuum of difference is perpetuated by various policy initiatives in Canada that have arisen from the Multiculturalism Act, such as heritage-language classes and classes for English-language learners (ELL). Differences that are problematic or present a potential impediment to Canadian unity are overtly addressed, such as ELL classes that focus on standardizing dialects.

Let's explore the allure of Canada's multiculturalism and the promise of success for all that is embedded within the Act.

### The possibilities of multiculturalism

"Why don't you Canadians stop lying to us immigrants?" a student in my socio-cultural course demanded in class one day. "You tell us we can come here to this country, that it is accepting of all races and faces, and we can practise our profession but that's not true! Your immigration website is full of lies!" Her white teacher-candidate counterparts stared at her in disbelief. For every "but," she had a rebuttal. When the "myth of meritocracy" raised its ugly head, she responded with a terse, "Canada is a racist society. When are you going to own that?" This ITC was an anomaly.[4] She took risks and stepped outside the expectations for ITCs, speaking up in ways that ostracized her from her colleagues and disrupted the model-minority expectations (Suzuki, 2002). Her outrage at Canadians' complacency and blind acceptance of Canada's Multiculturalism Act was strongly voiced. The Multiculturalism Act, Bill C-93 (1988), states in part that

> It is ... the policy of the Government of Canada to ... recognize and promote the understanding that multiculturalism reflects the cultural and racial diversity of Canadian society and acknowledges the freedom of all members of Canadian society to preserve, enhance and share their cultural heritage. (p. 3)

The Act would have Canadians believe that the fabric of our nation reflects diversity, the celebrated concept of the cultural mosaic. Through the decades leading up to the passing of the Act in 1988, Canadian citizenship and multicultural policies were increasingly focused on issues of identity. The public education system was seen as the ideal catalyst for promoting the idea that the Canadian identity is defined by multiculturalism (Joshee, 2004). Current multicultural education policies in Canada can trace their roots back to citizenship-education policies that, beginning in 1847, were designed to instill patriotism in Canadian youth and ensure that new immigrants and Indigenous people understood what it meant to be good Canadian citizens (Joshee, 2004). At the same time, those groups deemed unsuitable for assimilation were shunted into segregated schools—for example, schools for African-Canadian children in Nova Scotia and Ontario and schools for Asian children in British Columbia (Burnet & Palmer, 1989; Walker, 1997). On the policy level we may perceive a shift from assimilative policies to policies that stress diversity and the recognition of difference, but a closer look reveals that perhaps the shift has not been so momentous.

While Canada is often applauded for its progressive and forward-thinking multicultural policy of 1971 and the subsequent Multiculturalism Act of 1988, Canada has simultaneously been criticized for encouraging the very act of assimilation the policies and Act profess to discourage. The Multiculturalism Act builds upon the Canadian Charter of Rights and Freedoms (1981) to declare that the Canadian government

> recognizes the diversity of Canadians as regards race, national or ethnic origin, colour and religion as a fundamental characteristic of Canadian society and is committed to a policy of multiculturalism designed to preserve and enhance the multicultural heritage of Canadians while working to achieve the equality of all Canadians in the economic, social, cultural and political life of Canada. (Canadian Multiculturalism Act, 1985, c. 24)

While the outspoken student in my class railed against the Multiculturalism Act, many ITCs in my project relied on the Act to support their acceptance in schools.

As Rajni writes,

> As my very first foray into a Canadian academic setting, I was initially (and perhaps understandably) racked with trepidation, not quite knowing how I would "fit in." I had, in fact, been advised by fellow Indians in [the city] that the only way I *could* fit in would be to eclipse my "Indian-ness" and become as much like everyone else as I could; a prospect which never held much appeal. How delighted I was, therefore, to discover that one of the pillars of Teacher's College at [the university] is celebrating cultural diversity! Indeed, respectfulness and a willingness to accommodate diverse and specialized needs, inclusive of celebrating multifarious cultures or sexual orientations, proved to be the bedrock of the entire program. (Personal narrative, December 2008, original emphasis)

While Rajni was initially advised to shed her markers of difference, she holds fast to the multicultural discourse that permeates educational rhetoric in Ontario and the institution in which this project was conducted. For the ITCs in my project, believing in the multicultural discourse becomes a necessary and desirable tool. To acknowledge that anything else is going on would mean shattering the immigration dream: to be successful and welcomed to your new country. And so, to keep the dream alive, many ITCs accept, either consciously or unconsciously, the ways in which they are required to fit in and eclipse their markers of difference and the ways in which they are stripped of their markers of difference, little by little, until what is left more closely resembles the construction of the prototypical teacher. When conformity cannot occur or markers of difference cannot be stripped away, ITCs may face a lack of job prospects or a lack of success in the program.

Some ITCs in my project expressed a lack a knowledge of Canadian pop and youth culture and a desire to learn more. Rajni told us she didn't know who "Sponge Bob" was, so she spent time watching cartoons to fill in some of her gaps:

> I thought, 'Oh my god, I don't know any of these characters and that's all the children know'. Like I couldn't tell them about Mowgli or stories from the Ali Baba, that I read when I was a child because they wouldn't connect with that. So, I started watching more of cartoons and taking my own time to get more acquainted in cartoons with what they are interested in as well as their video games. (Focus Group 2, July 29, 2009)

As an instructor I hear many prototypical teacher candidates express uncertainty regarding their lack of knowledge of children's popular culture, but they do not seem to have the same drive or desire to educate themselves in this regard. Their limited knowledge will not be used against them in the same way it will be accentuated as another marker of difference for ITCs. This is another example of how ITCs are continually proving themselves in relation to their prototypical counterparts. Rajni assumes her childhood memories and stories will not be of any use in the Canadian classroom, and so she may omit them from her teaching repertoire in exchange for more Canadian stories and characters. Rajni's stories of Mowgli and lack of knowledge of Sponge Bob, for example, draw attention to her difference. As a way to protect and defend herself from criticism, she is eager to educate herself on Western children's popular culture. Rajni wants to refuse the "less than" position she finds herself in by increasing her knowledge of Western culture perhaps at the expense of her own childhood memories that she feels are ill suited for the Canadian classroom.

In contrast to the premise of multiculturalism, ITCs strive to minimize or erase cultural or ethnic markers to gain entrance into the public school sector. Many of the participants in my project were asked to give up ownership over where they born such as in this writing by Elke:

> Whenever I started to teach in a new class, I encouraged students to let me know if they would have problems understanding me—but not one child did. On the contrary, some came up to me in order to proudly share that they had been to Europe, or that a relative has connections to Europe; one student even explained that he had lived in Ireland for a few years and would therefore easily understand me. (Personal narrative, December 2008)

While it seems positive that students make these geographic connections, it is the children's experiences of visiting Europe that make Elke more approachable, less of a threat. Given the age of the students, we may infer only good intentions in their responses. The challenge is that this kind of response is not critiqued for the touristic response to diversity that is implied. Rather than engaging with someone who has immigrated from a country with which you are not familiar, or have not visited, there is strong desire to connect with someone *because* you have visited their home country as a tourist. It is a way for prototypical Canadians to claim geographic space from a superior position because they have had the luxury to visit and so have knowledge about that country or place. It is another way that ITCs are stripped of identity: they are asked to give up or at least share the ownership over where they were born because a prototypical Canadian has visited there. Elke does not seem offended by the student's assertion that he can understand her because he spent some time living in Ireland, which bears no resemblance to Elke's home country of Germany. The implication is that they have lived in a country where people speak English with an L1[5] dialect that differs from the L1 dialect spoken in Ontario. This assertion homogenizes difference related to dialect and silences Elke's experiences with linguicism. Elke's narrative reveals the ways in which the nuances of language are made invisible and also reveals some of the teachable moments with children that are not capitalized on.

## Conclusion

Underemployment or mal-employment of newly certified immigrant teachers is at an unacceptably high level in Ontario. Several of the ITCs in my project do not fit into rigid so-called Canadian identity expectations: some are brown, some speak with a non-standard dialect, some wear a *hijab*, a *sari*, and/or a *bindi*. The ITCs perceived that the discourse of multiculturalism was serving their interests and facilitating their entrance into the teaching profession; however, the underemployment statistics for teachers who are immigrants does not reflect this belief. I argue that the tools to disrupt the dominant discourse (of which the multicultural discourse is a key component) are missing from teacher education programs in Ontario and the various governing bodies. Faculty, teachers, and government policy-makers are perhaps more comfortable discussing the ideals of multiculturalism and, at best, suggesting an anti-racist discourse than critically examining the inequities in the system. Teachers who have immigrated to Canada, whose experiences reveal the racism embedded in our system, are likewise reluctant to disrupt the system because they want to be able to carve out a space for themselves within the existing structures of schooling. They need to believe in the system and the promise of immigration in spite of how it rejects or strives to mould them. As Makarim states,

> I think, if they [the university] accept ESL students, then they have to have more support. Even in the school right now I want to improve my English. I'd really like to have lots of support but I'm not sure if I'm going to or if I can get that. But for sure I'm going to ask.... The government has to help more immigrant teachers to have more subsidy, help them to be able to be a better teacher so they can be competitive, they can be in the same level as a White teacher. (Interview, July 30, 2009)

Makarim's desire to have the government provide subsidies so ITCs can be more competitive with their White counterparts reveals the ways in which the myth of meritocracy is infused in dominant ideologies around teaching: if you just have the right skills and knowledge, you will be successful. Makarim's request to have government financial support for ITCs is compelling. Rather than looking at how we can (re)imagine the construct of teacher, Makarim is questioning ways in which ITCs can be on a level playing field with prototypical teachers. Recognizing that the playing field is not level, she is suggesting that additional supports be provided so more ITCs can enter the profession. One might ask, conversely, what supports are in place for prototypical teachers already in the profession, particularly those in the position to hire new teachers, to be more accepting of ITCs?

## NOTES

1 Two primary–junior candidates were full-time students and two were part-time. The only male in the study was also a part-time primary–junior candidate.
2 He indicated he was enrolled in English as a Second Dialect classes when he arrived in Canada as he spoke a non-standard dialect of English.
3 The prototypical "teacher" is a profile I define as White, female, Christian, and English-speaking with a standard "Canadian" dialect.
4 It should be noted that the student was not a participant in my study; we met after the data collection had been completed.
5 An L1 dialect refers to the accent of a native speaker of English. There are structural variations of language, and as Lippi-Green (1997) asserts, all language has a dialect, no matter how unmarked the language may seem. An L2 dialect refers to the way language is accented by a person's first language.

## REFERENCES

Bogdan, R., & Biklen, S. (1998). *Qualitative research for education: An introduction to theory and methods* (3rd ed.). Toronto, ON: Allyn & Bacon.

Burnet, J., & Palmer, H. (1989). *Coming Canadians: An introduction to the history of Canada's peoples.* Toronto: McClelland & Stewart.

Canadian Multiculturalism Act, R.S.C. (1985) c. 24 (4th Supp). Retrieved 2011 from http://laws-lois.justice.gc.ca/PDF/C-18.7.pdf

Causey, V., Thomas, C., & Armento, B. (2000). Cultural diversity is basically a foreign term to me: The challenges of diversity for preservice teacher education. *Teaching and Teacher Education, 16,* 33–45. http://dx.doi.org/10.1016/S0742-051X(99)00039-6

Cho, C. (2010). "Qualifying" as teacher: Immigrant teacher candidates' counter-stories. *Canadian Journal of Educational Administration and Policy: Special Issue: Educational Policy and Internationally Educated Teachers (IETs) 100.*

Cho, C. (2013a). Performing the innocent stranger: Exploring immigrant identities and education. In C. Broom (Ed.), *Citizenship Education Research Network (CERN) Collection 2012, 76*–89.

Cho, C. (2013b). What does it mean to be a "Canadian" teacher? Experiences of immigrant teacher candidates. In L. Thomas (Ed.), *What is Canadian about Canadian teacher education?* Ottawa: Canadian Association for Teacher Education.

Cockrell, K.S., Placier, P.L., Cockrell, D.H., & Middleton, J.N. (1999). Coming to terms with "diversity" and "multiculturalism" in teacher education: Learning about our students, changing our practice. *Teaching and Teacher Education, 15*(4), 351–366. http://dx.doi.org/10.1016/S0742-051X(98)00050-X

Echols, C., & Stader, D. (2002). Education majors' attitudes about diversity. *Education Leadership Review, 3*(2), 1–7.

James, C.E., & Schecter, S.R. (2000). Mainstreaming and marginalization: Two national strategies in the circumscription of difference. *Pedagogy, Culture & Society, 8*(1), 23–41. http://dx.doi.org/10.1080/14681360000200078

Joshee, R. (2004). Citizenship and multicultural education in Canada: From assimiliation to social cohesion. In J. Banks (Ed.), *Diversity and citizenship education: Global perspectives* (pp. 127–156). San Francisco: Jossey-Bass.

Lippi-Green, R. (1997). *English with an accent: Language, ideology, and discrimination, in the United States.* New York: Routledge.

McIntyre, F. (2011). Determined new teachers face increased wait times. *Transition to Teaching: Professionally Speaking.*

OCT (2011). *Requirements for becoming a general education teacher in Ontario.* Retrieved March 2012 from http://www.oct.ca/become_a_teacher/registration_guides/general_education_teacher_e.pdf

Olmedo, I. (1997). Challenging old assumptions: Preparing teachers for inner city schools. *Teaching and Teacher Education, 13*(3), 245–258. http://dx.doi.org/10.1016/S0742-051X(96)00019-4

Pollock, K. (2006). Access to the teaching profession: Internationally educated teachers (IETs) experiences. *WALL Network.* 1–6. http://www.wallnetwork.ca/resources/Pollock_Internationally_Trained_Teachers_WALL2006.pdf

Suzuki, B. (2002). Revisiting the model minority stereotype: Implications for student affairs practice and higher education. *New Directions for Student Services, 2002*(97), 21–32. http://dx.doi.org/10.1002/ss.36

Walker, J.W. (1997). *Race, rights and the law in the Supreme Court of Canada.* Waterloo, ON: The Osgoode Society and Wilfrid Laurier University Press.

# Contributor biographies

**Neda Asadi** is a PhD student in the Department of Policy Studies, Faculty of Education, at the University of Alberta. She is interested in the topics of education, international politics, and health as they relate to marginalized populations and in particular those marginalized due to various forms of migration.

**Caroline Beauregard** is a trained art educator and art therapist. Her doctoral studies focus on the role of visual arts in the identity construction of immigrant children. She is part of the Transcultural Research and Intervention Team and participates in carrying out creative expression programs in Montreal's schools.

**Courtney Anne Brewer** is a part-time instructor at Nipissing University's Brantford campus in the Faculty of Arts and Science and at the Schulich School of Education. She is presently pursuing doctoral studies at the University of Western Ontario in London, Ontario. Her research interests include the support of families as they prepare for school after resettling in Canada, as well as studies of critical friendship.

**Elizabeth Burgess-Pinto** is a faculty member in the Bachelor of Science program in the Faculty of Health and Community Studies, MacEwan University, where she teaches population health and research methods. She has been involved in research with immigrant and refugee families.

**Catherine Caufield** taught at the University of Alberta from 2002 to 2013, where she served in the Faculty of Nursing and the Faculty of Arts' Religious Studies and Latin American Studies programs. With her work in plural contexts, her research integrates religion and nursing concerns for attaining and maintaining health.

**K. Jacky Chan** is a graduate student in clinical psychology at the University of Ottawa. His research interests include immigrant and refugee adjustment, psychological trauma, and well-being. Jacky also has interests in community mental health programming and evaluation.

**Christine L. Cho** is an assistant professor at Nipissing University's Schulich School of Education in Brantford, Ontario. Christine's research in teacher education explores the constructions and understandings of teacher identity within the structures of schools and contributes to current educational conversations on racial, ethnic, and linguistic representation in schools.

**Nancy Clark** is a PhD candidate at the University of British Columbia School of Nursing and a community mental health nurse in Vancouver. Her research interests include immigrant and refugee mental health, and her dissertation is focused on Karen refugee resettlement in BC. Her work examines community capacity to support Karen refugee women's mental health and well-being in the context of resettlement in Canada. Nancy has a special interest in the intersections of gender, migration, and mental health.

**Darcey M. Dachyshyn** is an associate professor of early childhood education. She teaches in the master of education program and the Centre for Continuing Education and Life Long Learning at Aga Khan University Institute for Educational Development, East Africa. Her teaching and research interests focus on interculturalism and how contextual ways of being hybridize and intersect with globalization.

**Mahdieh Dastjerdi** is an assistant professor at York University, School of Nursing. She is actively involved with different research projects on immigrant and refugee populations as primary investigator or co-investigator. At present, she is doing a pan-Canadian study on aging, well-being, and the quality of life of Iranian seniors living in Canada.

**Martha K. Ferede** earned her doctorate in higher education policy from Harvard University. She was a Presidential Scholar and a 2010–2013 Canada Research Fellow at Harvard's Weatherhead Center for International Affairs. She is a former teacher with the Toronto District School Board, where she taught many first- and second-generation immigrant and refugee students in a high-needs urban school in the Jane and Finch community.

**Darcy Fleming** was a postdoctoral fellow at the Community–University Partnership for the Study of Children, Youth, and Families when the research for Chapter 6 took place. His doctoral and postdoctoral work focused on issues related to early childhood development from an ecological perspective.

**Marie-France Gauthier** is an arts psychotherapist who works in a multi-ethnic milieu and is interested in developing preventive creative expression programs for immigrant and refugee children and families. She has been part of the Transcultural Research and Intervention Team for 13 years. She also has a private practice.

**Kimberly Hird-Bingeman** is an educator and administrator with the Waterloo Region District School Board. She has worked in some of the most multiculturally diverse schools in the region. She is a strong advocate for inclusive education for all students and has worked diligently to support the needs of refugee and immigrant students throughout the region. Outside of her daily responsibilities, Kim is a part-time faculty member of Wilfrid Laurier University's Faculty of Education, where she teaches and mentors the educators of tomorrow.

**Carl E. James** teaches courses on adolescents, urban education, and foundations of education in the Faculty of Education and the Graduate Program in Sociology. He is the current director of the York Centre for Education and Community. His research interests include exploration of identity/identification in relation to race, ethnicity, class, gender, and immigrant status; educational access and equity for marginalized youth; and the complementary and contradictory nature of sports in the schooling and educational attainments of racialized students. His most recent publications include *Life at the Intersection: Community, Class and Schooling* (2012).

**Anna Kirova** is a professor of early childhood education in the Faculty of Education, University of Alberta. Her research focuses on the need for understanding the school experiences of culturally and linguistically diverse families with young children, and the possibility such an understanding offers for culturally responsive pedagogy. Her international work in this area has resulted in the book *Global Migration and Education: Schools, Children, and Families* (2007).

**Ashley Korn** works with the newcomer settlement programs at the YMCA of Greater Toronto. She is an active contributor to the Student Refugee Program, providing orientations and integration assistance in both Malawi and Canada. She has also assisted the International Organization for Migration in Kenya, helping to develop the Canadian Orientation Abroad Refugee Youth Curriculum.

**Michelle Manks** is a senior program officer for the Student Refugee Program at the World University Service of Canada. She is responsible for providing post-secondary student, faculty, and staff volunteers with refugee-resettlement training, and coordinates the support given to refugee students once in Canada.

**Christine Massing** is a former teacher who has worked in schools in Asia, Africa, Latin America, and Canada. Currently, she is a doctoral candidate in the Department of Elementary Education at the University of Alberta, specializing in early childhood education. She also instructs part time in the early learning and child care program at MacEwan University. For her doctoral work, she has been conducting ethnographic research into immigrant and refugee women's experiences studying in an early-childhood teacher-education program. Her other research interests include cross-cultural guidance and communication practices, professionalism, immigrant/refugee families' involvement in early childhood settings, parent–child interactions, arts-based research, and early literacy.

**Michael McCabe** teaches at the Schulich School of Education at Nipissing University in Brantford, Ontario. His research focuses on community engagement in the schooling process, and he has published work related to parent involvement in mathematics learning and to the use of technology to assist in the process of engaging parents in schooling. Other research efforts include the study of community engagement in HIV/AIDS and character education programs in schools as well as issues related to mental health awareness in teachers. This current project, although new in focus, builds on the concepts associated with inclusive schools and efforts to make the wider community genuine partners in the schooling process.

**Linda Ogilvie** is a professor in the Faculty of Nursing at the University of Alberta. She was co-director of the Prairie Metropolis Centre from 2007 to 2012. She provides consultation in nursing education and research at the University of Ghana and the Aga Khan University of East Africa.

**Lucenia Ortiz** was the co-executive director of the Multicultural Health Brokers Co-op from 1998 to 2009, where she led various health initiatives with immigrant and refugee communities. She is currently a planner involved with social development projects with the City of Edmonton and remains passionate about immigrant issues.

**Patti Pente** is an artist and an associate professor in the Faculty of Education at the University of Alberta. She researches the pedagogical shifts that occur when examining philosophical texts through art process. Her interests include contemporary notions of subjectivity, with particular emphasis on educational potential within relationality and materiality. She continues to investigate the aesthetic nature of physical and virtual relationships to space and place through various disciplines and within different populations.

**Sandra Rastin** is completing her doctoral dissertation in sociology at the University of Alberta, researching government organizational change and its impact on public sector unions.

**Cécile Rousseau** is a professor of psychiatry at McGill University. She has developed and evaluated school-based prevention programs for immigrant and refugee children using different creative expression modalities. Her research also focuses on the evaluation of collaborative care models in youth mental health for multi-ethnic neighbourhoods.

**Lisa Sadler** began working with refugees as a volunteer with the Karen Initiative, a non-profit organization whose purpose was to advocate for refugees and fill gaps in service through volunteer initiatives. The Karen Initiative was recognized by the province of British Columbia with the 2009 Nesika Award for Excellence in Multiculturalism. Lisa has also been working directly with refugee and immigrant families in the Langley School District since 2008. Lisa recently completed a master of arts in community development at the University of Victoria. Her research is focused on the barriers that refugee students face in accessing post-secondary education.

**Jacqueline Strecker** is the ICT Innovations and Education Specialist at UNHCR, working with both UNHCR Innovation and the Education Unit. She has volunteered with the Student Refugee Program since 2004, facilitating and developing pre-departure orientations for refugee students in Kenya, as well as post-arrival sessions in Ottawa.

**Sam Tecle** is currently a PhD candidate in sociology at York University. Sam's research interests include disaporan and Black cultural studies, and educational issues as they relate to racialized youth. For the past decade, Sam has worked with community organizations across Toronto as a facilitator dealing with topics ranging from educational attainment to the personal and career development of youth. As a teacher with the Toronto District School

Board, Sam taught in high and middle schools as well as in alternative educational programs. He brings to his work his commitment to advocating for equitable education opportunities and outcomes for families from lower-income or impoverished areas.

**Taunya Wideman-Johnston** is a part-time instructor at Nipissing University's Brantford campus in the Faculty of Arts and Science and at the Schulich School of Education. She is a currently a doctoral student at Nipissing University in North Bay, Ontario. Her research focus is centred in the stories of people with chronic illness, particularly using fiction as a research practice. She is also interested in the development of critical friendship and the doctoral experience.

**Marta Young** is a registered psychologist and an associate professor in the clinical psychology program at the University of Ottawa. She graduated in 1991 with a PhD from the University of Western Ontario. She is past chair of the International and Cross-Cultural Section of the Canadian Psychological Association and served as Deputy Secretary-General of the International Association for Cross-Cultural Psychology. Dr. Young's teaching and research interests include the psychology of trauma, multicultural assessment and counselling, and the psychosocial adaptation of immigrants and refugees. Ethno-cultural communities surveyed include Somalis, South and East Indians, Ukrainians, Haitians, Filipinos, Chileans, Hong Kong Chinese, and Bosnians. Dr. Young is currently conducting a large-scale, cross-cultural study examining the relationships between acculturation, family conflict, and sexuality in young adults born in Canada of immigrant parents. Dr. Young is also actively involved in training clinical graduate students with respect to multicultural issues. Her private practice focuses on providing psycho-legal assessments and psychotherapy to migrants as well as consultation to resettlement workers, immigration lawyers, social workers, and ESL teachers.